Speeches that Reshaped the World

Speeches that Reshaped the World

Concise Edition

Alan J Whiticker

NEW
HOLLAND

First published in Australia in 2009 by
New Holland Publishers (Australia) Pty Ltd
Sydney • Auckland • London • Cape Town

www.newholland.com.au

1/66 Gibbes Street Chatswood NSW 2067 Australia
218 Lake Road Northcote Auckland New Zealand
86 Edgware Road London W2 2EA United Kingdom
80 McKenzie Street Cape Town 8001 South Africa

National Library of Australia Cataloguing-in-Publication entry

    Whiticker, Alan.
    Speeches that reshaped the world/Alan Whiticker.
    Concise edition
    9781741108446
    Speeches, addresses, etc.
    Communication.

    808.85

Publisher: Fiona Schultz
Publishing Manager: Lliane Clarke
Editor: Niamh Kenny
Project Editor: Ashlea Wallington
Cover Design: Hayley Norman
Text Design: Karl Roper, Natasha Hayles
Production Manager: Olga Dementiev
Printer: McPhersons Printing Group, Maryborough, Victoria

Front Cover: Democratic presidential candidate Barack Obama addresses supporters during his election
night victory rally at Grant Park on November 4, 2008 in Chicago, Illinois. Americans emphatically
elected Obama as their first black president in a transformational election. (Getty Images)

Back cover: Cuban President and revolutionary, Fidel Castro delivers a speech during a rally at the Plaza
de la Revolucion in Havana, 29 April, 2006, just under two years before he retires from Presidency.

Dedication

For all the teachers I have had the pleasure to work with
over the course of my 30 years in education—
thank you for your professionalism, friendship and collegiality.

Contents

Acknowledgements

I would like to thank Fiona Schultz, Lliane Clarke,
Niamh Kenny and all the team at New Holland Publishers for their
faith and support in this project. Thank you to everyone who wrote
to me from different parts of the world with their feedback regarding
Speeches That Shaped the Modern World (2005 and 2007, Concise Edition).
Your views, corrections and criticisms are much valued.

Introduction:

The Power of Oratory

And this, O men of Athens, is the truth and the whole truth;
I have concealed nothing, I have dissembled nothing. And yet I know that
this plainness of speech makes them hate me, and what is their hatred
but a proof that I am speaking the truth?
Socrates, as quoted by Plato in *The Apology*

This 'Concise Edition' of *Speeches that Reshaped the World* is a collection of some of the greatest speeches of modern times—speeches that not only shaped and changed the world but also moved us to action—emotionally, politically and socially. The speeches in this volume have been grouped under the following headings—War, Peace and Reconciliation, Revolution, Civil Rights, Politics and most importantly, Great Women. Starting in 1901 at the dawn of a new century and concluding with several speeches from the start of the new millennium, these speeches ring out across the decades.

The speeches in this book refect the lives of the famous and the infamous—Gandhi, Churchill, Castro, Malcolm X and Mandela. There are speeches that moved us closer to war—Hitler, Roosevelt, Truman and Bush (Senior and Junior—and speeches that have attempted to reconcile—Wilson, Atatürk, Yeltsin, Blair and Rudd. Many of these speeches have become iconic signposts in the passage of time—Winston Churchill's 'We Will Fight Them on the Beaches', Franklin Roosevelt's 'A Day That Will Live in Infamy' and John Kennedy's 'Ask Not What Your Country Can Do For You'—while others have remained relatively unknown—Bishop Romero's 'Final Sermon', Cesar Chavez's 'Lessons of Dr Martin Luther King' and New Zealand Prime Minister David Lange's speech against 'Nuclear Disarmament'.

As was the case with the first volume of great speeches I edited in 2005, *Speeches that Shaped the Modern World*, this collection is once again dominated by American rhetoric. Included here are some of the greatest orators America has produced—Twain, Darrow, King, and John and Robert Kennedy, to name but a few. Ten US Presidents are represented in this edition, including the victory speech given by President-elect Barack Obama in November 2008, but they are balanced by voices from around the world—France's Edouard Daladier, England's Margaret Thatcher and Australia's Paul Keating,

Adding an extra dimension to this volume of great speeches is a section devoted to female voices—speeches of immense clarity and hope. There are a dozen speeches by female orators—including heads of state, such as Queen Elizabeth II, Israel's Golda Meir and the late Benazir Bhutto; famous names such as Helen Keller, Eleanor Roosevelt and Hillary Clinton; and the unsung voices of Carrie Chapman, Elizabeth Glaser and Aun San Suu Kyi.

It would have been remiss of me not to include some of history's worst dictators and monsters in this volume, men such as Mussolini, Hitler and Milosoviç. They too have to the power to persuade, inspire and move us to action—disastrously, as history shows. The passing of time allows many speeches to take a deeper meaning and poignancy, for example Chaim Herzog's defence of 'Zionism' and Benino Aquino's 'Assassination Speech' that was never delivered, while several speeches delivered since the year 2000, such as Julian Bond's 'Eulogy for Rosa Parks' and Australian Prime Minister Kevin Rudd's 'Apology to the Stolen Generation,' will surely stand the test of time.

Speeches that Reshaped the World (Concise Edition) continues the tradition of the hardcover volume—modern history's greatest speeches placed in an historical and biographical context.

Alan J Whiticker

Politics

King George V

'The Eyes of the Whole Empire Are On Ireland'

Belfast, Ireland, 22 June 1921

King George V (1865–1936), the grandfather of Queen Elizabeth II, was also the first king of the Irish Free State which was established in 1922.

During his reign (1910–36) the 'troubles' in Ireland saw the British and Irish people in constant conflict. Moves towards 'Home Rule' in Ireland had gathered momentum since 1912. Despite its becoming law in 1914, Ulster Unionists made it clear they would resist any moves towards 'Home Rule' for the entire island.

Easter 1916 saw an uprising to reclaim Dublin for the Irish Republic but it was brutally quashed by British troops. The ringleaders were executed. Under the Government of Ireland Act in 1920, two Home Rule parliaments were established—one for Southern Ireland, based in Dublin (which the political party, Sinn Fein, refused to recognise because it did not represent all of Ireland), and the other for the six counties of Ulster, in Belfast. While Northern Ireland did not necessarily want its own parliament, partition allowed the Unionists to remain independent from Dublin rule and still be part of the British Empire.

Ignoring the threat of assassination, King George V and Queen Mary rode through three miles of Belfast streets 'at foot pace' to City Hall, where they opened the first North of Ireland Parliament on 22 June 1921. Britain was determined to seek a democratic solution to the 'troubles'. The final hope of ending generations of conflict lay with cooperation between the two Irish parliaments, or perhaps, future unity under one parliament.

‘Members of the Senate and of the House of Commons—for all who love Ireland, as I do with all my heart, this is a profoundly moving occasion in Irish history. My memories of the Irish people date back to the time when I spent many happy days in Ireland as a midshipman. My affection for the Irish people has been deepened by successive visits since that time, and I have watched with constant sympathy the course of their affairs. I could not have allowed myself to give Ireland by deputy alone my earnest prayers and good wishes in the new era which opens with this ceremony, and I have therefore come in person, as the Head of the Empire, to inaugurate this Parliament on Irish soil. I inaugurate it with deep-felt hope and I feel assured that you will do your utmost to make it an instrument of happiness and good government for all parts of the community which you represent.

'...for all who love Ireland, as I do with all my heart, this is a profoundly moving occasion in Irish history.'

This is a great and critical occasion in the history of the six counties, but not for the six counties alone, for everything which interests them touches Ireland, and everything which touches Ireland finds an echo in the remotest parts of the Empire. Few things are more earnestly desired throughout the English-speaking world than a satisfactory solution of the age-long Irish problems which for generations embarrassed our forefathers, as they now weigh heavily upon us. Most certainly there is no wish nearer my own heart than that every man of Irish birth, whatever be his creed and wherever be his home, should work in loyal cooperation with the free communities on which the British Empire is based.

I am confident that the important matters entrusted to the control and guidance of the Northern Parliament will be managed with wisdom and with moderation, with fairness and due regard to every faith and interest, and with no abatement of that patriotic devotion to the Empire which you proved so gallantly in the Great War. Full partnership in the United Kingdom and religious freedom Ireland has long enjoyed. She now has conferred upon her the duty of dealing with all the essential tasks of domestic legislation and government; and I feel no misgiving as to the spirit in which you who stand here today will carry out the all-important functions entrusted to your care.

'I am confident that the important matters entrusted to the control and guidance of the Northern Parliament will be managed with wisdom and with moderation...'

My hope is broader still. The eyes of the whole Empire are on Ireland today—that

Empire in which so many nations and races have come together in spite of ancient feuds—and in which new nations have come to birth within the lifetime of the youngest in this hall. I am emboldened by that thought to look beyond the sorrow and the anxiety which have clouded of late my vision of Irish affairs. I speak from a full heart when I pray that my coming to Ireland today may prove to be the first step towards an end of strife amongst her people, whatever their race or creed. In that hope, I appeal to all Irishmen to pause, to stretch out the hand of forbearance and conciliation, to forgive and to forget and to join in making for the land which they love a new era of peace, contentment and good will. It is my earnest desire that in Southern Ireland too there may ere long take place a parallel to what is now passing in this hall; that there, a similar occasion may present itself and a similar ceremony he performed.

For this, the Parliament of the United Kingdom has in the fullest measure provided the powers; for this, the Parliament of Ulster is pointing the way. The future lies in the hands of my Irish people themselves. May this historic gathering be the prelude of a day in which the Irish people, North and South, under one Parliament or two, as those Parliaments may themselves decide, shall work together in common love for Ireland upon the sure foundation of mutual justice and respect. ♪

Newspapers of the day praised the king for his speech and reflected on the great risk the royal couple had taken in coming to Northern Ireland. It was a move which the Northern Ireland 'News Letter' labelled as an 'act of genius'. The historian A.J.P Taylor (1906–90) described it as 'perhaps the greatest service performed by a British monarch in modern times'— but history shows it did not bring a diplomatic end to the 'troubles'.

The Irish Free State Treaty of December 1921 attempted to legalise partition, but this ultimately led to further bloodshed and outright civil war in Northern Ireland between Catholics (anti-partition) and Protestants (pro-partition).

On 22 December 1922 the Irish Free State was established as a Dominion (an autonomous community of the British Empire) under the Anglo-Irish Treaty. On the same day, Northern Ireland exercised its right under the terms of the treaty to 'opt out' of the new state.

The Irish Free State replaced Southern Ireland and became the self-proclaimed Irish Republic (which had been established on 21 January 1919).

It was not until 1948, that the Irish Free State was granted full independence from Britain under the terms of the Republic of Ireland Act.

The six Ulster counties, however, remained part of the United Kingdom, ensuring a further six decades of social, political and religious conflict until Prime Minister Tony Blair brokered a peace plan in 1998.

Richard M. Nixon

'The "Checkers" Speech'

Los Angeles, California, 23 September 1952

Richard Milhous Nixon (1913–94) was the 37th President of the United States of America (1969–74). He is renowned for the Watergate scandal, which led to his resignation from office to avoid impeachment. Twenty years before this, Nixon was involved in another scandal while campaigning as Dwight D. Eisenhower's running mate in the 1952 Presidential race. While the Republicans were holding their National Convention in September, the New York Post broke a story alleging that a 'slush fund' had kept Nixon in financial style far beyond his congressional salary.

There was immediate pressure to remove the 39-year-old Senator from the Republican ticket, but, in a brilliant move, Nixon appeared on national television from California to explain his financial situation to the American people. Now known as 'The "Checkers" Speech' because of his reference to a pet dog given to his daughters by a Republican supporter, Nixon's speech was a political triumph.

'My Fellow Americans,
I come before you tonight as a candidate for the Vice-Presidency and as a man whose honesty and integrity has been questioned.

Now, the usual political thing to do when charges are made against you is to either ignore them or to deny them without giving details. I believe we have had enough of that in the United States, particularly with the present administration in Washington DC.

To me, the office of the Vice-Presidency of the United States is a great office, and I feel that the people have got to have confidence in the integrity of the men who run for that office and who might attain it.

I have a theory, too, that the best and only answer to a smear or an honest misunderstanding of the facts is to tell the truth. And that is why I am here tonight. I want to tell you my side of the case.

I am sure that you have read the charges, and you have heard that I, Senator Nixon, took $18,000 from a group of my supporters.

Now, was that wrong? And let me say that it was wrong. I am saying, incidentally, that it was wrong, just not illegal, because it isn't a question of whether it was legal or illegal, that isn't enough. The question is, was it morally wrong? I say that it was morally wrong if any of that $18,000 went to Senator Nixon, for my personal use. I say that it was morally wrong if it was secretly given and secretly handled.

'...you will find that the purpose of the fund simply was to defray political expenses that I did not feel should be charged to the government.'

And I say that it was morally wrong if any of the contributors got special favors for the contributions that they made.

To answer those questions let me say this—not a cent of the $18,000 or any other money of that type ever went to me for my personal use. Every penny of it was used to pay for political expenses that I did not think should be charged to the taxpayers of the United States.

It was not a secret fund. As a matter of fact, when I was on "Meet the Press"—some of you may have seen it last Sunday—Peter Edson came up to me after the program, and he said: "Dick, what about this fund we hear about?" And I said: "Well, there is no secret about it. Go out and see Dana Smith who was the administrator of the fund," and I gave him his address. And I said, you will find that the purpose of the fund simply was to defray political expenses that I did not feel should be charged to the government.

And third, let me point out, and I want to make this particularly clear, that no contributor to this fund, no contributor to any of my campaigns, has ever received any consideration that he would not have received as an ordinary constituent.

I just don't believe in that, and I can say that never, while I have been in the Senate of the United States, as far as the people that contributed to this fund are concerned, have I made a telephone call to an agency, nor have I gone down to an agency on their behalf.

And the records will show that—the records which are in the hands of the administration.

Well, then, some of you will say, and rightly: "Well, what did you use the fund for, Senator? Why did you have to have it?"

Let me tell you in just a word how a Senate office operates. First of all, the Senator gets $15,000 a year in salary. He gets enough money to pay for one trip a year, a round trip that is, for himself and his family between his home and Washington DC. And then he gets an allowance to handle the people that work in his office to handle his mail.

The allowance for my State of California is enough to hire thirteen people. And let me say, incidentally, that this allowance is not paid to the Senator. It is paid directly to the individuals that the Senator puts on his payroll, but all of these people and all of these allowances are for strictly official business, for example, when a constituent writes in and wants you to go down to the Veterans' Administration and get some information about his GI policy—items of that type for example. But there are other expenses that are not covered by the government. And I think I can best discuss those expenses by asking you some questions.

Do you think that when I or any other Senator makes a political speech and has it printed we should charge the printing of that speech and the mailing of that speech to the taxpayers?

Do you think, for example, when I or any other Senator makes a trip to his home state to make a purely political speech that the cost of that trip should be charged to the taxpayers?

Do you think when a Senator makes political broadcasts on radio or television, that the expense of those broadcasts should be charged to the taxpayers?

I know what your answer is. It is the same answer that audiences give me whenever I discuss this particular problem. The answer is no. The taxpayers should not be required to finance items which are not official business but which are primarily political business.

Well, then the question arises, you say: "Well, how do you pay for these and how can you do it legally?" And there are several ways that it can be done, incidentally, and it is done legally in the United States Senate and in the Congress.

The first way is to be a rich man. So I couldn't use that.

Another way that is used is to put your wife on the payroll. Let me say, incidentally, that my opponent, my opposite number for the Vice-Presidency on the Democratic ticket, does have his wife on the payroll and has had her on his payroll for the past ten years. Now let me just say this—that is his business and I am not critical of him for doing that. You will have to pass judgment on that particular point, but I have never done that for this reason:

I have found that there are so many deserving stenographers and secretaries in Washington that needed the work that I just didn't feel it was right to put my wife on the payroll.... my wife sitting over there.

She is a wonderful stenographer. She used to teach stenography and she used to teach shorthand in high school. That was when I met her. And I can tell you folks that she has worked many hours on Saturdays and Sundays in my office and she has done a fine job, and I am proud to say tonight that in the six years I have been in the Senate of the United States, Pat Nixon has never been on the government payroll.

What are the other ways that these finances can be taken care of? Some who are lawyers, and I happen to be a lawyer, continue to practice law. But I haven't been able to do that.

I am so far away from California and I have been so busy with my senatorial work that I have not engaged in any legal practice. Also, as far as law practice is concerned, it seemed to me that the relationship between an attorney and the client was so personal that you couldn't possibly represent a man as an attorney and then have an unbiased view when he presented his case to you in the event that he had one before government.

And so I felt that the best way to handle these necessary political expenses of getting my message to the American people and the speeches I made— the speeches I had printed for the most part concerned this one message of exposing this administration, the Communism in it, the corruption in it—the only way I could do that was to accept the aid which people in my home state of California, who contributed to my campaign and who continued to make these contributions after I was elected, were glad to make.

And let me say that I am proud of the fact that not one of them has ever asked me for a special favor. I am proud of the fact that not one of them has ever asked me to vote on a bill other than my own conscience would dictate. And I am proud of the fact that the taxpayers, by subterfuge or otherwise, have never paid one dime for expenses which I thought were political and should not be charged to the taxpayers.

Let me say, incidentally, that some of you may say: "Well, that is all right, Senator, that is your explanation, but have you got any proof?" And I would like to tell you this evening that just an hour ago we received an independent audit of this entire fund. I suggested to Governor Sherman Adams, who is the chief

'The taxpayers should not be required to finance items which are not official business but which are primarily political business.'

'I am proud of the fact that not one of them has ever asked me to vote on a bill other than my own conscience would dictate.'

of staff of the Eisenhower campaign, that an independent audit and legal report be obtained, and I have that audit in my hand.

It is an audit made by Price Waterhouse & Co. and the legal opinion by Gibson, Dunn, & Crutcher, lawyers in Los Angeles, the biggest law firm and, incidentally, one of the best ones in Los Angeles.

I am proud to report to you tonight that this audit and legal opinion is being forwarded to General Eisenhower and I would like to read to you the opinion that was prepared by Gibson, Dunn, & Crutcher, based on all the pertinent laws and statutes, together with the audit report prepared by the certified public accountants.

"It is our conclusion that Senator Nixon did not obtain any financial gain from the collection and disbursement of the funds by Dana Smith; that Senator Nixon did not violate any federal or state law by reason of the operation of the fund; and that neither the portion of the fund paid by Dana Smith directly to third persons, nor the portion paid to Senator Nixon, to reimburse him for office expenses, constituted income in a sense which was either reportable or taxable as income under income tax laws.

Signed—Gibson, Dunn, & Crutcher, by Elmo Conley"

That is not Nixon speaking, but it is an independent audit which was requested because I want the American people to know all the facts and I am not afraid of having independent people go in and check the facts, and that is exactly what they did.

But then I realized that there are still some who may say, and rightly so— and let me say that I recognize that some will continue to smear regardless of what the truth may be—but that there has been, understandably, some honest misunderstanding on this matter, and there are some that will say: "Well, maybe you were able, Senator, to fake the thing. How can we believe what you say—after all, is there a possibility that maybe you got some sums in cash? Is there a possibility that you might have feathered your own nest?"

And so now, what I am going to do—and incidentally this is unprecedented in the history of American politics—I am going at this time to give to this television and radio audience, a complete financial history, everything I have earned, everything I have spent and everything I own, and I want you to know the facts.

I will have to start early. I was born in 1913. Our family was one of modest circumstances, and most of my early life was spent in a store out in East Whittier. It was a grocery store, one of those family enterprises.

The only reason we were able to make it go was because my mother and dad had five boys and we all worked in the store. I worked my way through college and, to a great extent, through law school. And then in 1940, probably the best thing that ever happened to me happened. I married Pat who is sitting over here.

We had a rather difficult time after we were married, like so many of the young couples who might be listening to us. I practiced law. She continued to teach school.

Then, in 1942, I went into the service. Let me say that my service record was not a particularly unusual one. I went to the South Pacific. I guess I'm entitled to a couple of battle stars. I got a couple of letters of commendation. But I was just there when the bombs were falling. And then I returned. I returned to the United States and, in 1946, I ran for Congress. When we came out of the war—Pat and I—Pat during the war had worked as a stenographer, and in a bank, and as an economist for a government agency—and when we came out, the total of our savings, from both my law practice, her teaching and all the time I was in the war, the total for that entire period was just less than $10,000. Every cent of that, incidentally, was in government bonds. Well, that's where we start, when I go into politics.

Now, whatever I earned since I went into politics—well, here it is. I jotted it down. Let me read the notes.

First of all, I have had my salary as a Congressman and as a Senator.

Second, I have received a total in this past six years of $1,600 from estates which were in my law firm at the time that I severed my connection with it. And, incidentally, as I said before, I have not engaged in any legal practice and have not accepted any fees from business that came into the firm after I went into politics.

I have made an average of approximately $1,500 a year from non-political speaking engagements and lectures.

And then, unfortunately, we have inherited little money. Pat sold her interest in her father's estate for $3,000 and I inherited $1,500 from my grandfather. We lived rather modestly. For four years we lived in an apartment in Parkfairfax, Alexandria, Virginia. The rent was $80 a month. And we saved for a time when we could buy a house. Now that was what we took in.

What did we do with this money? What do we have today to show for it? This will surprise you because it is so little, I suppose, as standards generally

> *'...I am proud of the fact that the taxpayers, by subterfuge or otherwise, have never paid one dime for expenses which I thought were political and should not be charged to the taxpayers.'*

go of people in public life.

First of all, we've got a house in Washington, which cost $41,000 and on which we owe $20,000.

We have a house in Whittier, California, which cost $13,000, on which we owe $3,000 [Nixon meant to say $10,000]. My folks are living there at the present time. I have just $4,000 in life insurance, plus my GI policy which I have never been able to convert and which will run out in two years.

I have no life insurance whatever on Pat. I have no life insurance on our two youngsters, Patricia and Julie.

I own a 1950 Oldsmobile car. We have our furniture. We have no stocks and bonds of any type. We have no interest, direct or indirect, in any business. Now that is what we have. What do we owe?

Well, in addition to the mortgages, the $20,000 mortgage on the house in Washington and the $10,000 mortgage on the house in Whittier, I owe $4,000 to the Riggs Bank in Washington DC with an interest at four per cent.

I owe $3,500 to my parents and the interest on that loan, which I pay regularly, because it is a part of the savings they made through the years they were working so hard—I pay regularly four per cent interest. And then I have a $500 loan, which I have on my life insurance. Well, that's about it. That's what we have. And that's what we owe. It isn't very much.

But Pat and I have the satisfaction that every dime that we have got is honestly ours. I should say this, that Pat doesn't have a mink coat. But she does have a respectable Republican cloth coat, and I always tell her she would look good in anything.

One other thing I probably should tell you, because if I don't they will probably be saying this about me, too. We did get something, a gift, after the election.

A man down in Texas heard Pat on the radio mention the fact that our two youngsters would like to have a dog and, believe it or not, the day before we left on this campaign trip we got a message from Union Station in Baltimore, saying they had a package for us. We went down to get it. You know what it was?

It was a little cocker spaniel dog, in a crate that he had sent all the way from Texas, black and white, spotted, and our little girl Tricia, the six year old, named it Checkers.

And you know, the kids, like all kids, loved the dog, and I just want to say this, right now, that regardless of what they say about it, we are going to keep it.

'It isn't easy to come before a nationwide audience and bare your life, as I have done.'

It isn't easy to come before a nationwide audience and bare your life, as I have done. But I want to say some things before I conclude, that I think most of you will agree on.

Mr Mitchell, the Chairman of the Democratic National Committee, made this statement that if a man couldn't afford to be in the United States Senate, he shouldn't run for the Senate. And I just want to make my position clear.

I don't agree with Mr Mitchell when he says that only a rich man should serve his government in the United States Senate or Congress. I don't believe that represents the thinking of the Democratic Party, and I know it doesn't represent the thinking of the Republican Party.

I believe that it's fine that a man like Governor Stevenson, who inherited a fortune from his father, can run for President. But I also feel that it is essential in this country of ours that a man of modest means can also run for President, because, you know—remember Abraham Lincoln—you remember what he said: "God must have loved the common people, he made so many of them …" ♪

With his wife Pat sitting by his side, Richard Nixon portrayed himself to be an American 'everyman' and turned the last part of his speech into a political attack against Democratic candidate, Adlai E. Stevenson, and the finances of his opponents. Although there was never really any mechanism for the Republican Party to vote whether they wanted Nixon to remain their candidate's running mate, Dwight Eisenhower was impressed and kept him on the ticket.

The Republican Party went on to win the election by a landslide and 'Tricky Dick' Nixon served eight years as Vice-President (1953–61) before being narrowly beaten by John Kennedy in the 1960 presidential race. Like a bad penny Nixon would return in 1968 and capture the Republican nomination and the presidency.

The 1972 Watergate scandal, in which Nixon's White House administration was found guilty of covering up the burglary of the Democratic Headquarters, led to the President's resignation in August 1974.

Dwight D. Eisenhower
'Farewell to the White House'
Washington DC, 17 January 1961

On 17 January 1961, in a nationally televised address, Dwight D. Eisenhower (1890–1969) spoke to the American people for the last time as US President. In a speech that was almost prophetic, considering the events of the Vietnam War, Eisenhower warned against the unfettered growth of 'military-industrial' interests and called for diplomacy and compassion in future dealings with the Soviet Union.

'Good evening, my fellow Americans:
First, I should like to express my gratitude to the radio and television networks for the opportunity they have given me over the years to bring reports and messages to our nation. My special thanks go to them for the opportunity of addressing you this evening.

Three days from now, after a half century of service to our country, I shall lay down the responsibilities of office as, in traditional and solemn ceremony, the authority of the Presidency is vested in my successor.

This evening I come to you with a message of leave-taking and farewell, and to share a few final thoughts with you, my countrymen. Like every other citizen, I wish the new President, and all who will labor with him, God speed. I pray that the coming years will be blessed with peace and prosperity for all.

Our people expect their President and the Congress to find essential agreement on questions of great moment, the wise resolution of which will better shape the future of the nation.

My own relations with Congress, which began on a remote and tenuous basis when, long ago, a member of the Senate appointed me to West Point, have since ranged to the intimate during the war and immediate post-war period, and finally to the mutually interdependent during these past eight years.

'So my official relationship with Congress ends in a feeling, on my part, of gratitude that we have been able to do so much together.'

In this final relationship, the Congress and the Administration have, on most vital issues, cooperated well, to serve the nation well rather than mere partisanship, and so have assured that the business of the nation should go forward. So my official relationship with Congress ends in a feeling, on my part, of gratitude that we have been able to do so much together.

We now stand ten years past the midpoint of a century that has witnessed four major wars among great nations. Three of these involved our own country. Despite these holocausts, America is today the strongest, the most influential and most productive nation in the world. Understandably proud of this pre-eminence, we yet realize that America's leadership and prestige depend not merely upon our unmatched material progress, riches and military strength, but on how we use our power in the interests of world peace and human betterment.

Throughout America's adventure in free government, such basic purposes have been to keep the peace; to foster progress in human achievement; and to enhance liberty, dignity and integrity among peoples and among nations. To strive for less would be unworthy of a free and religious people. Any failure traceable to arrogance or our lack of comprehension or readiness to sacrifice would inflict upon us a grievous hurt, both at home and abroad.

Progress toward these noble goals is persistently threatened by the conflict now engulfing the world. It commands our whole attention, absorbs our very beings. We face a hostile ideology, global in scope, atheistic in character, ruthless in purpose and insidious in method. Unhappily, the danger it poses promises to be of indefinite duration. To meet it successfully, there is called for, not so much the emotional and transitory sacrifices of crisis, but rather those which enable us to carry forward steadily, surely and without complaint, the burdens of a prolonged and complex struggle—with liberty the stake. Only thus shall we remain, despite every provocation, on our charted course toward permanent peace and human betterment.

Crises there will continue to be. In meeting them, whether foreign or domestic, great or small, there is a recurring temptation to feel that some spectacular and costly action could become the miraculous solution to all current difficulties. A huge increase in the newer elements of our defenses;

'Throughout America's adventure in free government, such basic purposes have been to keep the peace; to foster progress in human achievement; and to enhance liberty, dignity and integrity among peoples and among nations.'

development of unrealistic programs to cure every ill in agriculture; a dramatic expansion in basic and applied research—these and many other possibilities, each possibly promising in itself, may be suggested as the only way to the road we wish to travel.

But each proposal must be weighed in light of a broader consideration, the need to maintain balance in and among national programs; balance between the private and the public economy; balance between the cost and hoped for advantages; balance between the clearly necessary and the comfortably desirable; balance between our essential requirements as a nation and the duties imposed by the nation upon the individual; balance between the actions of the moment and the national welfare of the future. Good judgment seeks balance and progress. Lack of it eventually finds imbalance and frustration.

The record of many decades stands as proof that our people and their government have, in the main, understood these truths and have responded to them well in the face of threat and stress.

But threats, new in kind or degree, constantly arise.

Of these, I mention two only.

A vital element in keeping the peace is our military establishment. Our arms must be mighty, ready for instant action, so that no potential aggressor may be tempted to risk his own destruction.

Our military organization today bears little relation to that known by any of my predecessors in peacetime, or indeed by the fighting men of World War II or Korea.

Until the latest of our world conflicts, the United States had no armaments industry. American makers of plowshares could, with time and as required, make swords as well. But now we can no longer risk emergency improvisation of national defense. We have been compelled to create a permanent armaments industry of vast proportions. Added to this, three and a half million men and women are directly engaged in the defense establishment. We annually spend on military security more than the net income of all United States corporations.

This conjunction of an immense military establishment and a large arms industry is new in the American experience. The total influence—economic, political, even spiritual—is felt in every city, every State House, every office of the federal government. We recognize the imperative need for this development. Yet we must not fail to comprehend its grave implications. Our toil, resources and livelihood are all involved; so is the very structure of our society. In the councils of government, we must guard against the acquisition of unwarranted influence, whether sought or unsought, by the military-industrial complex. The potential for the disastrous rise of misplaced power exists and will persist.

'Akin to, and largely responsible for the sweeping changes in our industrial-military posture, has been the technological revolution during recent decades.'

We must never let the weight of this combination endanger our liberties or democratic processes. We should take nothing for granted. Only an alert and knowledgeable citizenry can compel the proper meshing of the huge industrial and military machinery of defense with our peaceful methods and goals, so that security and liberty may prosper together.

Akin to, and largely responsible for the sweeping changes in our industrial-military posture, has been the technological revolution during recent decades. In this revolution, research has become central, it also becomes more formalized, complex, and costly. A steadily increasing share is conducted for, by, or at the direction of the federal government.

Today, the solitary inventor, tinkering in his shop, has been overshadowed by taskforces of scientists in laboratories and testing fields. In the same fashion, the free university, historically the fountainhead of free ideas and scientific discovery, has experienced a revolution in the conduct of research. Partly because of the huge costs involved, a government contract becomes virtually a substitute for intellectual curiosity. For every old blackboard there are now hundreds of new electronic computers.

The prospect of domination of the nation's scholars by federal employment, project allocations and the power of money is ever present—and is gravely to be regarded.

Yet, in holding scientific research and discovery in respect, as we should, we must also be alert to the equal and opposite danger that public policy could itself become the captive of a scientific-technological elite. It is the task of statesmanship to mold, to balance and to integrate these and other forces, new and old, within the principles of our democratic system—ever aiming toward the supreme goals of our free society.

Another factor in maintaining balance involves the element of time. As we peer into society's future, we—you and I, and our government—must avoid the impulse to live only for today, plundering, for our own ease and convenience, the precious resources of tomorrow. We cannot mortgage the material assets of our grandchildren without asking the loss also of their political and spiritual heritage. We want democracy to survive for all generations to come, not to become the insolvent phantom of tomorrow.

Down the long lane of the history yet to be written, America knows that this world of ours, ever growing smaller, must avoid becoming a community of dreadful fear and hate and be, instead, a proud confederation of mutual trust and respect. Such a confederation must be one of equals. The weakest must come to the conference table with the same confidence as do we, protected as we are by our moral, economic, and military strength. That table, though scarred by many past frustrations, cannot be abandoned for the certain agony of the battlefield.

Disarmament, with mutual honor and confidence, is a continuing imperative. Together we must learn how to resolve differences, not with arms, but with intellect and decent purpose. Because this need is so sharp and apparent, I confess that I lay down my official responsibilities in this field with a definite sense of disappointment. As one who has witnessed the horror and the lingering sadness of war—as one who knows that another war could utterly destroy this civilization which has been so slowly and painfully built over thousands of years—I wish I could say tonight that a lasting peace is in sight.

Happily, I can say that war has been avoided. Steady progress toward our ultimate goal has been made. But so much remains to be done. As a private citizen, I shall never cease to do what little I can to help the world advance along that road.

So, in this my last good night to you as your President—I thank you for the many opportunities you have given me for public service in war and peace. I trust that in that service you find some things worthy. As for the rest of it, I know you will find ways to improve performance in the future.

You and I—my fellow citizens—need to be strong in our faith that all nations, under God, will reach the goal of peace with justice. May we be ever unswerving in devotion to principle, confident but humble with power, diligent in pursuit of the nation's great goals.

To all the peoples of the world, I once more give expression to America's prayerful and continuing aspiration: We pray that peoples of all faiths, all races, all nations, may have their great human needs satisfied; that those now denied opportunity shall come to enjoy it to the full; that all who yearn for freedom may experience its spiritual blessings; that those who have freedom will understand, also, its heavy responsibilities; that all who are insensitive to the needs of others will learn charity; that the scourges of poverty, disease and ignorance will be made to disappear from the earth, and that, in the fullness of time, all peoples will come to live together in a peace guaranteed by the binding force of mutual respect and love.

Now, on Friday noon, I am to become a private citizen. I am proud to do so. I look forward to it.

Thank you, and good night.

The first year of Eisenhower's Presidency brought the armistice that ended the Korean War (1950–53) but the remainder of the 1950s saw an intensification of the 'Cold War' between East and West. The USA (and her allies) and the USSR (and Eastern Bloc Communist countries) continued the build-up of strategic defensive weapons during the decade, while the 'cold' diplomatic relations between the two nations ensured that the fears of a nuclear attack was never far from public consciousness.

As a conservative Republican, however, Dwight D. Eisenhower didn't believe the expansion of a government sponsored 'military-industrial' complex was to blame for the Cold War—that was the fault of the Communists. While a 'Third World War' was averted—most notably by Eisenhower's successor, John F. Kennedy, in the 'Cuban Missile Crisis of 1962,—Eisenhower's fears of the growth of a 'military-industrial' complex were realised with the escalation of the Vietnam War during the 1960s.

John F. Kennedy

'Ask Not What Your Country Can Do For You...'

Washington DC, 20 January 1961

John F. Kennedy (1917–63) was the second son of self-made millionaire, Joseph Kennedy, the US Ambassador to England at the outbreak of World War II.

'JFK', as he became known, was a Harvard graduate and a World War II naval hero before fulfilling the family legacy and entering politics (Kennedy's older brother, Joe, who had already been earmarked for a political career had been killed during the war). A Democratic Representative (1947) and Senator for Massachusetts (1952), Kennedy married Jacqueline Bouvier in 1953. The Kennedys were the closest thing Americans had to royalty in the 1950s.

In 1960, John Kennedy overcame concerns about his youth (at 43 he was the youngest president elected) and religion (Kennedy was also the first Catholic president) to defeat Republican Vice President Richard M. Nixon. Kennedy won by a mere 119,000 votes out of nearly 70 million votes cast (Nixon carried four more states). A charismatic speaker with youthful good looks, Kennedy used the medium of television to charm and convince the American public, while his millionaire father ensured he had the money and the political connections to secure the narrowest (0.02 per cent) of victories.

On a cold January morning in 1961, John F. Kennedy took the oath of office as the 35th President of the United States of America. His inauguration speech—with a bold challenge for all Americans and the 'citizens of the world'—signalled the birth of a new frontier in the 1960s, which many referred to as Camelot.

'Vice President Nixon, President Eisenhower, revered clergy, fellow citizens...

We observe today not a victory of party but a celebration of freedom, symbolizing an end as well as a beginning, signifying renewal as well as change. For I have sworn before you and Almighty God the same solemn oath our forebears prescribed nearly a century and three-quarters ago.

The world is very different now. For man holds in his mortal hands the power to abolish all forms of human poverty and all forms of human life. And yet the same revolutionary belief for which our forebears fought is still at issue around the globe, the belief that the rights of man come not from the generosity of the state but from the hand of God.

We dare not forget today that we are the heirs of that first revolution. Let the word go forth from this time and place, to friend and foe alike, that the torch has been passed to a new generation of Americans, born in this century, tempered by war, disciplined by a hard and bitter peace, proud of our ancient heritage, and unwilling to witness or permit the slow undoing of these human rights to which this nation has always been committed, and to which we are committed today at home and around the world.

Let every nation know, whether it wishes us well or ill, that we shall pay any price, bear any burden, meet any hardship, support any friend, oppose any foe, to assure the survival and the success of liberty.

This much we pledge—and more.

To those old allies whose cultural and spiritual origins we share, we pledge the loyalty of faithful friends. United, there is little we cannot do in a host of cooperative ventures. Divided, there is little we can do, for we dare not meet a powerful challenge at odds and split asunder.

To those new states whom we welcome to the ranks of the free, we pledge our word that one form of colonial control shall not have passed away merely to be replaced by a far more iron tyranny. We shall not always expect to find them supporting our view. But we shall always hope to find them strongly supporting their own freedom, and to remember that, in the past, those who foolishly sought power by riding the back of the tiger, ended up inside.

To those peoples in the huts and villages of half the globe struggling to break the bonds of mass misery, we pledge our best efforts to help them help themselves, for whatever period is required, not because the Communists may be doing it, not because we seek their votes, but because it is right. If a free society cannot help the many who are poor, it cannot save the few who are rich.

To our sister republics south of our border, we offer a special pledge: To convert our good words into good deeds, in a new alliance for progress, to assist free men and free governments in casting off the chains of poverty. But this peaceful revolution of hope cannot become the prey of hostile powers. Let all our neighbors know that we shall join with them to oppose aggression or subversion anywhere in the Americas. And let every other power know that this hemisphere intends to remain the master of its own house.

To that world assembly of sovereign states, the United Nations, our last best hope in an age where the instruments of war have far outpaced the instruments of peace, we renew our pledge of support: To prevent it from becoming merely a forum for invective; to strengthen its shield of the new and the weak; and to enlarge the area in which its writ may run.

Finally, to those nations who would make themselves our adversary, we offer not a pledge but a request: That both sides begin anew the quest for peace, before the dark powers of destruction unleashed by science engulf all humanity in planned or accidental self-destruction.

We dare not tempt them with weakness. For only when our arms are sufficient beyond doubt can we be certain beyond doubt that they will never be employed.

But neither can two great and powerful groups of nations take comfort from our present course—both sides overburdened by the cost of modern weapons, both rightly alarmed by the steady spread of the deadly atom, yet both racing to alter that uncertain balance of terror that stays the hand of mankind's final war.

So let us begin anew, remembering on both sides that civility is not a sign of weakness and sincerity is always subject to proof. Let us never negotiate out of fear, but let us never fear to negotiate.

Let both sides explore what problems unite us instead of belaboring those problems which divide us.

Let both sides, for the first time, formulate serious and precise proposals for the inspection and control of arms and bring the absolute power to destroy other nations under the absolute control of all nations.

Let both sides seek to invoke the wonders of science instead of its terrors. Together let us explore the stars, conquer the deserts, eradicate disease, tap the ocean depths and encourage the arts and commerce.

Let both sides unite to heed in all corners of the earth the command of Isaiah to "undo the heavy burdens... (and) let the oppressed go free." And if a beachhead of cooperation may push back the jungle of suspicion, let both sides join in creating a new endeavor, not a new balance of power, but a new world of law, where the strong are just, the weak secure and the peace preserved.

All this will not be finished in the first one hundred days. Nor will it be finished in the first one thousand days, nor in the life of this Administration, nor even perhaps in our lifetime on this planet. But let us begin.

In your hands, my fellow citizens, more than mine, will rest the final success or failure of our course. Since this country was founded, each generation of Americans has been summoned to give testimony to its national loyalty. The graves of young Americans who answered the call to service surround the globe.

Now the trumpet summons us again—not as a call to bear arms, though arms we need; not as a call to battle, though embattled we are; but a call to bear the burden of a long twilight struggle, year in and year out, "rejoicing in hope, patient in tribulation," a struggle against the common enemies of man, tyranny, poverty, disease and war itself.

Can we forge against these enemies a grand and global alliance, North and South, East and West, that can assure a more fruitful life for all mankind? Will you join in that historic effort?

In the long history of the world, only a few generations have been granted the role of defending freedom in its hour of maximum danger. I do not shrink from this responsibility, I welcome it. I do not believe that any of us would exchange places with any other people or any other generation. The energy, the faith, the devotion which we bring to this endeavor will light our country and all who serve it and the glow from that fire can truly light the world.

And so, my fellow Americans, ask not what your country can do for you, ask what you can do for your country. My fellow citizens of the world, ask not what America will do for you, but what together we can do for the freedom of man.

Finally, whether you are citizens of America or citizens of the world, ask of us here the same high standards of strength and sacrifice which we ask of you. With a good conscience our only sure reward, with history the final judge of our deeds, let us go forth to lead the land we love, asking His blessing and His help, but knowing that here on earth, God's work must truly be our own. ♪

Kennedy was young, bright and a cultural icon of the 1960s. On 23 November 1963, while campaigning in Dallas, Texas, for a second term in the White House, John Kennedy was cut down by an assassin's bullet as he rode in a motorcade with wife Jackie, Texan Governor John Connally and Vice President Lyndon Johnson. He had been in office for just 1036 days.

Harold Holt

'All the Way with LBJ'

Washington DC, 29 June 1966

Harold Edward Holt (1908–67) succeeded the longest serving Australian Prime Minister, Sir Robert Menzies, in January 1966. Holt, grey-haired, hard-working and personally charming, faced the difficult task of leading the Liberal Party into that year's election after 17 years in government. The 1960s was also a period of social, cultural and political upheaval and Australia's involvement in the Vietnam War was threatening to derail Holt's tenure as Prime Minister from the very beginning.

Australian personnel had been involved in Vietnam as early as 1962, but by November 1964, following America's escalating involvement in the conflict, Prime Minister Robert Menzies had introduced the National Service Scheme (NSS)—the balloted conscription of eligible 20-year-old males.

In April 1965, the 1st Battalion of the Royal Australian Regiment was dispatched to Vietnam. A year later, Harold Holt announced the dispatch of a taskforce consisting of two battalions and support services to replace the 1st RAR which was based in Nui Dat, Phouc Tuy province. The taskforce included conscripts who had been called up under the NSS in 1964.

In June 1966, Harold Holt and his wife Zara visited Washington DC to discuss Australia's increasing commitment to the war in Vietnam and were warmly greeted by US President Lyndon Johnson and his wife. The President spoke at 12.25 pm on the South Lawn of the White House, where Prime Minister Harold Holt was welcomed with full military honours. The Prime Minister, whose trip to the United States was described as a working visit, responded to the President's welcome with one of the most famous slogans of the 1960s.

'Mr President and Mrs Johnson:

Thank you for your warm welcome, Mr President. You have said warm and generous things about Australia and its people.

What a memorable morning for the Australian people and for an Australian Prime Minister. I thank you for the honor which, by this ceremonial, you have accorded to my country and you have accorded to me. What has been done will be appreciated deeply by my people as it is by myself as head of my government.

We meet, Mr President, as heads of government while our two nations are again comrades in arms. This is at least the fourth time in this century that Americans and Australians have combined together with other friendly forces to resist aggression.

We fought alongside each other in two World Wars and then Australia was the first country, I believe, to announce itself beside you when America made the historic decision to bring its strength to the aid of South Korea.

I say historic decision advisedly, because I believe that to have been, Mr President, one of the turning points in human history. I believe at that critical point of time was decided the issue of whether we handed Asia over to penetrating, aggressive Communism, or whether we kept intact a large part of Asia as member countries of the company of free people throughout the world.

Australia was with you when you made the decision, critical also to you and to us, in South Vietnam, another battleground against Communist aggression.

You have spoken of the taskforce of Australians which is now assembled in Saigon. You will be aware, Mr President, that in other parts of Southeast Asia, Australia is making a military contribution, small by the standards of your own great country, but useful in the company in which we find ourselves there.

I know that this taskforce in South Vietnam will acquit itself with distinction. The men that are serving there are men of quality. They are well-trained. The 1st Battalion was accorded the highest commendation by your own leaders and by the leaders of South Vietnam. The taskforce which follows them will acquit themselves with no less courage and distinction.

'This is at least the fourth time in this century that Americans and Australians have combined together with other friendly forces to resist aggression.'

The outcome of this struggle is critical for the hopes that you and we share for a better and more secure way of life for the free people of Asia.

You have spoken of the vital free Asia that is emerging. I can speak of this from some personal experience, because not merely do we have a view from "Down Under" which is perhaps a different perspective from that of others in different parts of the world, but it has been my own good fortune in recent times to have travelled over several of these countries of Southeast Asia.

What has occurred over recent years is a transformation. To go through Thailand, Malaysia, and even South Vietnam itself, and see the massive support being rendered there, see the security, the progress which has been found possible by these other countries where Communism has successfully been held in check—to see these things is to give heartening encouragement to go on with the job of resisting aggression where we find it.

But it does not take a war to bring Americans and Australians close together. We like each other. Friendships form quickly between us. We have many mutually beneficial links: Our trade with each other; the investment that you make with us with your capital. We cooperate in many constructive international interests and causes.

You mentioned, Mr President, your time in Australia 25 years ago. A new Australia has arisen since then. When can we see you there again? And this time we hope with Mrs Johnson, and perhaps the whole family.

You will be encouraged to see the national growth in which many American skills and resources have assisted.

Mr. President, we recognize all too clearly in my own country that on you, personally, falls the heavy and at times lonely responsibility of free world leadership. On your country these burdens have been assumed in comparatively recent times in terms of modern history. But America has shouldered those burdens firmly, and you have inspired and encouraged us all by the strength of your own resolution.

You know that in Australia you have an understanding friend. I am here, sir, not asking for anything—an experience which I am sure you value at times when it is not so frequent as it might be.

You have in us not merely an understanding friend, but one staunch in the belief of the need for our presence with you in Vietnam. We are not there because of our friendship; we are there because, like you, we believe it is right to be there, and, like you, we shall stay there as long as seems necessary in order to achieve the purposes of the South Vietnamese Government and the purposes that we join in formulating and progressing together.

And so, sir, in the lonelier and perhaps even more disheartening moments which come to any national leader, I hope there will be a corner of your mind and heart which takes cheer from the fact that you have an admiring friend, a staunch friend that will be "all the way with LBJ."

'All the Way with LBJ' was Johnson's campaign slogan in the 1964 Presidential election, but coming from Holt's lips to the ears of the Australian public it took on a new resonance. While to many it meant that Australia's fortunes in Vietnam would be forever tied to America's ability to win the war, there is no doubt that the comment was an expression of what Zara Holt termed her husband's 'most spectacular friendship' with the US President.

President Johnson made good on Holt's invitation to visit Australia and became the first US President to visit 'Down Under' when he arrived in Sydney in October 1966. Faced by anti-Vietnam War protesters lying in the streets, NSW Premier Robert Askin, who was travelling with President Johnson, famously told his driver to 'run the bastards over!'

Harold Holt's government was returned to power in the November 1966 election which, despite the burgeoning anti-war movement, was seen as a vindication of the Australian-American alliance in Vietnam.

A year later, while snorkelling on the unpatrolled Cheviot Beach in Victoria, Harold Holt disappeared in treacherous surfing conditions. His body was never found. President Lyndon Johnson came to Australia a third and final time for the memorial service for his friend Harold Holt on 22 December 1967.

Lyndon B. Johnson

'I Shall Not Seek, Nor Will I Accept, the Nomination'

Washington DC, 31 March 1968

Lyndon Baines Johnson (1908–73) was a Democratic Representative for ten years before being elected to the US Senate in 1948. The Senate majority leader when he became the unlikely choice as John Kennedy's running mate in the 1960 Presidential election, Johnson was a restless Vice President to the handsome, articulate JFK. On Friday, 22 November 1963, President Kennedy was killed by an assassin's bullet as he rode in a motorcade through Dallas, Texas. Vice President Lyndon Johnson took the oath of office aboard Air Force One at 2.38 pm in the presence of his wife, Lady Bird, and Kennedy's widow, Jackie, with the body of the slain president on board.

Johnson was elected President in his own right in 1964, but any gains he made on civil rights issues during his first full term in office (1965–69) were brought undone by the escalation of the Vietnam War. In July 1965, Johnson committed a further 100,000 troops to the conflict but buried the announcement in a non-televised statement concerning Supreme Court appointments. The following year he sent another 120,000 troops to Vietnam but concealed the actual number by announcing 10,000-strong troop deployments each month for the next 12 months.

In January 1968, as American forces in the Vietnam War neared their peak of 535,000, North Vietnamese troops attacked 36 provincial capitals and five major cities in South Vietnam. Included was an attack on the US embassy in Saigon and the presidential palace. Known as the Tet'Offensive (because it was the Vietnamese New Year holiday), the attack reinforcedthe North Vietnamese determination to win the civil war. Just as importantly, uncensored news coverage shown on nightly news programs and in American newspapers reinforced the growing perception that this was not a winnable war.

Congressional opposition, media scrutiny and domestic unrest—especially among young students—brought President Lyndon Johnson to make the gravest of decisions. With the mounting death toll and the continuing erosion of popular and political support for the war, President Johnson gave a long televised speech concerning the situation in Vietnam. He then stunned the world at the end of the speech with a surprise announcement.

‘Good evening, my fellow Americans:

Tonight I want to speak to you of peace in Vietnam and Southeast Asia.

No other question so preoccupies our people. No other dream so absorbs the 250 million human beings who live in that part of the world. No other goal motivates American policy in Southeast Asia ...

One day, my fellow citizens, there will be peace in Southeast Asia.

It will come because the people of Southeast Asia want it—those whose armies are at war tonight, and those who, though threatened, have thus far been spared.

Peace will come because Asians were willing to work for it, to sacrifice for it and to die by the thousands for it.

But let it never be forgotten, peace will come also because America sent her sons to help secure it.

It has not been easy—far from it. During the past four and a half years, it has been my fate and my responsibility to be Commander in Chief. I have lived—daily and nightly—with the cost of this war. I know the pain that it has inflicted. I know, perhaps better than anyone, the misgivings that it has aroused.

Throughout this entire, long period, I have been sustained by a single principle: That what we are doing now, in Vietnam, is vital not only to the security of Southeast Asia, but it is vital to the security of every American.

Surely we have treaties which we must respect. Surely we have commitments that we are going to keep. Resolutions of the Congress testify to the need to resist aggression in the world and in Southeast Asia.

But the heart of our involvement in South Vietnam—under three different presidents, three separate administrations—has always been America's own security.

The larger purpose of our involvement has always been to help the nations of Southeast Asia become independent and stand alone, self-sustaining, as members of a great world community, at peace with themselves, and at peace with all others.

With such an Asia, our country, and the world, will be far more secure than it is tonight.

I believe that a peaceful Asia is far nearer to reality because of what America has done in Vietnam. I believe that the men who endure the dangers of battle— fighting there for us tonight—are helping the entire world avoid far greater conflicts, far wider wars, far more destruction, than this one.

The peace that will bring them home some day will come. Tonight I have offered the first in what I hope will be a series of mutual moves toward peace.

I pray that it will not be rejected by the leaders of North Vietnam. I pray that they will accept it as a means by which the sacrifices of their own people may be ended. And I ask your help and your support, my fellow citizens, for this effort to reach across the battlefield toward an early peace.

Finally, my fellow Americans, let me say this:

Of those to whom much is given, much is asked. I cannot say, and no man could say, that no more will be asked of us.

Yet I believe that now, no less than when the decade began, this generation of Americans is willing to "pay any price, bear any burden, meet any hardship, support any friend, oppose any foe to assure the survival and the success of liberty."

Since those words were spoken by John F. Kennedy, the people of America have kept that compact with mankind's noblest cause.

And we shall continue to keep it.

Yet I believe that we must always be mindful of this one thing, whatever the trials and the tests ahead. The ultimate strength of our country and our cause will lie not in powerful weapons or infinite resources or boundless wealth, but will lie in the unity of our people.

This I believe very deeply.

Throughout my entire public career I have followed the personal philosophy that I am a free man, an American, a public servant and a member of my party, in that order always and only.

For 37 years in the service of our nation, first as a Congressman, as a Senator, and as Vice President, and now as your President, I have put the unity of the people first. I have put it ahead of any divisive partisanship.

And in these times, as in times before, it is true that a house divided against itself by the spirit of faction, of party, of region, of religion, of race, is a house that cannot stand.

There is division in the American house now. There is divisiveness among us all tonight. And holding the trust that is mine, as President of all the people, I cannot disregard the peril to the progress of the American people and the hope and the prospect of peace for all peoples.

So I would ask all Americans, whatever their personal interests or concerns, to guard against divisiveness and all its ugly consequences.

Fifty-two months and 10 days ago, in a moment of tragedy and trauma, the duties of this office fell upon me. I asked then for your help and God's, that we might continue America on its course, binding up our wounds, healing our history, moving forward in new unity, to clear the American agenda and to keep the American commitment for all of our people.

United we have kept that commitment. United we have enlarged that commitment.

Through all time to come, I think America will be a stronger nation, a more just society, and a land of greater opportunity and fulfilment because of what we have all done together in these years of unparalleled achievement.

Our reward will come in the life of freedom, peace and hope that our children will enjoy through ages ahead.

What we won when all of our people united must not now be lost in suspicion, distrust, selfishness and politics among any of our people.

Believing this as I do, I have concluded that I should not permit the Presidency to become involved in the partisan divisions that are developing in this political year.

With America's sons in the fields far away, with America's future under challenge right here at home, with our hopes and the world's hopes for peace in the balance every day, I do not believe that I should devote an hour or a day of my time to any personal partisan causes or to any duties other than the awesome duties of this office—the Presidency of your country.

Accordingly, I shall not seek, and I will not accept, the nomination of my party for another term as your President.

But let men everywhere know, however, that a strong, a confident and a vigilant America stands ready tonight to seek an honorable peace—and stands ready tonight to defend an honored cause—whatever the price, whatever the burden, whatever the sacrifice that duty may require.

Thank you for listening.
Good night and God bless all of you.

Lyndon Johnson was so unpopular when he made this speech that he would not seek re-election in the 1968 presidental race, he really had no other option. Winning the Vietnam War meant a further escalation of troops. There was no way to seek an honourable peace with an enemy that held the upper hand. Johnson will always be remembered for the commitment with which he used government force to solve domestic civil rights issues, but his legacy with many Americans is that of being the only US President to 'lose' a war—if not on the battle field, certainly in the court of popular opinion—during his term in office. He died in 1973, aged just 64, from heart disease brought on by years of heavy smoking and stress.

Robert Kennedy

'California Primary Victory Speech'

Ambassador Hotel, Los Angeles, California, 4 June 1968

In March 1968, five years after his brother John was slain in Dallas, Texas, former Attorney General and New York Senator Robert Francis Kennedy (1925–68) announced to a disheartened American public that he would run for the US Presidency. When incumbent President Lyndon Johnson announced later that month that he would not accept the nomination of his Party—his Presidency ruined by the Vietnam War and internal social unrest—Kennedy still faced a huge task to defeat Vice-President Hubert Humphrey and Senator Eugene McCarthy to be the Democratic nominee for the 1968 Presidential election. Kennedy's radical policies of social and economic justice, his opposition to the Vietnam War and, most importantly, the hope that he would fulfil his brother's political legacy, saw his campaign gain widespread support.

By the time he arrived in California in June, Kennedy had won the Indiana and Nebraska primaries but had lost in Oregon. He needed to win California to knock Senator McCarthy out of the race, while a win in South Dakota, which was held on the same day as the California primary, would go a long way to bridging the gap with front-runner Hubert Humphrey (Humphrey was born in South Dakota). Kennedy won in both California and South Dakota, setting up a showdown with Humphrey in the National Convention in Chicago where the Democratic Party delegates would choose their nominee.

Just before midnight on 4 June 1968, Bobby Kennedy took to the podium at the ballroom of the Ambassador Hotel, his Californian headquarters, and gave a short victory speech. The room was full of cheering Kennedy supporters, staff, workers and volunteers, and the Presidential candidate had to wait several minutes before he could start his speech. Kennedy thanked numerous people—his campaign managers and staff; his wife and family (including his dog Freckles); various labour leaders including Mexican-American civil rights leader César Chávez; African-American sports stars, Rafer Johnson and Rosie Greer, who had joined his campaign; and Dodgers baseballer Don Drysdale, who pitched his sixth straight shut-out that night. 'I hope that we have as good fortune in our campaign,' Kennedy said.

He then began what would become his final speech.

‘I think we can end the divisions within the United States. What I think is quite clear is that we can work together in the last analysis. And that what has been going on with the United States over the period of the last three years, the divisions, the violence, the disenchantment with our society, the divisions—whether it's between blacks and whites, between the poor and the more affluent, or between age groups, or in the war in Vietnam—that we can start to work together. We are a great country, an unselfish country and a compassionate country. And I intend to make that my basis for running in the period over the next few months.

Ladies and gentlemen, if I can take a moment of your time, because everyone must be dying from the heat... but what I think all of the primaries have indicated and all the party caucuses have indicated, whether they occurred in Colorado or Idaho or Iowa—wherever they occurred—it was that the people in the Democratic party and the people in the United States wanted change... and that change can come about only if those who are delegates in Chicago recognise the importance of what has happened here in California, what has happened in South Dakota, what happened in New Hampshire, what happened across the rest of the country.

The country wants to move in a different direction—we want to deal with our own problems in our own country—and we want peace in Vietnam.

I congratulate Senator McCarthy and those who have been associated with him on the efforts they have started in New Hampshire and carried through to the primary here in the State of California. The fact is, all of us involved in the great effort and it is a great effort, not on behalf of the Democratic Party, it's a great effort on behalf of the United States, on behalf of our own people, on behalf of mankind, all the people around the globe and the next generation of Americans.

And I would hope now that the California primary is finished, now that the primary is over, that we can now concentrate on having a dialogue, or a debate, I hope, between the Vice President and perhaps myself, on what direction we want to go in the United States… what we are going to do in the rural areas of our country, what we are going to do for those who still suffer within the United States from hunger, what we are going to do around the rest of the globe and whether we are going to continue the policies that have been so unsuccessful in Vietnam…of American troops and American marines carrying the major burden of that conflict. I do not want to and I think we can move in a different direction. ♪

Bobby Kennedy then thanked his campaign workers, saying that he had been a campaign manager eight years ago—a reference to his brother's 1960 election win—and made a joke that Los Angeles Mayor Samuel Yorty had complained that they 'had been here too long already…' His final public utterance was: 'Thanks to all of you and now it's on to Chicago and let's win there…'

Kennedy then headed to a press conference in another part of the hotel, but against the advice of his bodyguards took a short cut through the kitchen to shake the hands of hotel workers. At 12.23 am, just two and a half minutes after he left the ballroom with the crowd still chanting his name, Kennedy was shot twice by Jordanian immigrant, Sirhan Bishara Sirhan. Kennedy was hit in the armpit and behind the right ear, as his supporters wrestled the gunman to the ground. Five other bystanders were wounded as Sirhan emptied the eight bullets in his gun. The 24-year-old migrant was allegedly upset by Kennedy's support of Israel in the Six Day War the previous year.

Kennedy was rushed to the Good Samaritan Hospital where he underwent a three hour and forty minute operation to remove a bullet from his brain. The following day, some 25 hours after being shot, surrounded by family and friends, he passed away. A week later, Kennedy's body was interred at Arlington War Cemetery in a night-time ceremony (as with his brother John, Bobby had served in the navy in World War II).

While it is unsure whether Kennedy would have defeated Humphrey for the 1968 ticket—the Vice President was almost assured that he had the required number of votes to gain the nomination before he went to Chicago—the United States, and the world, had lost one of its brightest lights. Considering the victory by Republican candidate Richard Nixon later that year, the escalation of the Vietnam War and the Watergate scandal in 1972, one can only wonder what the world would be like today if Bobby Kennedy had lived.

Queen Elizabeth II

'The Opening of the New Parliament House'

Canberra, Australia, 9 May 1988

The year 1988 marked the 200th anniversary of the foundation of Australia. On 28 January 1788 a British colony comprising soldiers, free settlers and convict labour stepped ashore at Port Jackson and raised the Union Jack. The colony at Sydney Cove in New South Wales, as Britain named the eastern side of the 'uninhabited' continent, was foremost a penal settlement—statehood and the establishment of a nation called Australia would come much later. Australia was part of the British Empire—as it remains to this day— and the Head of State of the new Parliament is still the Queen.

Following the Federation of the Commonwealth of Australia in 1901, the national capital of Canberra, situated roughly halfway between rival cities Sydney and Melbourne, was established. The then Duke of York, later King George V, opened the first sitting of Parliament in Melbourne (a compromise by Sydney) on 9 May 1901. It was not until 9 May 1927, however, that his son, who later became King George VI upon the abdication of King Edward VIII in 1936, opened Parliament House in Canberra.

The original austere white building was only a provisional home for both Houses of Parliament. It was another 61 years—to the day— before Queen Elizabeth II followed in the footsteps of her father and grandfather and opened the new Parliament House of the Commonwealth of Australia.

'In this bicentenary year, Australians are looking back over the events of the last two hundred years. This is well worth while because the events link together to tell a story of remarkable achievement.

'I am sure that they had every hope that the new federal constitution would be a success...'

Of course, we do not know what was going through the mind of Captain Phillip when he stepped ashore at Sydney Cove, but I am sure he could never have imagined such an event as this, or the scene before us today.

I also rather doubt that the founding fathers of the Australian Federation could have foreseen that their work would be crowned by such a confident expression of Australia's faith in parliamentary democracy.

I am sure that they had every hope that the new federal constitution would be a success, but neither they, nor anyone else, could have predicted that no less than three important national parliamentary occasions would fall on the same day of the year and involve three generations of my family.

It was also on this same day in 1927 that the provisional Parliament House was opened here in the new capital of Canberra by my father. So, in the bicentennial year of the arrival of the First Fleet, and in the seventy-fifth anniversary year of the foundation of Canberra, there can surely be no more appropriate day for the opening of this magnificent new home for the Commonwealth Parliament.

The completion of this splendid building has put the finishing touch to Walter Burley Griffin's grand design chosen by the Australian Government seventy-six years ago. It is as if all the other buildings of the great national institutions had been waiting for his, the greatest of them all, to take its rightful place as their centre and focus.

This is a special occasion for the Parliament, but it is also a very important day for all the people of Australia. After eighty-seven years of Federation, a permanent home has been provided for Parliament, which is both the living expression of that Federation and the embodiment of the democratic principles of freedom, equality and justice.

Parliamentary democracy is a compelling ideal, but it is a fragile institution. It cannot be imposed and it is only too easily destroyed. It needs the positive dedication of the people as a whole and of their elected representatives, to make it work.

The earliest free settlers brought their ideals of a democratic society with them, and succeeding generations of Australians have inherited those principles

> *'Commitment to parliamentary democracy lies at the heart of this nation's maturity, tolerance and humanity.'*

and put them to work in what we know as the parliamentary system.

Commitment to parliamentary democracy lies at the heart of this nation's maturity, tolerance and humanity. This is surely one of the characteristics that has attracted so many people to come to Australia from countries which do not enjoy the benefits of the parliamentary system in such large measure.

This new Parliament House will become the work place for the men and women into whose hands Australians choose to place legislative and executive responsibility. The chambers will become the centres for debate on all the pressing issues of government and future generations of Australians will look to those who work here for national security, wise legislation and fair administration.

I am sure that many members will feel a pang of regret as they leave the old and familiar Parliament House. I have many happy recollections of events in the simple elegance of its hall and chambers, but it has been obvious for years that a larger building with more modern facilities was needed.

It was equally obvious that it would never be easy to make the decision to build a new House. I can only say that I am deeply impressed by the speed and skill with which this site has been transformed into such an impressive and functional home for the national Parliament.

I had the opportunity to visit the site at an early stage in the construction and I am delighted to be here today to see it complete. I offer my warmest congratulations to the architects, to the members of the Parliament House Construction Authority, to the contractors and sub-contractors and to the artists and crafts people whose creative talents enrich the interior and, particularly, to Michael Tjakamarra Nelson, whose mosaic is in the forecourt.

Together they have given the whole complex a distinctive Australian character. More than ten thousand men and women can take great pride in the parts they have played in the creation of this symbol of Australian unity and democracy.

The laws of the Commonwealth of Australia are enacted in the name of the Queen and the two Houses of Parliament. It is fitting, therefore, and a great pleasure for me, to offer my best wishes to all those who will be giving their service to the nation within these walls, and to declare open the new Parliament House of the Commonwealth of Australia. ♪

In the 1990s, under the leadership of Paul Keating's Labor Government (1991–96), the ideal of an Australian Republic—effectively replacing Queen Elizabeth II as Head of State—gathered momentum. Prime Minister Keating established the Republic Advisory Committee to investigate a number of different options that would lead Australia to becoming a republic by 1 January 2001; the Centenary of Australian Federation. The preferred option was the replacement of the Queen's nominee, the Governor General, with a 'President nominated' by the Prime Minister and appointed by a two-thirds majority of both House of Parliament. Keating's government was voted out of office, however, before these changes could be put to the Australian people.

Liberal Prime Minister John Howard (1996–2007) held a 'Constitutional Convention' in Canberra in February 1998 where 152 delegates debated the issues and drafted a referendum that would be voted on by the Australian people. The number of staunch monarchists appointed as delegates by the Liberal federal government was seen to contribute to its failure but so did the rival 'models' of Presidential election.

The question put forward at the referendum on 6 November 1999—whether Australia should become a republic with a President appointed by Parliament—was an unsatisfactory compromise that effectively shut the Australian public out of the election process. It was rejected by a 55–45% majority, ensuring that Queen Elizabeth II remained as Head of State of the Commomwealth of Australia.

It's interesting to note that her speech on this day contained only a hint of Australian self-determination or the republican issue.

F.W. de Klerk

'Nelson Mandela Released'

Johannesburg, South Africa, 10 February 1990

Frederik Willem de Klerk (b. 1936) succeeded South African President P.W. Botha, in September 1989, and almost immediately entered into negotiations with minor political parties regarding the dismantling of the black and white segregation system of apartheid. International sanctions in protest to the country's inequity and oppression of its majority black population had cost the country $4 billion between 1988 and 1990.

Enforcing the apartheid goal of congregating blacks into separate homelands had proved impossible to maintain and the social and political alienation of its native population had made the minority white South African government an international pariah. Having articulated a peaceful solution to the problem of power sharing at the opening of Parliament on 2 February 1990, F.W. de Klerk lifted the ban on the outlawed African National Congress (ANC), the Pan African Congress and the South African Communist Party. He also made his first public commitment to release ANC leader Nelson Mandela from prison.

The day after this press conference on 10 February 1990, 71-year-old Nelson Mandela, the symbolic focus of an international protest movement, was released after 27 years in prison.

‘In pursuance of my opening address to Parliament, I am now in a position to announce that Mr Nelson Mandela will be released at the Victor Verster Prison on Sunday, February 11, 1990, at about 3 o'clock.

Yesterday evening I met with Mr. Mandela in Cape Town together with ministers Gerrit Viljoen and Kobie Coetsee. During the meeting, Mr Mandela was informed of the Government's decision regarding his release.

We would all like Mr Mandela's release to take place in a dignified and orderly manner. To attain this, government officials are at the moment involved in discussions with parties concerned in order to afford them the opportunity to make suitable arrangements.

'We would all like Mr Mandela's release to take place in a dignified and orderly manner.'

Two issues were also raised during the discussions between me and Mr. Mandela, namely the state of emergency and the position of persons serving sentences for politically motivated crimes, as well as those who have committed such crimes and who are now outside the country.

I stressed the importance of creating conditions which would enable me to lift the state of emergency without jeopardizing the maintenance of law and order. Regarding the position of persons involved in politically motivated crimes, I indicated that while this is a matter that should be dealt with in negotiations, exploratory discussions could take place in the meantime.

I want to emphasize that there can no longer be any doubt about the Government's sincerity to create a just dispensation based on negotiations. I call upon Mr Mandela and all other interested parties to make their contribution toward a positive climate for negotiations.

The eyes of the world are presently focused on all South Africans. All of us now have an opportunity and the responsibility to prove that we are capable of a peaceful process in creating a new South Africa.

Ladies and gentlemen, this announcement and tomorrow will bring us to the end of a long chapter. What I've announced today was started by my predecessor a number of years ago. Since the moment that Mr Mandela met him at Townhouse and, since the moment that in that discussion Mr. Mandela clearly stated his commitment, also, to peaceful solutions, it has become a certainty that he would be released.

Also in my two discussions with him, late last year and last evening, I came to the conclusion that he is committed to a peaceful solution and a peaceful process. The Government is committed to negotiation. The Government is committed to bringing about, through negotiation, a new constitution which is fair and just to all the people of South Africa.

'The eyes of the world are presently focused on all South Africans. All of us now have an opportunity and the responsibility to prove that we are capable of a peaceful process in creating a new South Africa.'

I hope that now that this chapter is ended, the world and more especially all the people of South Africa will grasp the opportunity and play whatever supportive role can be played toward a peaceful conclusion of the process which has started. ♪

In answering questions from the press after his speech, de Klerk stated that his government had a mandate from the minority white population after its 1987 election victory to 'grant full class-A citizenships to all South Africans irrespective of race or colour'.

De Klerk remarked: 'We are doing what we sincerely believe to be in the best interests of South Africa' and confirmed that the discussions with Nelson Mandela 'took place in good spirits'. He said: 'He's an elderly man. He's a dignified man. And he's an interesting man... '

But the state of emergency would remain in force. There was still a long way to go before democratic elections could be held.

Nelson Mandela led the ANC in its negotiations with other minority black parties and the white South African government to bring an end to apartheid and to finally establish a multiracial government.

In September 1992, Mandela and de Klerk signed the 'Record of Understanding' which promised to formally investigate the role of the police in propagating violence between ethnic groups and to establish an elected constitutional assembly to develop a new South African constitution. In 1993, Mandela and de Klerk shared the Nobel Peace Prize for their peaceful efforts to bring non-racial democracy to South Africa.

Black South Africans voted for the first time in the 1994 election and the ANC won 252 of the 400 seats in the country's first free elections, with Nelson Mandela elected president of South Africa's first multiracial government. F.W. de Klerk, a man of courage and conviction, was named Nelson Mandela's Deputy alongside Thabo Mbeki.

Mandela retired in 1999 and was succeeded by Thabo Mbeki.

Barack Obama

'Presidential Election Victory Speech'

Manassas, Virginia November 3, 2008

More than forty-five years after Rev. Martin Luther King Jnr. told the world, 'I have a dream ...' Democratic nominee Barack Obama stood before a crowd of more than 100,000 supporters at the Prince William County Fairgrounds in Manassas, Virginia, and acknowledged his victory in the 2008 US Presidential race. He had easily defeated the Republican candidate, Vietnam veteran John McCain. Obama's win was historic in that he had become the first African American to garner his country's top office but that night, before a worldwide television audience, the President-elect also showed he had that rare ability to seize the moment and unite the American people with his own dream for the future.

'If there is anyone out there who still doubts that America is a place where all things are possible; who still wonders if the dream of our founders is alive in our time; who still questions the power of our democracy, tonight is your answer. It's the answer told by lines that stretched around schools and churches in numbers this nation has never seen; by people who waited three hours and four hours, many for the very first time in their lives, because they believed that this time must be different; that their voice could be that difference. It's the answer spoken by young and old, rich and poor, Democrat and Republican, black, white, Latino, Asian, Native American, gay, straight, disabled and not disabled ... Americans who sent a message to the world that we have never been a collection of Red States and Blue States: we are, and always will be, the United States of America. It's the answer that led those who have been told for so long by so many to be cynical, and fearful, and doubtful of what we can achieve to put their hands on the arc of history and bend it once more toward the hope of a better day.

It's been a long time coming, but tonight, because of what we did on this day, in this election, at this defining moment, change has come to America.

I just received a very gracious call from Senator McCain. He fought long and hard in this campaign, and he's fought even longer and harder for the country he loves. He has endured sacrifices for America that most of us cannot begin to imagine, and we are better off for the service rendered by this brave and selfless leader. I congratulate him and Governor Palin for all they have achieved, and I look forward to working with them to renew this nation's promise in the months ahead.

I want to thank my partner in this journey, a man who campaigned from his heart and spoke for the men and women he grew up with on the streets of Scranton and rode with on that train home to Delaware, the Vice President-elect of the United States, Joe Biden.

I would not be standing here tonight without the unyielding support of my best friend for the last sixteen years, the rock of our family and the love of my life, our nation's next First Lady, Michelle Obama. Sasha and Malia, I love you both so much, and you have earned the new puppy that's coming with us to the White House. And while she's no longer with us, I know my grandmother is watching, along with the family that made me who I am. I miss them tonight, and know that my debt to them is beyond measure.

To my campaign manager David Plouffe, my chief strategist David Axelrod, and the best campaign team ever assembled in the history of politics ... you made this happen, and I am forever grateful for what you've sacrificed to get it done.

But above all, I will never forget who this victory truly belongs to ... it belongs to you.

I was never the likeliest candidate for this office. We didn't start with much money or many endorsements. Our campaign was not hatched in the halls of Washington ... it began in the backyards of Des Moines and the living rooms of Concord and the front porches of Charleston.

It was built by working men and women who dug into what little savings they had to give five dollars and ten dollars and twenty dollars to this cause. It grew strength from the young people who rejected the myth of their generation's apathy; who left their homes and their families for jobs that offered little pay and less sleep; from the not-so-young people who braved the bitter cold and scorching heat to knock on the doors of perfect strangers; from the millions of Americans who volunteered, and organized, and proved that more than two centuries later, a government of the people, by the people and for the people has not perished from this Earth. This is your victory.

I know you didn't do this just to win an election and I know you didn't do it for me. You did it because you understand the enormity of the task that lies ahead. For even as we celebrate tonight, we know the challenges that tomorrow will bring are the greatest of our lifetime ... two wars, a planet in peril, the worst financial crisis in a century. Even as we stand here tonight, we know there are brave Americans waking up in the deserts of Iraq and the mountains of Afghanistan to risk their lives for us. There are mothers and fathers who will lie awake after their children fall asleep and wonder how they'll make the mortgage, or pay their doctor's bills, or save enough for college. There is new energy to harness and new jobs to be created; new schools to build and threats to meet and alliances to repair.

The road ahead will be long. Our climb will be steep. We may not get there in one year or even one term, but America ... I have never been more hopeful than I am tonight that we will get there. I promise you ... we as a people will get there.

There will be setbacks and false starts. There are many who won't agree with every decision or policy I make as President, and we know that government can't solve every problem. But I will always be honest with you about the challenges we face. I will listen to you, especially when we disagree. And above all, I will ask you join in the work of remaking this nation the only way it's been done in America for two-hundred and twenty-one years ... block by block, brick by brick, calloused hand by calloused hand.

What began twenty-one months ago in the depths of winter must not end on this autumn night. This victory alone is not the change we seek ... it is only the chance for us to make that change. And that cannot happen if we go back to the way things were. It cannot happen without you.

So let us summon a new spirit of patriotism; of service and responsibility where each of us resolves to pitch in and work harder and look after not only ourselves, but each other. Let us remember that if this financial crisis taught us anything, it's that we cannot have a thriving Wall Street while Main Street suffers ... in this country, we rise or fall as one nation; as one people.

Let us resist the temptation to fall back on the same partisanship and pettiness and immaturity that has poisoned our politics for so long. Let us remember that it was a man from this state who first carried the banner of the Republican Party to the White House ... a party founded on the values of self-reliance, individual liberty, and national unity. Those are values we all share, and while the Democratic Party has won a great victory tonight, we do so with a measure of humility and determination to heal the divides that have held back our progress. As Lincoln said to a nation far more divided than ours, "We are not enemies, but friends ...though passion may have strained it must not break our bonds of affection." And to those Americans whose support I have yet to earn ... I may not have won your vote, but I hear your voices, I need your help, and I will be your President too.

.And to all those watching tonight from beyond our shores, from parliaments and palaces to those who are huddled around radios in the forgotten corners of our world ... our stories are singular, but our destiny is shared, and a new dawn of American leadership is at hand. To those who would tear this world down ... we will defeat you. To those who seek peace and security ... we support you. And to all those who have wondered if America's beacon still burns as bright ... tonight we proved once more that the true strength of our nation comes not from our the might of our arms or the scale of our wealth, but from the enduring power of our ideals: democracy, liberty, opportunity, and unyielding hope.

For that is the true genius of America ... that America can change. Our union can be perfected. And what we have already achieved gives us hope for what we can and must achieve tomorrow.

This election had many firsts and many stories that will be told for generations. But one that's on my mind tonight is about a woman who cast her ballot in Atlanta. She's a lot like the millions of others who stood in line to make their voice heard in this election except for one thing ... Ann Nixon Cooper is 106 years old.

She was born just a generation past slavery; a time when there were no cars on the road or planes in the sky; when someone like her couldn't vote for two reasons ... because she was a woman and because of the color of her skin.

And tonight, I think about all that she's seen throughout her century in America ... the heartache and the hope; the struggle and the progress; the times we were told that we can't, and the people who pressed on with that American creed: Yes we can.

At a time when women's voices were silenced and their hopes dismissed, she lived to see them stand up and speak out and reach for the ballot. Yes we can.

When there was despair in the dust bowl and depression across the land, she saw a nation conquer fear itself with a New Deal, new jobs and a new sense of common purpose. Yes we can.

When the bombs fell on our harbor and tyranny threatened the world, she was there to witness a generation rise to greatness and a democracy was saved. Yes we can.

She was there for the buses in Montgomery, the hoses in Birmingham, a bridge in Selma, and a preacher from Atlanta who told a people that "We Shall Overcome." Yes we can.

A man touched down on the moon, a wall came down in Berlin, a world was connected by our own science and imagination. And this year, in this election, she touched her finger to a screen, and cast her vote, because after 106 years in America, through the best of times and the darkest of hours, she knows how America can change. Yes we can.

America, we have come so far. We have seen so much. But there is so much more to do. So tonight, let us ask ourselves ... if our children should live to see the next century; if my daughters should be so lucky to live as long as Ann Nixon Cooper, what change will they see? What progress will we have made?

This is our chance to answer that call. This is our moment. This is our time ... to put our people back to work and open doors of opportunity for our kids; to restore prosperity and promote the cause of peace; to reclaim the American Dream and reaffirm that fundamental truth ... that out of many, we are one; that while we breathe, we hope, and where we are met with cynicism, and doubt, and those who tell us that we can't, we will respond with that timeless creed that sums up the spirit of a people:

Yes We Can. Thank you, God bless you, and may God Bless the United States of America. ♪

Barack Hussein Obama II, the son of a Kenyan father and Ann Dunham, a teenage anthropology student from Wichita Kansas, was born in Honolulu, Hawaii, in 1961. Obama's parents, who had met at the University of Hawaii, separated when Barack was just two years old and his mother later married an Indonesian national, Lolo Soetoro, and had another child (a daughter, Maya). Barack Obama went to school in Jakarta until the age of ten before returning to Honolulu to live with his maternal grandparents. His mother returned to Hawaii in 1977 when her second marriage ended but Barack only met his Kenyan father on one other occasion before Obama Senior was killed in a car accident in 1982. Obama's mother died of ovarian cancer in 1995, at the age of 53.

Barack Obama attended Columbia College in New York City, where he majored in political science, before going on to Harvard Law School. He later worked as a civil rights attorney in Chicago before being elected to the Illinois State Senate in 1996 (he emerged as the only candidate after legally challenging the validity of his four competitors.) Re-elected in 1998 (and again in 2002), he failed to secure the Democratic nomination for the US House of Representatives in 2000. In January 2003 Obama announced his intention to run for the US Senate and his national profile was boosted by his selection to deliver the keynote address to the Democratic National Convention in Boston in July 2004. Despite being a vocal opponent to President Bush's War in Iraq, Obama was elected to the US Senate in a landslide, garnering a staggering 70% of the vote. He was only the third African-American to be popularly elected to Congress.

A best-selling author (*'Dreams of My Father: A Story of Race and Inheritance'* in 1995 and *'The Audacity of Hope: Thoughts in Reclaiming the American Dream'* in 2006) Obama announced his candidacy for President of the United States on February 10, 2007. After a bitter and hard-fought battle against favourite Hillary Rodham Clinton, Obama secured the Democratic nomination in June 2008 and named Senator Joe Biden as his running mate. Having overcome issues of gender, religion and youth, Obama transcended the divisive issue of race and spoke out about the war in Iraq and the country's deepening economic crisis.

Civil Rights

Mark Twain

'Women's Suffrage'

Annual Meeting of the Hebrew Technical School for Girls, New York, 20 January 1901

Women's suffrage—the right to vote—was one of the most divisive issues at the end of the 19th century. The call for women's suffrage in the United States of America had begun from the first drafting of the Constitution (which contained the sentence 'all men are created equal'). While New Zealand was the first country to give women the vote, in 1898, closely followed by Australia (1902), Britain and the US—the two greatest democracies in the world—held out for some years.

It took famed American author and humorist Mark Twain (born Samuel Clemens, 1835–1910) to bring a common sense approach—and an old-world sense of humour—to the cause. Twain is rightly regarded as America's most successful author. His books, including The Adventures of Tom Sawyer (1876), The Adventures of Huckleberry Finn (1884) and A Connecticut Yankee in King Arthur's Court (1889) became classics in his own lifetime.

Financially ruined after a series of failed business speculations, Twain spent the last 16 years of his life travelling the world on the lucrative public speaking circuit in order to pay his debtors.

On 20 January 1901—just three weeks into the new century that held so much promise—Mark Twain addressed a public meeting at the Hebrew Technical School in New York. When the subject of women's suffrage was tabled by one of the other speakers at the venue, Mark Twain—the voice of America—took centre stage.

'Ladies and Gentlemen... It is a small help that I can afford, but it is just such help that one can give as coming from the heart through the mouth.

Referring to woman's sphere in life, I'll say that woman is always right. For twenty-five years I've been a woman's rights man. I have always believed, long before my mother died, that, with her grey hairs and admirable intellect, perhaps she knew as much as I did. Perhaps she knew as much about voting as I.

I should like to see the time come when women shall help to make the laws. I should like to see that whiplash, the ballot, in the hands of women. As for this city's government, I don't want to say much, except that it is a shame—a shame. But if I should live twenty-five years longer—and there is no reason why I shouldn't—I think I'll see women handle the ballot. If women had the ballot today, the state of things in this town would not exist.

If all the women in this town had a vote today, they would elect a mayor at the next election and they would rise in their might and change the awful state of things now existing here.

Mark Twain never did get his wish. He passed away in 1910 and the United States of America did not amend its constitution to grant women the fundamental right to vote until 1920. By that time, the world had been involved in the most disastrous war in the history of mankind—World War I (1914–18)—following which the Treaty of Versailles and the establishment of the League of Nations laid the foundations for World War II (1939–45).

One can only imagine the course history could have taken had women's suffrage been granted before the conscription of America's sons to the fields of France in 1917 and, as Mark Twain first suggested, women were put in charge of the government and changed 'the awful state of things'.

Mohandas K. Gandhi

'The Great Trial'

Ahmedabad, India, 18 April 1922

In 1914, lawyer and journalist Mohandas Karamchand Gandhi (1869–1948) became the dominant figure of the Indian National Congress movement for Home Rule—the complete withdrawal of English imperial interests from India. Gandhi was the son of the chief minister of the province of Poorbandar, West India, and his fourth wife. A deeply religious Hindu, Gandhi's policies of non-violent defiance of unfair laws had been developed during his time as a lawyer in South Africa at the turn of the century and had earned him international recognition.

At the height of India's civil disobedience campaign, however, nearly 400 people were massacred by British soldiers at Amritsar on 13 April 1919.

Gandhi was consequently arrested for conspiracy relating to the publication of three articles criticising 'the repressive measure adopted by the government to put down the struggle.' The historic trial of Mahatma Gandhi and Shri Shankarlal Ghelabhai (banker, editor, printer and publisher of the 'Young India' newspaper) on charges under Section 124A of the Indian Penal Code, began on 18 March 1922, in Ahmedabad.

The following month, Gandhi addressed the court and argued his case on the grounds of 'law versus conscience'.

'Before I read this statement, I would like to state that I entirely endorse the learned Advocate-General's remarks in connection with my humble self I think that he has made. Because it is very true and I have no desire whatsoever to conceal from this court the fact that to preach disaffection towards the existing system of government has become almost a passion with me, and the

Advocate-General is entirely in the right when he says that my preaching of disaffection did not commence with my connection with Young India but that it commenced much earlier.

In the statement that I am about to read, it will be my painful duty to admit before this court that it commenced much earlier than the period stated by the Advocate-General. It is a painful duty with me, but I have to discharge that duty knowing the responsibility that rests upon my shoulders.

I wish to endorse all the blame that the learned Advocate-General has thrown on my shoulders in connection with the Bombay occurrences, Madras occurrences and the Chauri Chuara occurrences. Thinking over these things deeply and sleeping over them night after night, it is impossible for me to dissociate myself from the diabolical crimes of Chauri Chaura or the mad outrages of Bombay. He is quite right when he says that, as a man of responsibility, a man having received a fair share of education, having had a fair share of experience of this world, I should have known the consequences of every one of my acts. I know them. I knew that I was playing with fire. I ran the risk and if I was set free I would still do the same. I have felt it this morning that I would have failed in my duty if I did not say what I said here just now.

I wanted to avoid violence. Non-violence is the first article of my faith. It is also the last article of my creed. But I had to make my choice. I had either to submit to a system which I considered had done an irreparable harm to my country, or incur the risk of the mad fury of my people bursting forth when they understood the truth from my lips. I know that my people have sometimes gone mad. I am deeply sorry for it and I am, therefore, here to submit not to a light penalty but to the highest penalty. I do not ask for mercy. I do not plead any extenuating act. I am here, therefore, to invite and cheerfully submit to the highest penalty that can be inflicted upon me for what, in law, is a deliberate crime and what appears to me to be the highest duty of a citizen. The only course open to you, the Judge, is, as I am going to say in my statement, either to resign your post, or inflict on me the severest penalty if you believe that the system and law you are assisting to administer are good for the people. I do not accept that kind of conversion. But by the time I have finished with my statement you will have a glimpse of what is raging within my breast to run this maddest risk which a sane man can run.

[Gandhi then read out the written statement:]

I owe it perhaps to the Indian public and to the public in England, to placate which this prosecution is mainly taken up, that I should explain why from a staunch loyalist and cooperator, I have become an uncompromising disaffectionist and non-cooperator. To the court too I should say why I plead guilty to the charge of promoting disaffection towards the Government established by law in India.

My public life began in 1893 in South Africa in troubled weather. My first contact with British authority in that country was not of a happy character.

I discovered that as a man and an Indian, I had no rights. More correctly, I discovered that I had no rights as a man because I was an Indian.

But I was not baffled. I thought that this treatment of Indians was an excrescence upon a system that was intrinsically and mainly good. I gave the Government my voluntary and hearty cooperation, criticizing it freely where I felt it was faulty, but never wishing its destruction.

Consequently, when the existence of the Empire was threatened in 1899 by the Boer challenge, I offered my services to it, raised a volunteer ambulance corps and served at several actions that took place for the relief of Ladysmith. Similarly in 1906, at the time of the Zulu revolt, I raised a stretcher bearer party and served till the end of the rebellion. On both occasions I received medals and was even mentioned in dispatches. For my work in South Africa, I was given by Lord Hardinge, a Kaisar-i-Hind gold medal.

When the war broke out in 1914 between England and Germany, I raised a volunteer ambulance corps in London, consisting of then resident Indians in London, chiefly students. Its work was acknowledged by the authorities to be valuable. Lastly, in India, when a special appeal was made at the War Conference in Delhi in 1918 by Lord Chelmsford for recruits, I struggled at the cost of my health to raise a corps in Kheda. The response was being made when the hostilities ceased and orders were received that no more recruits were wanted. In all these efforts at service, I was actuated by the belief that it was possible by such services to gain a status of full equality in the Empire for my countrymen.

The first shock came in the shape of the Rowlatt Act—a law designed to rob the people of all real freedom. I felt called upon to lead an intensive agitation against it. Then followed the Punjab horrors, beginning with the massacre at Jallianwala Bagh and culminating in crawling orders, public flogging and other indescribable humiliations. I discovered, too, that the plighted word of the Prime Minister to the Mussalmans of India regarding the integrity of Turkey and the holy places of Islam was not likely to be fulfilled. But in spite of the forebodings and the grave warnings of friends, at the Amritsar Congress in 1919, I fought for cooperation and the working of the Montagu-Chelmsford reforms, hoping that the Prime Minister would redeem his promise to the Indian Mussalmans, that the Punjab wound would be healed and that the reforms, inadequate and unsatisfactory though they were, marked a new era of hope in the life of India.

'I fought for cooperation and the working of the Montagu-Chelmsford reforms, hoping that the Prime Minister would redeem his promise to the Indian Mussalmans...'

But all that hope was shattered. The Khilafat promise was not to be redeemed. The Punjab crime was whitewashed and most culprits went not only unpunished but remained in service. Some continued to draw pensions from the Indian revenue and in some cases were even rewarded. I saw too that not only did the reforms not mark a change of heart, they were only a method of further draining India of her wealth and of prolonging her servitude.

I came reluctantly to the conclusion that the British connection had made India more helpless than she ever was before, politically and economically.

A disarmed India has no power of resistance against any aggressor if she wanted to engage in an armed conflict with him. So much is this the case that some of our best men consider that India must take generations before she can achieve Dominion status.

She has become so poor that she has little power of resisting famines. Before the British advent, India spun and wove in her millions of cottages, just the supplement she needed for adding to her meagre agricultural resources. This cottage industry, so vital for India's existence, has been ruined by incredibly heartless and inhuman processes as described by English witnesses.

Little do town dwellers know how the semi-starved masses of India are slowly sinking to lifelessness. Little do they know that their miserable comfort represents the brokerage they get for the work they do for the foreign exploiter, that the profits and the brokerage are sucked from the masses. Little do they realize that the Government established by law in British India is carried on for this exploitation of the masses.

No sophistry, no jugglery in figures, can explain away the evidence that the skeletons in many villages present to the naked eye. I have no doubt whatsoever that both England and the town dweller of India will have to answer, if there is a God above, for this crime against humanity, which is perhaps unequalled in history. The law itself in this country has been used to serve the foreign exploiter.

My unbiased examination of the Punjab Marital Law cases has led me to believe that at least ninety-five per cent of convictions were wholly bad. My experience of political cases in India leads me to the conclusion, in nine out of every ten, the condemned men were totally innocent. Their crime consisted in the love of their country. In ninety-nine cases out of a hundred, justice has been denied to Indians as against Europeans in the courts of India.

This is not an exaggerated picture. It is the experience of almost every Indian who has had anything to do with such cases. In my opinion, the administration of the law is thus prostituted, consciously or unconsciously, for the benefit of the exploiter.

The greater misfortune is that the Englishmen and their Indian associates in the administration of the country do not know that they are engaged in the crimes I have attempted to describe. I am satisfied that many Englishmen and Indian officials honestly believe that they are administering one of the best systems devised in the world and that India is making steady, though slow progress. They do not know that a subtle but effective system of terrorism and an organized display of force on the one hand, and the deprivation of all powers of retaliation or self-defense on the other, have emasculated the people and induced in them the habit of simulation. This awful habit has added to the ignorance and the self-deception of the administrators.

Section 124A, under which I am happily charged, is perhaps the prince among the political sections of the Indian Penal Code designed to suppress the liberty of the citizen. Affection cannot be manufactured or regulated by law. If one has no affection for a person or system, one should be free to give the fullest expression to his disaffection, so long as he does not contemplate, promote, or incite to violence.

But the section under which mere promotion of disaffection is a crime. I have studied some of the cases tried under it. I know that some of the most loved of India's patriots have been convicted under it. I consider it a privilege, therefore, to be charged under that section. I have endeavored to give in their briefest outline the reasons for my disaffection. I have no personal ill-will against any single administrator, much less can I have any disaffection towards the King's person. But I hold it to be a virtue to be disaffected towards a Government which in its totality has done more harm to India than any previous system. India is less manly under the British rule than she ever was before. Holding such a belief, I consider it to be a sin to have affection for the system. It has been a precious privilege for me to be able to write what I have in the various articles tendered in evidence against me.

In fact, I believe that I have rendered a service to India and England by showing in non-cooperation the way out of the unnatural state in which both are living. In my opinion, non-cooperation with evil is as much a duty as is cooperation with good. But in the past, non-cooperation has been deliberately expressed in violence to the evil-doer. I am endeavoring to show to my countrymen that violent non-cooperation only multiplies evil and that as evil can only be sustained by violence, withdrawal of support of evil requires complete abstention from violence.

Non-violence implies voluntary submission to the penalty for non-cooperation with evil. I am here, therefore, to invite and submit cheerfully to the highest penalty that can be inflicted upon me for what in law is a deliberate crime and what appears to me to be the highest duty of a citizen. The only course open to you, the Judge and the assessors, is either to resign your posts and thus dissociate yourselves from evil, if you feel that the law you are called upon to administer is an evil and that in reality I am innocent, or to inflict on me the severest penalty, if you believe that the system and the law you are assisting to administer are good for the people of this country and that my activity is, therefore, injurious to the Commonwealth.

Gandhi was found guilty of sedition and was sentenced to six years in prison. He served less than two years and was released in February 1924 to recover from an operation to remove his appendix.

On his release from jail, the Hindu and Muslim members of the National Congress refused to find common ground and warring between factions aligned to the two religious groups led to bloodshed. Unable to reason with either side, Gandhi undertook a three-week fast that not only restored the non-violent aims of the Home Rule campaign but also promoted this personal act of spiritual cleansing. By 1928, Gandhi was again elected head of India's National Congress.

Following a non-violent 200km march to the sea in defiance of the English government monopoly on the production and taxing of salt, more than 60,000 people were arrested. Among them was Mohandas Gandhi, who was again jailed for three years.

The dream of Indian self-determination was not fulfilled until after World War II, and not before further bloodshed and political upheaval with the separation of Pakistan into a separate Muslim state and the First Kashmir War (1947–48).

On 30 January 1948, following his last great fast to end the social and religious conflict Mahatma Gandhi—'the great soul'—was assassinated by Hindu extremists.

Will Rogers

'I Am Here Tonight Representing Poverty'

Columbia University, New York, 4 December 1924

William Penn 'Will' Rogers (1879–1933), America's 'cowboy sage', became the country's leading humourist—reading the newspapers from the stage of the Ziegfeld Follies and commenting upon events of the day. Originally billed as the Cherokee Kid in Wild West Shows at the turn of the century, Rogers' homespun philosophies made him famous on Broadway in 1915 before he moved into silent films, radio and contributed articles to the Saturday Evening Post. Rogers' common man approach and his rustic, simple commentary on topical events, social and political issues and the powerful personalities of the period, made him something of a folk hero.

However, Rogers was also one of the first of a new breed of mass media celebrity to use his public drawing power to focus attention on the needs of the poor. At a formal dinner in December 1924, a memorial to Alexander Hamilton arranged by Columbia University President, Nicholas Murray Butler, Rogers spoke to the wealth of the Columbia alumni among whom he sat as 'the poor boy' from Claremore, Oklahoma.

'President Butler paid me a compliment a while ago in mentioning my name in his introductory remarks and he put me ahead of the Columbia graduates. I am glad he did that because I got the worst of it last week. The Prince of Wales last week, in speaking of the sights of America, mentioned the Woolworth Building, the subway, the slaughterhouse, Will Rogers and the Ford factory. He could at least put me ahead of the hogs.

Everything must be in contrast at an affair like this. You know, to show anything off properly you must have the contrast. Now, I am here tonight representing poverty. We have enough wealth right here at this table, right here at the speaker's table alone—their conscience should hurt them, which I doubt it does—so that we could liquidate our national debt. Every rich man reaches a time in his career when he comes to a turning point and starts to give it away. I have heard that of several of our guests here tonight, and that is one of the reasons I am here. I would like to be here at the psychological moment.

'You know, to show anything off properly you must have the contrast. Now, I am here tonight representing poverty. We have enough wealth right here at this table, right here at the speaker's table alone...'

We are here, not only to keep cool with Coolidge, but to do honor to Alexander Hamilton. He was the first Secretary of the Treasury. The reason he was appointed that was because he and Washington were the only men in America at that time who knew how to put their names on a check. Signing a check has remained the principal qualification of a US Secretary of the Treasury.

I am glad President Butler referred to it in this way. The principal reason, of course, was that the man he fought against wanted to be President. He was a Princeton man—or I believe it was Harvard—anyway it was one of those primary schools. In fighting a duel, he forgot that in America our men over here could shoot. So, unfortunately, one of them was killed, which had never happened in the old country. So they did away with dueling. It was alright to protect your honor, but not to go as far as you like.

If you are speaking of finance here tonight, I do not believe that you could look further than President Butler. Butler is the word—to dig up the dough. Columbia was nothing twenty years ago. Now, he has gone around and got over a hundred buildings and has annexed Grant's Tomb. He was the first man to go around to the graduates and explain to them that by giving money to Columbia it would help on the income tax and also perpetuate their names.

We have an Alexander Hamilton Building. He landed these buildings and ran the place up to ninety millions or something like that.

There are more students in the university than there are in any other in the world. It is the foremost university. There are thirty-two hundred courses. You spend your first two years in deciding what courses to take, the next two years in finding the building that these courses are given in and the rest of your life wishing you had taken another course. And they have this wonderful society called the Alumni Association, a bunch of men who have gone to school and after they have come out, formed a society to tell the school how to run it. ♪

The irony that Will Rogers had himself long ago joined the ranks of millionaires was not lost on the gathering that night, nor in newspaper reports of the speech that he gave. In courageously drawing attention to those less fortunate than himself, he publicly ran the risk of appearing to be a hypocrite—worse than that, an actor merely feigning concern for the poor in order to build a platform for his own self-promotion. Neither was true and generations of celebrities—from the late John Lennon to actor Paul Newman—have endeavoured to use their positions to promote social justice causes.

When Will Rogers perished in a plane crash in Alaska along with close friend and aviator, Wiley Post, in 1933, he was one of the film industry's most popular actors.

Clarence Darrow

'The History of the Negro Race'

Detroit, Michigan, 11 May 1926

Famed lawyer Clarence Darrow (1857–1938) is best known for his defence of thrill killers, Leopold and Loeb (1924) and of Southern teacher, John T. Scopes, who dared to teach Darwinism (the Scopes 'Monkey' Trial, 1925). He also he had long championed the cause of African Americans.

From the early promotion of 'the sacred cause of abolition' in the late 1800s to his support of the National Association for the Advancement of Colored People (NAACP) in the early 1900s, Darrow often took up the unpopular cause of ensurng black Americans received the same level of justice afforded white Americans in a white-dominated society.

In 1925 Darrow was the defence attorney in the 'Sweet' Murder Trial. Doctor Ossian Sweet tried to escape the institutionalised bigotry of the South by moving his black family to live in a white neighbourhood of Detroit. During a family gathering on the night of 9 September, a mob gathered outside Sweet's home and rocks were thrown through the windows. Scared for their lives, the family fired shots at the mob and two men were wounded. One of the mob, Leon Breiner, later died and Dr Sweet and ten members of his family were charged with murder.

The Sweets were first tried as a group and the prosecution presented a number of witnesses who told the all-white jury that Leon Breiner was shot by a black mob while he chatted to a neighbour. While Darrow painted a vastly different picture of the 'mob', his defence was not only about the events of that night but of the history of suffering by black America.

'If I thought any of you had any opinion about the guilt of my clients, I wouldn't worry, because that might be changed,' Darrow trumpeted. 'What I'm worried about is prejudices. They are harder to change. They come with your mother's milk and stick like the colour of the skin. I know that if these defendants had been a white group defending themselves from a coloured mob, they never would have been arrested or tried. My clients are charged with murder, but they are really charged with being black.'

The trial resulted in a hung jury and the defendants were retried separately. The following May, at the trial of Henry Sweet, the brother of Ossie Sweet, who admitted firing the fatal shot, Clarence Darrow's closing statement—which lasted seven hours—concluded with an impassioned speech on the history of the Negro race.

'Gentlemen, I feel deeply on this subject; I cannot help it. Let us take a little glance at the history of the Negro race. It only needs a minute. It seems to me that the story would melt hearts of stone. I was born in America. I could have left it if I had wanted to go away.

Some other men, reading about this land of freedom that we brag about on the fourth of July, came voluntarily to America. These men, the defendants, are here because they could not help it. Their ancestors were captured in the jungles and on the plains of Africa, captured as you capture wild beasts, torn from their homes and their kindred; loaded into slave ships, packed like sardines in a box, half of them dying on the ocean passage; some jumping into the sea in their frenzy, when they had a chance to choose death in place of slavery. They were captured and brought here. They could not help it. They were bought and sold as slaves, to work without pay, because they were black.

They were subjected to all of this for generations, until finally they were given their liberty, so far as the law goes—and that is only a little way—because, after all, every human being's life in this world is inevitably mixed with every other life and, no matter what laws we pass, no matter what precautions we take, unless the people we meet are kindly and decent and human and liberty-loving, then there is no liberty. Freedom comes from human beings, rather than from laws and institutions.

'These people are the children of slavery. If the race that we belong to owes anything to any human being, or to any power in this universe, they owe it to these black men.'

Now, that is their history. These people are the children of slavery. If the race that we belong to owes anything to any human being, or to any power in this universe, they owe it to these black men. Above all other men, they owe an obligation and a duty to these black men which can never be repaid. I never see one of them that I do not feel I ought to pay part of the debt of my race. And if you gentlemen feel as you should feel in this case, your emotions will be like mine.

Gentlemen, you were called into this case by chance. It took us a week to find you, a week of culling out prejudice and hatred. Probably we did not cull it all out at that, but we took the best and the fairest that we could find. It is up to you.

Your verdict means something in this case. It means something more than the fate of this boy. It is not often that a case is submitted to twelve men where the decision may mean a milestone in the progress of the human race. But this case does. I hope and I trust that you have a feeling of responsibility that will make you take it and do your duty as citizens of a great nation and as members of the human family, which is better still.

Let me say just a parting word for Henry Sweet, who has well nigh been forgotten. I am serious, but it seems almost like a reflection upon this jury to talk as if I doubted your verdict. What has this boy done? This one boy now that I am culling out from all of the rest and whose fate is in your hands, can you tell me what he has done? Can I believe myself? Am I standing in a Court of Justice, where twelve men on their oaths are asked to take away the liberty of a boy twenty-one years of age, who has done nothing more than what Henry Sweet has done?

Gentlemen, you may think he shot too quick; you may think he erred in judgment; you may think that Doctor Sweet should not have gone there, prepared to defend his home. But, what of this case of Henry Sweet? What has he done? I want to put it up to you, each one of you, individually. Doctor Sweet was his elder brother. He had helped Henry through school. He loved him. He had taken him into his home. Henry had lived with him and his wife; he had fondled his baby. The doctor had promised Henry money to go through school. Henry was getting his education, to take his place in the world, gentlemen—and this is a hard job. With his brother's help, he had worked himself through college up to the last year. The doctor had bought a home. He feared danger. He moved in with his wife and he asked this boy to go with him. And this boy went to help defend his brother and his brother's wife and his child and his home.

Do you think more of him or less of him for that? I never saw twelve men in my life—and I have looked at a good many faces of a good many juries—I never saw twelve men in my life that if you could get them to understand a human case, were not true and right.

> *'So, gentlemen, I am justified in saying that this boy is as kindly, as well disposed, as decent a man as any one of you twelve. Do you think he ought to be taken out of his school and sent to the penitentiary?'*

Should this boy have gone along and helped his brother? Or, should he have stayed away? What would you have done? And yet, gentlemen, here is a boy, and the President of his College came all the way here from Ohio to tell you what he thinks of him. His teachers have come here, from Ohio, to tell you what they think of him. The Methodist Bishop has come here to tell you what he thinks of him.

So, gentlemen, I am justified in saying that this boy is as kindly, as well disposed, as decent a man as any one of you twelve. Do you think he ought to be taken out of his school and sent to the penitentiary? All right, gentlemen, if you think so, do it. It is your job, not mine. If you think so, do it. But if you do, gentlemen, if you should ever look into the face of your own boy, or your own brother, or look into your own heart, you will regret it in sackcloth and ashes. You know, if he committed any offense, it was being loyal and true to his brother whom he loved. I know where you will send him, and it will not be to the penitentiary.

Now, gentlemen, just one more word and I am through with this case. I do not live in Detroit. But I have no feeling against this city. In fact, I shall always have the kindest remembrance of it, especially if this case results as I think and feel that it will. I am the last one to come here to stir up race hatred, or any other hatred. I do not believe in the law of hate. I may not be true to my ideals always, but I believe in the law of love and I believe you can do nothing with hatred.

I would like to see a time when man loves his fellow man, and forgets his color or his creed. We will never be civilized until that time comes.

I know the Negro race has a long road to go. I believe the life of the Negro race has been a life of tragedy, of injustice, of oppression. The law has made him equal, but man has not. And, after all, the last analysis is, what has man done—not what has the law done? I know there is a long road ahead of him before he can take the place which I believe he should take. I know that before him there is suffering, sorrow, tribulation and death among the blacks, and perhaps the whites. I am sorry. I would do what I could to avert it. I would advise patience; I would advise toleration; I would advise understanding; I would advise all of those things which are necessary for men who live together.

Gentlemen, what do you think is your duty in this case? I have watched, day after day, these black, tense faces that have crowded this court. These black faces that now are looking to you twelve whites, feeling that the hopes and fears of a race are in your keeping.

This case is about to end, gentlemen. To them, it is life. Not one of their color sits on this jury. Their fate is in the hands of twelve whites. Their eyes are fixed on you, their hearts go out to you and their hopes hang on your verdict.

This is all. I ask you, on behalf of this defendant, on behalf of these helpless ones who turn to you, and more than that—on behalf of this great state, and this great city which must face this problem, and face it fairly—I ask you, in the name of progress and of the human race, to return a verdict of not guilty in this case! ♪

Henry Sweet was aquitted of murder and the prosecution dropped the cases against the other ten defendants. The trials, which were presided over by the Honorable Frank Murphy, who went on to become Governor of Michigan and an Associate Justice of the Supreme Court of the United States, had a profound impact on civil rights in the United States.

As Clarence Darrow told the press after the 'Sweet' trial, 'The verdict meant simply that the doctrine that a man's house is his castle applied to the black man as well as the white man. If not the first time that a white jury had vindicated this principle, it was the first time that ever came to my notice.'

Martin Luther King

'I've Seen the Promised Land'

Mason Temple, Memphis, Tennessee, 3 April 1968

Dr Martin Luther King Jnr, born in Atlanta, Georgia in 1929, was a baptist minister and civil rights leader. He was at the crossroads of his public career in 1968.

After several high profile victories in the South—starting with the Alabama bus boycotts in the late 1950s, the voter registration demonstrations in the early 1960s and culminating in the march on Washington in 1963—Dr King was stung by criticism from militant blacks in the North, especially the followers of Malcolm X, who did not support his non-violent protest movement in the face of continued discrimination, injustice and violence.

When Dr King attempted to form a new coalition of equal support for civil rights and the peace movement against the Vietnam War, he drew criticism from his own supporters that he was spreading resources—and himself—far too thinly.

In April 1968, Dr King went to Memphis, Tennessee, to support striking sanitation workers. He gave this speech at the Mason Temple in Memphis on the evening of 3 April 1968—inviting his audience to share in the pain of the striking sanitary workers and suggesting they boycott city businesses that did not support the strike. In summoning all of the emotions of the moment, Martin Luther King became the prophet of his own death.

'Now, let me say as I move to my conclusion that we've got to give ourselves to this struggle until the end. Nothing would be more tragic than to stop at this point, in Memphis. We've got to see it through. And when we have our march, you need to be there. Be concerned about your brother. You may not be on strike. But either we go up together, or we go down together.

Let us develop a kind of dangerous unselfishness. One day a man came to Jesus; and he wanted to raise some questions about some vital matters in life. At points, he wanted to trick Jesus and show him that he knew a little more than Jesus knew and, through this, throw him off base. Now that question could have easily ended up in a philosophical and theological debate. But Jesus immediately pulled that question from mid-air, and placed it on a dangerous curve between Jerusalem and Jericho. And he talked about a certain man who fell among thieves.

You remember that a Levite and a priest passed by on the other side. They didn't stop to help him. And finally a man of another race came by. He got down from his beast and decided not to be compassionate by proxy. But with him, administered first aid and helped the man in need. Jesus ended up saying, this was the good man, because he had the capacity to project the "I" into the "thou" and to be concerned about his brother.

Now you know, we use our imagination a great deal to try to determine why the priest and the Levite didn't stop. At times we say they were busy going to church meetings—an ecclesiastical gathering—and they had to get on down to Jerusalem so they wouldn't be late for their meeting. At other times we would speculate that there was a religious law that "One who was engaged in religious ceremonials was not to touch a human body twenty-four hours before the ceremony."

And every now and then we begin to wonder whether maybe they were not going down to Jerusalem, or down to Jericho, rather to organize a "Jericho Road Improvement Association." That's a possibility. Maybe they felt that it was better to deal with the problem from the casual root rather than to get bogged down with an individual effort.

But I'm going to tell you what my imagination tells me. It's possible that these men were afraid. You see, the Jericho road is a dangerous road. I remember when Mrs King and I were first in Jerusalem. We rented a car and drove from Jerusalem down to Jericho. And as soon as we got on that road, I said to my wife: "I can see why Jesus used this as a setting for his parable." It's a winding, meandering road. It's really conducive for ambushing. You start out in Jerusalem, which is about 1200 miles, or rather 1200 feet above sea level. And by the time you get down to Jericho, fifteen or twenty minutes later, you're about 2200 feet below sea level. That's a dangerous road. In the day of Jesus it came to be known as the "Bloody Pass." And you know, it's possible that the priest and the Levite looked over that man on the ground and wondered if the robbers were still around. Or it's possible that they felt that the man

> *'The question is not, "If I stop to help this man in need, what will happen to me?" "If I do not stop to help the sanitation workers, what will happen to them?" That's the question.'*

on the ground was merely faking. And he was acting like he had been robbed and hurt, in order to seize them over there, lure them there for quick and easy seizure. And so the first question that the Levite asked was: "If I stop to help this man, what will happen to me?" But then the Good Samaritan came by. And he reversed the question: "If I do not stop to help this man, what will happen to him?"

That's the question before you tonight. Not, "If I stop to help the sanitation workers, what will happen to all of the hours that I usually spend in my office every day and every week as a pastor?"

The question is not, "If I stop to help this man in need, what will happen to me?"

"If I do not stop to help the sanitation workers, what will happen to them?" That's the question.

Let us rise up tonight with a greater readiness. Let us stand with a greater determination. And let us move on in these powerful days, these days of challenge to make America what it ought to be. We have an opportunity to make America a better nation. And I want to thank God, once more, for allowing me to be here with you.

You know, several years ago (in 1958), I was in New York City autographing the first book that I had written. And while sitting there autographing books, a demented black woman came up. The only question I heard from her was: "Are you Martin Luther King?"

And I was looking down writing, and I said yes. And the next minute I felt something beating on my chest. Before I knew it, I had been stabbed by this demented woman. I was rushed to Harlem Hospital. It was a dark Saturday afternoon. And that blade had gone through, and the X-rays revealed that the tip of the blade was on the edge of my aorta, the main artery. And once that's punctured, you drown in your own blood—that's the end of you.

It came out in the New York Times the next morning, that if I had sneezed, I would have died. Well, about four days later, they allowed me, after the operation, after my chest had been opened and the blade had been taken out, to move around in the wheelchair in the hospital. They allowed me to read some of the mail that came in- and from all over the States, and the world, kind letters came in. I read a few, but one of them I will never forget. I had received one from the President and the Vice-President. I've forgotten what those telegrams said. I'd received a visit and a letter from the Governor of New York, but I've forgotten what the letter said. But there was another letter that came from a little girl, a young girl who was a student at the White Plains High School. And I looked at that letter, and I'll never forget it. It said simply: "Dear Dr King: I am a ninth-grade student at the White Plains High School." She said: "While it should not matter, I would like to mention that I am a white girl. I read in the paper of your misfortune and of your suffering. And I read that if you had sneezed, you would have died. And I'm simply writing you to say that I'm so happy that you didn't sneeze."

And I want to say tonight, I want to say that I am happy that I didn't sneeze. Because if I had sneezed, I wouldn't have been around here in 1960, when students all over the South started sitting in at lunch counters. And I knew that as they were sitting in, they were really standing up for the best in the American dream. And taking the whole nation back to those great wells of democracy which were dug deep by the Founding Fathers in the Declaration of Independence and the Constitution.

If I had sneezed, I wouldn't have been around in 1962, when Negroes in Albany, Georgia, decided to straighten their backs up. And whenever men and women straighten their backs up, they are going somewhere, because a man can't ride your back unless it is bent.

If I had sneezed, I wouldn't have been here in 1963, when the black people of Birmingham, Alabama, aroused the conscience of this nation and brought into being the Civil Rights Bill.

If I had sneezed, I wouldn't have had a chance later that year, in August, to try to tell America about a dream that I had had.

If I had sneezed, I wouldn't have been down in Selma, Alabama, to see the great movement there. If I had sneezed, I wouldn't have been in Memphis to see a community rally around those brothers and sisters who are suffering.

I'm so happy that I didn't sneeze.

And they were telling me, now it doesn't matter. It really doesn't matter what happens now. I left Atlanta this morning, and as we got started on the plane, there were six of us, the pilot said over the public address system: "We are sorry for the delay, but we have Dr Martin Luther King on the plane. And to be sure that all of the bags were checked, and to be sure that nothing would be wrong with the plane, we had to check out everything carefully. And we've had the plane protected and guarded all night."

And then I got into Memphis. And some began to say that threats, or talk about the threats that were out. What would happen to me from some of our sick white brothers?

Well, I don't know what will happen now. We've got some difficult days ahead. But it doesn't matter with me now. Because I've been to the mountain top. And I don't mind. Like anybody, I would like to live a long life. Longevity has its place. But I'm not concerned about that now. I just want to do God's will. And He's allowed me to go up to the mountain. And I've looked over. And I've seen the Promised Land. I may not get there with you. But I want you to know tonight, that we, as a people, will get to the Promised Land. And I'm happy tonight. I'm not worried about anything. I'm not fearing any man. Mine eyes have seen the glory of the coming of the Lord. ♪

The following day, on the evening of 4 April 1968, Martin Luther King was shot and killed as he stood on the balcony of the black-owned Lorraine Hotel, just off Beale Street. King was talking to colleagues Ralph Abernathy and Jesse Jackson when he was struck in the neck at 6.01 pm and died at the scene soon after.

Almost perversely for a man of peace, Dr King died a violent death and his passing caused a wave of destruction in many major cities across the United States. He was only 39 years old but had accomplished so much in his brief life.

On 8 June 1968, 40-year-old escaped convict James Earl Ray was captured at London's Heathrow Airport carrying a forged Canadian passport and was charged with the murder of Dr King. Ray pleaded guilty to avoid the death penalty and was sentenced to 99 years in prison (he died from liver failure in 1998). Although he later recanted his guilty plea and maintained that he was a 'patsy'—the same defense Lee Harvey Oswald put forward after he was captured for the assassination of President John Kennedy—it is alleged that Ray was a known segregationist who had decided to kill King when the opportunity presented it when the high-profile civil rights leader announced that he would come to Memphis.

Chaim Herzog

'Response to "Zionism is Racism"'

General Assembly of the UN, 10 November 1975

Chaim Herzog (1918–97) was the Dublin-born son of the Chief Rabbi of the Irish Free State and later President of Israel from 1983 to 1993. Herzog emigrated to Palestine in 1935 and fought against the 'Great Arab Revolt', which rose against increased Jewish immigration to the area in the late 1930s. A British army and intelligence officer during World War II, 'Vivian' Herzog returned to Palestine and fought in the Arab-Israeli war in 1948. He left his military career as a major general in 1962, opened a law firm in Israel and was later made a military governor when the West Bank was captured in the Six-Day War (1967).

As a former military attaché to the Israeli embassy in Washington (1950–54), Chaim Herzog entered politics and was appointed Israeli Ambassador to the United Nations (1975–78). In the first year of his term, the United Nations adopted General Assembly Resolution 3379—'Zionism is Racism'—in response to concerns of increased Israeli nationalism in the Middle East. The resolution was passed by a margin of 75 to 35 (with 32 countries abstaining from voting) on 10 November 1975.

Herzog gave this stinging condemnation of the stance by those countries, which led to the United Nations adopting the resolution. He then symbolically tore the printed resolution in half.

‘I come here to denounce the two great evils which menace society in general and a society of nations in particular. These two evils are hatred and ignorance. These two evils are the motivating force behind the proponents of this resolution and their supporters. These two evils characterize those who would drag this world organization, the ideals of which were first conceived by the prophets of Israel, to the depths to which it has been dragged today.

The key to understanding Zionism is in its name. The easternmost of the two hills of ancient Jerusalem during the tenth century BCE was called Zion. In fact, the name Zion, referring to Jerusalem, appears 152 times in the Old Testament. The name is overwhelmingly a poetic and prophetic designation. The religious and emotional qualities of the name arise from the importance of Jerusalem as the Royal City and the City of the Temple. Mount Zion is the place where God dwells. Jerusalem, or Zion, is a place where the Lord is King, and where He has installed His king, David.

King David made Jerusalem the capital of Israel almost three thousand years ago, and Jerusalem has remained the capital ever since. During the centuries the term "Zion" grew and expanded to mean the whole of Israel. The Israelites in exile could not forget Zion. The Hebrew Psalmist sat by the waters of Babylon and swore: "If I forget thee, O Jerusalem, let my right hand forget her cunning." This oath has been repeated for thousands of years by Jews throughout the world. It is an oath which was made over seven hundred years before the advent of Christianity and over twelve hundred years before the advent of Islam.

Zion came to mean the Jewish homeland, symbolic of Judaism, of Jewish national aspirations.

While praying to his God, every Jew, wherever he is in the world, faces towards Jerusalem. For over two thousand years of exile, these prayers have expressed the yearning of the Jewish people to return to their ancient homeland, Israel. In fact, a continuous Jewish presence, in larger or smaller numbers, has been maintained in the country over the centuries.

Zionism is the name of the national movement of the Jewish people and is the modern expression of the ancient Jewish heritage. The Zionist ideal, as set out in the Bible, has been, and is, an integral part of the Jewish religion.

Zionism is to the Jewish people what the liberation movements of Africa and Asia have been to their own people.

Zionism is one of the most dynamic and vibrant national movements in human history. Historically it is based on a unique and unbroken connection, extending some four thousand years, between the People of the Book and the Land of the Bible.

In modern times, in the late nineteenth century, spurred by the twin forces of anti-Semitic persecution and of nationalism, the Jewish people organized the Zionist movement in order to transform their dream into reality. Zionism as a political movement was the revolt of an oppressed nation against the depredation and wicked discrimination and oppression of the countries in which anti-Semitism flourished. It is no coincidence that the co-sponsors and supporters of this resolution include countries

'These two evils are hatred and ignorance. These two evils are the motivating force behind the proponents of this resolution and their supporters.'

who are guilty of the horrible crimes of anti-Semitism and discrimination to this very day.

Support for the aim of Zionism was written into the League of Nations Mandate for Palestine and was again endorsed by the United Nations in 1947, when the General Assembly voted by overwhelming majority for the restoration of Jewish independence in our ancient land.

The re-establishment of Jewish independence in Israel, after centuries of struggle to overcome foreign conquest and exile, is a vindication of the fundamental concepts of the equality of nations and of self-determination. To question the Jewish people's right to national existence and freedom is not only to deny to the Jewish people the right accorded to every other people on this globe, but it is also to deny the central precepts of the United Nations.

As a former Foreign Minister of Israel, Abba Eban, has written:

"Zionism is nothing more—but also nothing less—than the Jewish people's sense of origin and destination in the land linked eternally with their name.

It is also the instrument whereby the Jewish nation seeks an authentic fulfilment of itself. And the drama is enacted in twenty states comprising a hundred million people in four and a half million square miles, with vast resources. The issue, therefore, is not whether the world will come to terms with Arab nationalism. The question is at what point Arab nationalism, with its prodigious glut of advantage, wealth and opportunity, will come to terms with the modest but equal rights of another Middle Eastern nation to pursue its life in security and peace."

The vicious diatribes on Zionism voiced here by Arab delegates may give this Assembly the wrong impression that while the rest of the world supported the Jewish national liberation movement, the Arab world was always hostile to Zionism. This is not the case. Arab leaders, cognizant of the rights of the Jewish people, fully endorsed the virtues of Zionism.

Sherif Hussein, the leader of the Arab world during World War I, welcomed the return of the Jews to Palestine. His son, Emir Feisal, who represented the

> *'It is perhaps pertinent at this point to recall that when the question of Palestine was being debated in the United Nations. in 1947, the Soviet Union strongly supported the Jewish independence struggle.'*

Arab world in the Paris Peace Conference, had this to say about Zionism:

"We Arabs, especially the educated among us, look with deepest sympathy on the Zionist movement.... We will wish the Jews a hearty welcome home.... We are working together for a reformed and revised Near East, and our two movements complement one another. The movement is national and not imperialistic. There is room in Syria for us both. Indeed, I think that neither can be a success without the other."

It is perhaps pertinent at this point to recall that when the question of Palestine was being debated in the United Nations in 1947, the Soviet Union strongly supported the Jewish independence struggle. It is particularly relevant to recall some of Andrei Gromyko's remarks:

"As we know, the aspirations of a considerable part of the Jewish people are linked with the problem of Palestine and of its future administration. This fact scarcely requires proof.... During the last war, the Jewish people underwent exceptional sorrow and suffering. Without any exaggeration, this sorrow and suffering are indescribable. It is difficult to express them in dry statistics on the Jewish victims of the Fascist aggressors. The Jews in the territories where the Hitlerites held sway were subjected to almost complete physical annihilation. The total number of Jews who perished at the hands of the Nazi executioners is estimated at approximately six million....

"The United Nations cannot and must not regard this situation with indifference, since this would be incompatible with the high principles proclaimed in its Charter, which provides for the defense of human rights, irrespective of race, religion or sex....

"The fact that no Western European state has been able to ensure the defence of the elementary rights of the Jewish people and to safeguard it against the violence of the Fascist executioners explains the aspirations of the Jews to establish their own state. It would be unjust not to take this into consideration and to deny the right of the Jewish people to realize this aspiration."

How sad it is to see here a group of nations, many of whom have but recently freed themselves of colonial rule, deriding one of the most noble liberation movements of this century, a movement which not only gave an example of encouragement and determination to the peoples struggling for independence, but also actively aided many of them either during the period of preparation for their independence or immediately thereafter.

Here you have a movement which is the embodiment of a unique pioneering spirit, of the dignity of labor, and of enduring human values; a movement which has presented to the world an example of social equality and open democracy being associated in this resolution with abhorrent political concepts.

'We in Israel have endeavored to create a society which strives to implement the highest ideals of society— political, social and cultural—for all the inhabitants of Israel, irrespective of religious belief, race or sex.'

We in Israel have endeavored to create a society which strives to implement the highest ideals of society—political, social and cultural—for all the inhabitants of Israel, irrespective of religious belief, race or sex.

Show me another pluralistic society in this world in which despite all the difficult problems, Jew and Arab live together with such a degree of harmony; in which the dignity and rights of man are observed before the law; in which no death sentence is applied; in which freedom of speech, of movement, of thought, of expression are guaranteed; in which even movements which are opposed to our national aims are represented in our Parliament.

The Arab delegates talk of racism. What has happened to the 800,000 Jews who lived for over two thousand years in the Arab lands, who formed some of the most ancient communities long before the advent of Islam? Where are they now?

The Jews were once one of the important communities in the countries of the Middle East, the leaders of thought, of commerce, of medical science. Where are they in Arab society today?

You dare talk of racism when I can point with pride to the Arab ministers who have served in my government; to the Arab deputy speaker of my Parliament; to Arab officers and men serving of their own volition in our border and police defense forces, frequently commanding Jewish troops; to the hundreds of thousands of Arabs from all over the Middle East crowding the cities of Israel every year; to the thousands of Arabs from all over the Middle East coming for medical treatment to Israel; to the peaceful co-existence which has developed; to the fact that Arabic is an official language in Israel on a par with Hebrew; to the fact that it is as natural for an Arab to serve in public office in Israel as it is incongruous to think of a Jew serving in any public office in an Arab country, indeed being admitted to many of them. Is that racism? It is not!

> **'Zionism is our attempt to build a society, imperfect though it may be, in which the visions of the prophets of Israel will be realized.'**

That, Mr President, is Zionism.

Zionism is our attempt to build a society, imperfect though it may be, in which the visions of the prophets of Israel will be realized. I know that we have problems. I know that many disagree with our government's policies. Many in Israel, too, disagree from time to time with the government's policies... and are free to do so because Zionism has created the first and only real democratic state in a part of the world that never really knew democracy and freedom of speech.

This malicious resolution, designed to divert us from its true purpose, is part of a dangerous anti-Semitic idiom which is being insinuated into every public debate by those who have sworn to block the current move towards accommodation and ultimately towards peace in the Middle East.

This, together with similar moves, is designed to sabotage the efforts of the Geneva Conference for peace in the Middle East and to deflect those who are moving along the road towards peace from their purpose. But they will not succeed, for I can but reiterate my Government's policy to make every move in the direction towards peace, based on compromise.

We are seeing here today but another manifestation of the bitter anti-Semitic, anti-Jewish hatred which animates Arab society. Who would have believed that in this year, 1975, the malicious falsehoods of the "Elders of Zion" would be distributed officially by Arab governments? Who would have believed that we would today contemplate an Arab society which teaches the vilest anti-Jewish hate in the kindergartens?

We are being attacked by a society which is motivated by the most extreme form of racism known in the world today. This is the racism which was expressed so succinctly in the words of the leader of the PLO, Yasser Arafat, in his opening address at a symposium in Tripoli, Libya: "There will be no presence in the region other than the Arab presence..."

In other words, in the Middle East, from the Atlantic Ocean to the Persian Gulf, only one presence is allowed, and that is an Arab presence. No other people, regardless of how deep are its roots in the region, is to be permitted to enjoy its right to self-determination.

Look at the tragic fate of the Kurds of Iraq. Look what happened to the black population in southern Sudan. Look at the dire peril in which an entire community of Christians finds itself in Lebanon. Look at the avowed policy of the PLO, which calls on its Palestine Covenant of 1964 for the destruction of the State of Israel, which denies any form of compromise on the Palestine issue and which, in the words of its representative only the other day in this building, considers Tel Aviv to be occupied territory.

Look at all this and you see before you the root cause of the twin evils of this world at work, the blind hatred of the Arab proponents of this resolution and the abysmal ignorance and wickedness of those who support them.

The issue before this Assembly is neither Israel nor Zionism. The issue is the fate of this organization. Conceived in the spirit of the prophets of Israel, born out of an anti-Nazi alliance after the tragedy of World War II, it has degenerated into a forum which was this last week described by Paul Johnson, one of the leading writers in a foremost organ of social and liberal thought in the West, as "rapidly becoming one of the most corrupt and corrupting creations in the whole history of human institutions... almost without exception those in the majority came from states notable for racist oppression of every conceivable hue." He goes on to explain the phenomenon of this debate:

"Israel is a social democracy, the nearest approach to a free socialist state in the world; its people and government have a profound respect for human life, so passionate indeed that, despite every conceivable provocation, they have refused for a quarter of a century to execute a single captured terrorist. They also have an ancient but vigorous culture and a flourishing technology. The combination of national qualities they have assembled in their brief existence as a state is a perpetual and embittering reproach to most of the new countries whose representatives swagger about the UN building. So Israel is envied and hated and efforts are made to destroy her. The extermination of the Israelis has long been the prime objective of the Terrorist International. They calculate that if they can break Israel, then all the rest of civilization is vulnerable to their assaults...

"The melancholy truth, I fear, is that the candles of civilisation are burning low. The world is increasingly governed not so much by capitalism, or Communism, or social democracy, or even tribal barbarism, as by a false lexicon of political clichés, accumulated over half a century and now assuming a kind of degenerate sacerdotal authority... We all know what they are..."

Over the centuries it has fallen to the lot of my people to be the testing agent of human decency, the touchstone of civilization, the crucible in which enduring human values are

'Over the centuries it has fallen to the lot of my people to be the testing agent of human decency, the touchstone of civilization, the crucible in which enduring human values are to be tested.'

to be tested. A nation's level of humanity could invariably be judged by its behavior towards its Jewish population.

Persecution and oppression have often enough begun with the Jews, but it has never ended with them. The anti-Jewish pogroms in Czarist Russia were but the tip of the iceberg which revealed the inherent rottenness of a regime that was soon to disappear in the storm of revolution. The anti-Semitic excesses of the Nazis merely foreshadowed the catastrophe which was to befall mankind in Europe....

On the issue before us, the world has divided itself into good and bad, decent and evil, human and debased. We, the Jewish people, will recall in history our gratitude to those nations who stood up and were counted and who refused to support this wicked proposition. I know that this episode will have strengthened the forces of freedom and decency in this world and will have fortified the free world in their resolve to strengthen the ideals they so cherish. I know that this episode will have strengthened Zionism as it has weakened the United Nations.

As I stand on this rostrum, the long and proud history of my people unravels itself before my inward eye. I see the oppressors of our people over the ages as they pass one another in evil procession into oblivion. I stand here before you as the representative of a strong and flourishing people which has survived them all and which will survive this shameful exhibition and the proponents of this resolution.

The great moments of Jewish history come to mind as I face you, once again outnumbered and the would-be victim of hate, ignorance and evil. I look back on those great moments. I recall the greatness of a nation which I have the honor to represent in this forum. I am mindful at this moment of the Jewish people throughout the world wherever they may be, be it in freedom or in slavery, whose prayers and thoughts are with me at this moment.

I stand here not as a supplicant. Vote as your moral conscience dictates to you. For the issue is neither Israel nor Zionism. The issue is the continued existence of this organization, which has been dragged to its lowest point of discredit by a coalition of despots and racists.

The vote of each delegation will record in history its country's stand on anti-Semitic racism and anti-Judaism. You yourselves bear the responsibility for your stand before history, for as such will you be viewed in history. We, the Jewish people, will not forget.

For us, the Jewish people, this is but a passing episode in a rich and event-filled history. We put our trust in our Providence, in our faith and beliefs, in our time-hallowed tradition, in our striving for social advance and human values and in our people wherever they may be. For us, the Jewish people, this resolution based on hatred, falsehood and arrogance, is devoid of any moral or legal value. ♪

It would be another generation until Resolution 3379 was finally revoked by the United Nations in 1991. In the more than three decades since Herzog's defence of 'Zionism', the Arab–Israeli 'question' has gone unanswered.

César Chávez

'Lessons of Dr Martin Luther King'

California, 12 January 1990

César Estrada Chávez (1927–94) was born in Yuma, Arizona, the grandson of Mexican immigrants and the son of a prosperous farmer and a deeply religious mother. When Chávez was ten years old, his parents lost their home and the family joined 300,000 California migrant workers picking crops in the San Joaquin Valley. Despite his love of education and books, Chávez dropped out of school to work in the fields to support his family. He enlisted in the Marines in 1944, where he experienced the hurt of racial discrimination, as he had in the classroom and fields. He returned to California and married Helen Fabela, a young woman who would share his life's work of pursuing social justice for the poor.

César Chávez was heavily influenced by the works of St. Francis of Assisi and his devotion to the poor; and the life of Mahatma Gandhi and his philosophy of non-violence. Asked by the local Community Services Organization (CSO) to inform migrant workers of their rights, Chávez recruited more than 2000 workers to the organisation during the late 1940s. He then quit his job picking apricots and during the next decade made the CSO the most effective Latino civil rights group of its day.

In 1962, Chávez resigned from the CSO and launched the United Farm Workers (UFW) organisation. For the next four years, Chávez and his family, (which had grown to include eight children), drove to farm worker camps and towns signing up members. During the ensuing years, the pursuit of 'La Causa' resulted in numerous non-violent boycotts, strikes and marches.

In the spirit of Mahatma Gandhi, Chávez also fasted as a form of political protest. In early 1968, he fasted for 25 days and only broke the fast when he was joined by Senator Robert F. Kennedy and 8000 farm workers to celebrate Catholic mass.

In 1973, when 10,000 farm workers walked off the grape fields over a contract dispute, many strikers were arrested, beaten and even killed. Fearing further violence, Chávez ended the strike and called for a boycott of table grapes. A total of 17 million Americans refused to buy grapes and the drop in revenue (estimated at 15 per cent) had an enormous impact on grape growers.

In 1975, the Agricultural Labor Relations Act was introduced after gaining support from California Governor, Jerry Brown. The new law protected the rights of farm workers to unionise and boycott and guaranteed secret ballots in farm workers' union elections. In the 1980s, Chávez focused attention on the dangers of pesticides, which had long caused illness among poor farm workers. In 1988, he fasted for 36 days to highlight 'the plague of pesticides on our land and our food' and was joined by the Reverend Jesse Jackson and many other civil rights leaders.

On 12 January 1990—the anniversary of the birthday of Martin Luther King—César Chávez spoke of the united struggle for civil rights in America and his own unique journey.

‘My friends, today we honor a giant among men, today we honor the Reverend Martin Luther King Junior.

Dr King was a powerful figure of destiny, of courage, of sacrifice and of vision. Few people in the long history of this nation can rival his accomplishment, his reason, or his selfless dedication to the cause of peace and social justice.

Today we honor a wise teacher, an inspiring leader and a true visionary, but to truly honor Dr King we must do more than say words of praise.

We must learn his lessons and put his views into practice, so that we may truly be free at last.

Who was Dr King?

Many people will tell you of his wonderful qualities and his many accomplishments, but what makes him special to me, the truth many people don't want you to remember, is that Dr King was a great activist, fighting for radical social change with radical methods.

While other people talked about change, Dr King used direct action to challenge the system. He welcomed it and used it wisely.

'Dr King was also radical in his beliefs about violence. He learned how to successfully fight hatred and violence with the unstoppable power of non-violence.'

In his famous letter from the Birmingham jail, Dr King wrote that "the purpose of direct action is to create a situation so crisis-packed that it will inevitably open the door to negotiation."

Dr King was also radical in his beliefs about violence. He learned how to successfully fight hatred and violence with the unstoppable power of non-violence.

He once stopped an armed mob, saying: "We are not advocating violence. We want to love our enemies. I want you to love our enemies. Be good to them. This is what we live by. We must meet hate with love."

Dr King knew that he very probably wouldn't survive the struggle that he led so well. But he said: "If I am stopped, the movement will not stop. If I am stopped, our work will not stop. For what we are doing is right. What we are doing is just and God is with us."

My friends, as we enter a new decade, it should be clear to all of us that there is an unfinished agenda, that we have miles to go before we reach the Promised Land.

The men who rule this country today never learned the lessons of Dr King, they never learned that non-violence is the only way to peace and justice.

Our nation continues to wage war upon its neighbors and upon itself.

The powers-that-be rule over a racist society, filled with hatred and ignorance.

Our nation continues to be segregated along racial and economic lines.

The powers-that-be make themselves richer by exploiting the poor. Our nation continues to allow children to go hungry and will not even house its own people. The time is now for people of all races and backgrounds to sound the trumpets of change. As Dr King proclaimed: "There comes a time when people get tired of being trampled over by the iron feet of oppression."

My friends, the time for action is upon us. The enemies of justice want you to think of Dr King as only a civil rights leader, but he had a much broader agenda. He was a tireless crusader for the rights of the poor, for an end to the war in Vietnam long before it was popular to take that stand and for the rights of workers everywhere.

Many people find it convenient to forget that Martin was murdered while supporting a desperate strike on that tragic day in Memphis, Tennessee. He died while fighting for the rights of sanitation workers.

Dr King's dedication to the rights of the workers who are so often exploited by the forces of greed has profoundly touched my life and guided my struggle.

'The United Farm Workers are dedicated to carrying on the dream of Reverend Martin Luther King Junior.'

During my first fast in 1968, Dr King reminded me that our struggle was his struggle too. He sent me a telegram which said: "Our separate struggles are really one. A struggle for freedom, for dignity and for humanity."

I was profoundly moved that someone facing such a tremendous struggle himself would take the time to worry about a struggle taking place on the other side of the continent.

Just as Dr King was a disciple of Gandhi and Christ, we must now be Dr King's disciples.

Dr King challenged us to work for a greater humanity. I only hope that we are worthy of his challenge.

The United Farm Workers are dedicated to carrying on the dream of Reverend Martin Luther King Junior. My friends, I would like to tell you about the struggle of the farm workers who are waging a desperate struggle for our rights, for our children's rights and for our very lives.

Many decades ago, the chemical industry promised the growers that pesticides would bring great wealth and bountiful harvests to the fields.

Just recently, the experts are learning what farm workers and the truly organized farmers have known for years.

The prestigious National Academy of Sciences recently concluded an exhaustive five-year study which determined that pesticides do not improve profits and do not produce more crops.

What, then, is the effect of pesticides? Pesticides have created a legacy of pain and misery and death for farm workers and consumers alike.

The crop which poses the greatest danger, and the focus of our struggle, is the table grape crop. These pesticides soak the fields, drift with the wind, pollute the water and are eaten by unwitting consumers.

These poisons are designed to kill and pose a very real threat to consumers and farm workers alike. The fields are sprayed with pesticides like Captan, Parathion, Phosdrin and Methyl Bromide. These poisons cause cancer, DNA mutation and horrible birth defects.

The Central Valley of California is one of the wealthiest agricultural regions in the world. In its midst are clusters of children dying from cancer.

The children live in communities surrounded by the grape fields that

> **'My friends, the suffering must end. So many children are dying, so many babies are born without limbs and vital organs, so many workers are dying in the fields.'**

employ their parents. The children come into contact with the poisons when they play outside, when they drink the water and when they hug their parents returning from the fields.

And the children are dying.

They are dying slow, painful, cruel deaths in towns called cancer clusters, in cancer clusters like McFarland, where the child cancer rate is 800 per cent above normal. A few months ago, the parents of a brave little girl in the agricultural community of Earlimart came to the United Farm Workers to ask for help.

The Ramirez family knew about our protests in nearby McFarland and thought there might be a similar problem in Earlimart. Our union members went door to door in Earlimart and found that the Ramirez family's worst fears were true. There are at least four other children suffering from cancer in the little town of Earlimart, a rate 1200 per cent above normal.

In Earlimart, little Jimmy Caudillo died recently from Leukaemia at the age of three.

Three other young children in Earlimart, in addition to Jimmy and Natalie, are suffering from similar fatal diseases that the experts believe are caused by pesticides.

These same pesticides can be found on the grapes you buy in the stores.

My friends, the suffering must end. So many children are dying, so many babies are born without limbs and vital organs, so many workers are dying in the fields.

We have no choice, we must stop the plague of pesticides.

The growers responsible for this outrage are blinded by greed, by racism and by power.

The same inhumanity displayed at Selma, in Birmingham, in so many of Dr King's battlegrounds, is displayed every day in the vineyards of California.

The farm labor system in place today is a system of economic slavery.

My friends, even those farm workers who do not have to bury their young children are suffering from abuse, neglect and poverty.

Our workers labor for many hours every day under the hot sun, often without safe drinking water or toilet facilities. Our workers are constantly subjected to incredible pressures and intimidation to meet excessive quotas.

The women who work in the fields are routinely subjected to sexual harassment and sexual assaults by the grower's thugs. When our workers complain, or try to organize, they are fired, assaulted and even murdered.

Just as Bull Connor turned the dogs loose on non-violent marchers in Alabama, the growers turn armed foremen on innocent farm workers in California.

The stench of injustice in California should offend every American. Some people, especially those who just don't care, or don't understand, like to think that the government can take care of these problems. The government should, but won't.

The growers used their wealth to buy good friends like Governor George Deukmajian, Ronald Reagan and George Bush (Senior).

My friends, if we are going to end the suffering, we must use the same people power that vanquished injustice in Montgomery, Selma and Birmingham.

I have seen many boycotts succeed. Dr King showed us the way with the bus boycott. And with our first boycott we were able to get DDT, Aldrin, and Dieldrin banned in our first contracts with grape growers. Now, even more urgently, we are trying to get deadly pesticides banned.

The growers and their allies have tried to stop us for years, with intimidation, with character assassination, with public relations campaigns, with outright lies and with murder.

But those same tactics did not stop Dr King and they will not stop us.

Once social change begins, it cannot be reversed.

You cannot uneducate the person who has learned to read. You cannot humiliate the person who feels pride. And you cannot oppress the people who are not afraid any more.

In our life and death struggle for justice we have turned to the court of last resort: The American people. And the people are ruling in our favor.

As a result, grape sales keep falling. We have witnessed truckloads of grapes being dumped because no one would stop to buy them. As demand drops, so do prices and profits.

The growers are under tremendous economic pressure.

We are winning, but there is still much hard work ahead of us. I hope that you will join our struggle. The simple act of refusing to buy table grapes laced with pesticides is a powerful statement that the growers understand.

Economic pressure is the only language

'You cannot uneducate the person who has learned to read. You cannot humiliate the person who feels pride. And you cannot oppress the people who are not afraid any more.'

the growers speak and they are beginning to listen.

Please, boycott table grapes. For your safety, for the workers and for the children, we must act together.

My friends, Dr King realized that the only real wealth comes from helping others.

I challenge each and every one of you to be a true disciple of Dr King, to be truly wealthy.

I challenge you to carry on his work by volunteering to work for a just cause you believe in.

Consider joining our movement because the farm workers, and so many other oppressed peoples depend upon the unselfish dedication of its volunteers, people just like you.

Thousands of people have worked for our cause and have gone on to achieve success in many different fields.

Our non-violent cause will give you skills that will last a lifetime. When Dr King sounded the call for justice, the freedom riders answered the call in droves. I am giving you the same opportunity to join the same cause, to free your fellow human beings from the yoke of oppression.

I have faith that in this audience there are men and women with the same courage and the same idealism that put young Martin Luther King Junior on the path to social change.

I challenge you to join the struggle of the United Farm Workers. And if you don't join our cause, then seek out the many organizations seeking peaceful social change.

Seek out the many outstanding leaders who will speak to you this week, and make a difference.

If we fail to learn that each and every person can make a difference, then we will have betrayed Dr King's life's work. The Reverend Martin Luther King Junior had more than just a dream, he had the love and the faith to act.

God Bless You. ♪

In April 1993, after days of testimony contesting a lawsuit filed in Arizona by lettuce farmers, César Chávez died of natural causes in the modest San Luis home of a friend while visiting Latino farmers. His funeral was conducted by Cardinal Roger Mahoney, (Pope John Paul II sent a message of condolence), and was attended by more than 50,000 mourners. President Bill Clinton, in posthumously awarding

Chávez the Medal of Freedom in 1994, said: 'César Chávez left our world better than he found it and his legacy inspires us still. He was, for his own people, a Moses figure. The farm workers who labored in the fields pinned their hopes on this remarkable man.'

Julian Bond

'Eulogy for Rosa Parks'

Washington DC, 30 October 2005

Rosa Parks (1913–2005) is regarded as the mother of the American civil rights movement. During the 1930s, Parks and her husband Raymond were active members of the National Association for the Advancement of Colored People (NAACP) in Montgomery, Alabama. Parks and many of her associates in the Congress of Racial Equality (CORE) were heavily influenced by Gandhi's non-violent civil disobedience campaign which had led India to independence.

Like most towns in the South, Montgomery had segregated bus travel. Rosa Parks and several other NAACP members had considered using Gandhi's methods to protest the socially enforced law that blacks had to travel at the back of the bus and give up their seat to a white person if the bus was full.

On several occasions during the 1940s, Parks, among many others, was thrown off buses for refusing to give up her seats. Despite the 1954 Supreme Court ruling overriding segregation in education, the leaders of the NAACP declined to take up an organised disobedience movement against bus travel for fear of provoking a violent backlash.

On 1 December 1955, Rosa Parks left the department store where she worked and moved to the back of the same bus she caught every night. When the bus became full, however, the bus driver instructed Parks to give up her seat to a white person. She calmly refused, was arrested by the police, found guilty of violating the segregation law and fined.

Parks approached the NAACP and volunteered to use her conviction as a test case to fight the unfair law in the Supreme Court. She was promptly sacked from her job as a tailor for taking a public stance.

The pastor at the local Baptist Church, 26-year-old Martin Luther

King Junior, agreed to organise protests against bus segregation.

For the next 13 months, 17,000 black people in Montgomery refused to use the buses until travel was completely integrated. Most walked to work or obtained lifts from the small car-owning black population of the city. The non-violent protest drew an extraordinary response. National attention was now focused on the civil rights movement. But Dr King was arrested and his house fire-bombed. Eventually, a decision by the Supreme Court and the loss of revenue forced the Montgomery Bus Company to accept integration. The boycott finally came to an end on 20 December 1956.

Rosa Parks died on 24 October 2005, aged 92. More than 40,000 people filed past her casket in the US Capitol Rotunda where her body lay in state (Parks was the first civilian and only second woman or African-American to be so honoured).

Almost 2500 mourners filled the Metropolitan African Methodist Episcopal (AME) Church in Washington DC for her memorial service. In a nice touch, a vintage Metropolitan bus dressed in black bunting followed the hearse, along with other city buses, to the AME Church.

Speakers at the two and a half hour memorial included broadcaster Oprah Winfrey, actress Cicely Tyson, civil rights pioneer Dorothy Height and Parks' childhood friend and Montgomery bus boycott veteran, Johnnie Carr. It was NAACP chair, Julian Bond, however, who caught the mood of the moment.

'We are gathered here to say goodbye and well done to Rosa Louise McCauley Parks. She leaves us as she lived her life, with honor and dignity. She was daughter, sister, wife, aunt and mother to the Movement. But she was more than that. She leaves us just short of the 50th anniversary of the day she showed the world you can stand up for your rights by sitting down. Her actions produced a movement and introduced America to a new leader. Dr King said she was anchored to that seat by the accumulated indignities of days gone by and the boundless aspirations of generations yet to come.

She wasn't the first to refuse to surrender to Montgomery's apartheid. There had been Claudette Colvin, there had been Mary

'She leaves us as she lived her life, with honor and dignity. She was daughter, sister, wife, aunt and mother to the Movement. But she was more than that.'

Louise Smith and countless others before her, those who believed they had rights just like any other citizen. But Rosa Parks was the first person to plead not guilty. For her, breaking Alabama law was obeying the Constitution. It was defending justice. She was tired, alright. She was tired of mistreatment. She was tired of second class citizenship. But, you know, she didn't want to be known as the bus woman. She was much, much more than that.

A historian writes: "Although Martin Luther King played a crucial role in transforming a local boycott into a social justice movement, he was, himself, transformed by a movement he did not initiate." In Montgomery, the boycott owed its success to what a historian calls the self-reliant NAACP stalwarts who acted on their own before King could lead. Rosa Parks was first among those NAACP stalwarts. She had been active with the NAACP for more than a decade before the boycott began. When it began, she was secretary to the Alabama NAACP state conference. She was secretary to the Montgomery branch of the NAACP. She was advisor to the youth council of the NAACP. She was secretary to the Alabama Voters League. But she was more than that.

She was secretary to the Montgomery branch of the Brotherhood of Sleeping Car Porters, the pioneering black union, led nationally by A. Philip Randolph and locally by ED Nixon. She writes in her biography that Mr Nixon once told her: "Women don't belong nowhere but in the kitchen." She said: "Mr Nixon, what about me?" He said: "You're a good secretary and I need one." But she was more than that.

She became such an icon in American history and popular culture that the Neville Brothers immortalized her. They sang, "Thank you, Ms. Rosa.

You were the spark that started our freedom movement. Thank you, Sister Rosa Parks."

She was a long-time fighter for justice in Alabama. She and her husband were strong defenders of the Scottsboro Boys. She fought for their freedom. She was active in the NAACP. But she was more than that.

Nine years ago she delivered the eulogy at the funeral for Robert Williams,

'She was a long-time fighter for justice in Alabama. She and her husband were strong defenders of the Scottsboro Boys. She fought for their freedom.'

much as we are eulogizing her today. For those of you who don't remember, Williams was the NAACP president in Monroe, North Carolina.

He answered Klan attacks bullet for bullet. For his courage, the NAACP expelled him. The State of North Carolina made him a criminal. And he found safety and sanctuary in Cuba and China. He became an all but forgotten man.

In 1996, an elderly Rosa Parks, the exemplar of non-violence, stood in a church pulpit in Monroe, North Carolina. She was glad, she said, to finally attend the funeral of a heroic black leader who had escaped the assassin's bullet and lived a long and happy life. The work that he did, she said, should go down in history and never be forgotten.

It was my great pleasure to have known her over the years, giving me precious memories of the time we were together. I was once speaking in Detroit. And when the event was over, my host asked me if I would like to go out for a drink with Rosa Parks. Of course, I said yes.

Mrs Parks had Coca-Cola. She turned to me, and she said: "Julian, what are you doing now? Where are you living?" I said, "Mrs Parks, I've moved to Washington DC. I just saw you on TV. You and Jesse Jackson were picketing the Greyhound bus station in support of the striking bus drivers."

And I said: "You know, Mrs Parks, I've just taken a job at the University of Virginia in Charlottesville. It's too close and too expensive to fly there. The train isn't convenient. The best way to get there from DC is by bus."

And in her sweet, calm, quiet, respectful, gentle manner Ms. Parks said, "Don't you ride that bus!"

Now, Mrs Parks was much, much more than the bus woman. She was much, much more than that. Eldridge Cleaver famously remarked that when she sat down that December day in Montgomery fifty years ago, somewhere in the universe a gear in the machinery had shifted. Rosa Parks shifted the gears of the universe all her life. Now she belongs to the universe.

Thank you, Sister Rosa. Thank you, Rosa Parks. ♪

Rosa Parks and her family moved to Detroit in 1957 after becoming the focus of continued harassment by white racists. She later became a special assistant to Democratic Congressman, John Conyers, and remained active in the NAACP. In 1987 she founded the Rosa and Raymond Parks Institute for Self-Development, which aimed to help the young and educate them about civil rights. The Southern Christian Leadership Conference (SCLC) also established an annual Rosa Parks Freedom Award.

War

Woodrow Wilson

'Fourteen-Point Peace Plan'

Washington DC, 8 January 1918

In January 1918, US President Woodrow Wilson (1856–1924) appeared before a joint session of the US Congress and outlined possible peace terms to end the so called Great War of 1914–1918. The fourteen points outlined in this speech served as both the basis for peace and the establishment of a League of Nations aimed at promoting 'post-war understanding and peaceful relations'.

The League of Nations would rise above national governments, Wilson maintained, and be the guardian of liberty for the people of the world. 'We must concert our best judgment,' he said, 'to make the League of Nations a vital thing—not merely a formal thing, not an occasional thing, not a thing sometimes called into life to meet an exigency—but always functioning in watchful attendance upon the interests of the nations, and that its continuity should be a vital continuity.'

❛ …It will be our wish and purpose that the processes of peace, when they are begun, shall be absolutely open and that they shall involve and permit henceforth no secret understandings of any kind. The day of conquest and aggrandizement is gone by. So is also the day of secret covenants entered into in the interest of particular governments and likely at some unlooked-for moment to upset the peace of the world. It is this happy fact, now clear to the view of every public man whose thoughts do not still linger in an age that is dead and gone, which makes it possible for every nation whose purposes are consistent with justice and the peace of the world to avow now or at any other time the objects it has in view.

'We entered this war because violations of right had occurred which touched us to the quick and made the life of our own people impossible...'

We entered this war because violations of right had occurred which touched us to the quick and made the life of our own people impossible unless they were corrected and the world secured once and for all against their recurrence.

What we demand in this war, therefore, is nothing peculiar to ourselves. It is that the world be made fit and safe to live in; and particularly that it be made safe for every peace-loving nation which, like our own, wishes to live its own life, determine its own institutions, be assured of justice and fair dealing by the other peoples of the world, as against force and selfish aggression.

All the peoples of the world are in effect partners in this interest and, for our own part, we see very clearly that unless justice be done to others it will not be done to us.

The program of the world's peace, therefore, is our program; and that program, the only possible program, all we see it, is this:

1. Open covenants of peace must be arrived at, after which there will surely be no private international action or rulings of any kind, but diplomacy shall proceed always frankly and in the public view.

2. Absolute freedom of navigation upon the seas, outside territorial waters, alike in peace and in war, except as the seas may be closed in whole or in part by international action for the enforcement of international covenants.

3. The removal, so far as possible, of all economic barriers and the establishment of equality of trade conditions among all the nations consenting to the peace and associating themselves for its maintenance.

4. Adequate guarantees given and taken that national armaments will be reduced to the lowest points consistent with domestic safety.

5. A free, open-minded and absolutely impartial adjustment of all colonial claims, based upon a strict observance of the principle that in determining all such questions of sovereignty, the interests of the population concerned must have equal weight with the equitable claims of the government whose title is to be determined.

6. The evacuation of all Russian territory and such a settlement of all questions affecting Russia as will secure the best and free-est cooperation of the other nations of the world in obtaining for her an unhampered and unembarrassed opportunity for the independent determination of her own political development and national policy, and assure her of a sincere welcome into the society of free nations under institutions of her own choosing; and, more than a welcome, assistance also of every kind that she may need and may herself desire. The treatment accorded Russia by her sister nations in the months to come will be the acid test of their good will, of their comprehension

of her needs as distinguished from their own interests, and of their intelligent and unselfish sympathy.

7. Belgium, the whole world will agree, must be evacuated and restored, without any attempt to limit the sovereignty which she enjoys in common with all other free nations. No other single act will serve, as this will serve, to restore confidence among nations in the laws which they have themselves set and determined for the government of their relations with one another. Without this healing act, the whole structure and validity of international law is forever impaired.

8. All French territory should be freed and the invaded portions restored and the wrong done to France by Prussia in 1871 in the matter of Alsace-Lorraine, which has unsettled the peace of the world for nearly fifty years, should be righted, in order that peace may once more be made secure in the interest of all.

9. A readjustment of the frontiers of Italy should be effected along clearly recognizable lines of nationality.

10. The peoples of Austria-Hungary, whose place among the nations we wish to see safeguarded and assured, should be accorded the free-est opportunity of autonomous development.

11. Romania, Serbia, and Montenegro should be evacuated; occupied territories restored; Serbia accorded free and secure access to the sea; and the relations of the several Balkan states to one another determined by friendly counsel along historically established lines of allegiance and nationality; and international guarantees of the political and economic independence and territorial integrity of the several Balkan states should be entered into.

12. The Turkish portions of the present Ottoman Empire should be assured a secure sovereignty, but the other nationalities which are now under Turkish rule should be assured an undoubted security of life and an absolutely unmolested opportunity of autonomous development; and the Dardanelles should be permanently opened as a free passage to the ships and commerce of all nations under international guarantees.

13. An independent Polish state should be erected which should include the territories inhabited by indisputably Polish populations, which should be assured free and secure access to the sea; and whose political and economic independence and territorial integrity should be guaranteed by international covenant.

14. A general association of nations must be formed under specific covenants for the purpose of affording mutual guarantees of political independence and

territorial integrity to great and small states alike.

In regard to these essential rectifications of wrong and assertions of right, we feel ourselves to be intimate partners of all the governments and peoples associated together against the imperialists. We cannot be separated in interest or divided in purpose. We stand together until the end.

'For such arrangements and covenants, we are willing to fight and to continue to fight until they are achieved...'

For such arrangements and covenants, we are willing to fight and to continue to fight until they are achieved; but only because we wish right to prevail and desire a just and stable peace such as can be secured only by removing the chief provocations to war, which this program does remove...'

We have no jealousy of German greatness and there is nothing in this program that impairs it. We grudge her no achievement or distinction of learning or of pacific enterprise such as have made her record very bright and very enviable. We do not wish to injure her or to block in any way her legitimate influence or power. We do not wish to fight her either with arms or with hostile arrangements of trade, if she is willing to associate herself with us and the other peace-loving nations of the world in covenants of justice and law and fair dealing.

We wish her only to accept a place of equality among the peoples of the world—the new world in which we now live—instead of a place of mastery.

Neither do we presume to suggest to her any alteration or modification of her institutions. But it is necessary, we must frankly say, and necessary as a preliminary to any intelligent dealings with her on our part, that we should know whom her spokesmen speak for when they speak to us, whether for the Reichstag majority or for the military party and the men whose creed is imperial domination.

We have spoken now, surely, in terms too concrete to admit of any further doubt or question. An evident principle runs through the whole program I have outlined. It is the principle of justice to all peoples and nationalities and their right to live on equal terms of liberty and safety with one another, whether they be strong or weak.

Unless this principle be made its foundation, no part of the structure of international justice can stand. The people of the United States could act upon no other principle; and to the vindication of this principle they are ready to devote their lives, their honor and everything that they possess. The moral climax of this, the culminating and final war for human liberty, has come; and they are ready to put their own strength, their own highest purpose, their own integrity and devotion to the test. ♪

The war dragged on until the end of 1918, when Germany's allies collapsed or surrendered and English, French and American troops were poised to invade Germany itself. In August, the Chancellor of Germany, Prince Max of Baden, appealed for an armistice based upon Wilson's 14 points, but by the time the war ended—at 11am on 11 November 1918—nearly 40 million people had perished in the conflict.

Wilson was forced to make compromise after compromise to bring his dream of a League of Nations into reality. Despite winning the Nobel Peace Prize in 1919, the Republican-dominated US Congress rejected the Treaty of Versailles and the US President suffered a complete breakdown.

It is now clear that a President who had lost the support of his own country had outlined his personal dream of future international security based upon an idealism for which the world was not yet ready.

Woodrow Wilson died a broken man in 1924.

Benito Mussolini

'Invasion of Abyssinia'

Rome, Italy, 2 October 1935

Benito Mussolini (1883–1945) was born in the northern Italian province of Emilia-Romagna, the eldest son of a socialist activist blacksmith and a Catholic schoolteacher. A journalist and editor for a socialist newspaper at the start of World War I, he was originally against the war but later fought in the Italian army on the side of the Allies and was wounded in 1917. After the War, Mussolini thought socialism was dead and formed the Milan fascio—a political group with strong nationalist leanings that cut across class boundaries.

After some political success with the National Fascist Party, Mussolini came to power in 1922 when the March on Rome by thousands of black-shirted fascist supporters resulted in King Victor Emmanuel III sacking his Prime Minister and handing power to Mussolini.

Although Mussolini was originally the leader of a multi-party coalition government, he quickly seized control and became Il Duce (the Leader) with dictatorial powers. Within three years, Italy had become a one-party police state through the implementation of a series of laws, enforced by a fascist militia (called Blackshirts or squadristri) and the use of propaganda, intimidation and even murder. Mussolini also utilised a dramatic speaking style—often bombastically striking a pose by jutting out his chin—to accentuate the flamboyantly nationalistic rhetoric of his speeches.

In spite of several assassination attempts in the 1920s, he remained in power and promoted a policy of military expansion into Greece, Albania, Libya and, finally, Ethiopia.

With colonies in neighbouring Eritrea and Italian Somaliland and with Italy having failed to conquer Abyssinia in the 1890s, Mussolini signed the Italo-Ethiopian Treaty of Friendship in 1928. After declaring a 20-year friendship between the two nations, border skirmishes threatened to escalate into all-out war.

In 1935, while the League of Nations tried unsuccessfully to achieve a diplomatic solution to the problem, Mussolini sent Italian troops to Eritrea and Italian Somaliland in preparation for an invasion. On 2 October 1935, Mussolini spoke to the Italian people, justifying war with Ethiopia.

'Black Shirts of the revolution! Men and women of all Italy! Italians spread throughout the world, beyond the mountains and beyond the seas! Hear me! A solemn hour is about to sound in the history of the fatherland. At this moment twenty million men occupy the public squares of all Italy. Never in the history of mankind has there been seen a more gigantic spectacle. Twenty million men, but one heart, one will, one decision. Their demonstration must and does show the world that Italy and Fascism constitute a perfect, absolute and unalterable identity. For many months the wheels of destiny have been moving toward their goal under the impulse of our calm determination. In the latter hours, their rhythm has become more swift and by now cannot be stopped. It is not only an army that strives toward its objectives but a whole people of 44 million souls against whom an attempt is being made to consummate the blackest of injustices, that of depriving us of some small place in the sun.

When, in 1915, Italy exposed itself to the risks of war and joined its destiny with that of the Allies, how much praise there was for our courage and how many promises were made! But after the common victory to which Italy had made the supreme contribution of 670,000 dead, 400,000 mutilated and a million wounded, around the hateful peace table, Italy received but a few crumbs from the rich colonial booty gathered by others. We have been patient for thirteen years, during which the circle of selfishness that strangles our vitality has become ever tighter. With Ethiopia we have been patient for forty years! It is time to say enough!

In the League of Nations, there is talk of sanctions instead of recognition of our rights. Until there is proof to the contrary, I shall refuse to believe that the real and generous people of France can support sanctions against Italy. Similarly, I refuse to believe that the real people of Great Britain, who have never had discords with Italy, are prepared to run the risk of hurling Europe along the road to catastrophe for the sake of defending an African country universally branded as a country without the slightest shadow of civilization.

We shall face economic sanctions with our discipline, our sobriety and our spirit of sacrifice. Against military sanctions we shall reply with military measures. To acts of war we shall reply with acts of war.

Let no one think that he can make us yield without a hard struggle. A people jealous of its honor can use no other language nor can it adopt a different attitude. But let it be said once more and in the most categorical manner—and at this moment I make before you a sacred pledge—that we shall do all that is possible to prevent this conflict of a colonial character from assuming the nature and scope of a European conflict. That might be desired by those who seek in a new war to avenge their fallen temples, but not by us. Never before as in this historical epoch has the Italian people revealed the quality of its spirit and the power of its character. It is against this people to whom humanity owes some of its greatest conquests and it is against this people of poets, of artists, of heroes, of saints, of navigators, of emigrants, it is against this people that one dares speak of sanctions. Italy, proletarian and fascist, Italy of Vittorio Veneto and of the Revolution, arise! Let the cry of your decision fill the heavens; let it be a comfort to the soldiers who wait in Africa, a spur to friends and a warning to enemies in every part of the world. A cry of justice, a cry of victory.

The following day, Mussolini's army in Eritrea invaded Ethiopia. Italian troops captured the Ethiopian capital of Addis Ababa the following spring and on 9 May 1936, King Victor Emmanuel III of Italy was proclaimed Emperor of Ethiopia.

Having already supported Franco in the Spanish Civil War (1935–39), Mussolini entered into an agreement with Hitler in October 1936 and coined the term Axis Powers to describe the alliance between Italy and Germany. Inexorably set on a course towards world war, Italy declared war on Britain and France in June 1940, just in time to support Germany's occupation of its northern neighbour.

Five years later, with Italy defeated, invaded and demoralised, Benito Mussolini (wearing a German uniform) was captured near Lake Como trying to escape to Switzerland.

On 26 April 1945, the former fascist dictator, his mistress and several other party leaders were executed by partisans in the little township of Giulino di Mezzegra. Their bodies were then unceremoniously hung upside down on meat hooks hanging from the roof of a gas station.

Adolf Hitler

'The Obersalzburg Speech'

Obersalzburg, Germany, 22 August 1939

Adolf Hitler's Obersalzburg Speech is one of the most important and controversial speeches leading up to the Second World War (1939–45). On 22 August 1939, at the castle fortress he kept in Obersalzburg, the fascist German dictator known as The Führer spoke to his Commanders-in-Chief of his plans to invade Poland. The contents of his first speech later came to light when files belonging to the Chief of the High Command of the Armed Forces (OKW) were captured by American troops in Saalfelden, Austria. The speech later became the chief document of the American prosecutor at Nuremberg as 'evidence in the course of the session concerned with the invasion of Poland'.

Two other versions of the speech, as noted in minutes written by Admiral Hermann Boehm, Chief of the High Seas Fleet, and the diary of General Franz Halder, Chief of Staff, were later used as evidence in the Nuremburg trials. Halder was one of a growing band of anti-Hitler officers concerned about Germany's course towards war (Hitler dismissed him in 1942) and his records, which correspond closely to Boehm's minutes, were seen as further evidence of the speech's veracity.

' I have called you together to give you a picture of the political situation, in order that you may have insight into the individual element on which I base my decision to act, and in order to strengthen your confidence. After this, we will discuss military details.

It was clear to me that a conflict with Poland had to come sooner or later.

I had already made this decision in the spring, but I thought I would first turn against the West in a few years, and only afterwards against the East.

But the sequence cannot be fixed.

One cannot close one's eyes before a threatening situation. I wanted to establish an acceptable relationship with Poland, in order to fight first against the West, but this plan, which was agreeable to me, could not be executed, since the essential points have changed. It became clear to me that Poland would attack us, in case of a conflict with the West. Poland wants access to the sea. The further development became obvious after the occupation of the Memel region, and it became clear to me that under the circumstances a conflict with Poland could arise at an inopportune moment. I enumerate as reasons for this reflection:

> *'It was clear to me that a conflict with Poland had to come sooner or later. I had already made this decision in the spring, but I thought I would first turn against the West in a few years, and only afterwards against the East.'*

First of all, two personal constitutions: My own personality and that of Mussolini.

Essentially, it depends on me, my existence, because of my political activities. Furthermore, the fact that probably no one will ever again have the confidence of the whole German people as I do. There will probably never again be a man in the future with more authority than I have. My existence is, therefore, a factor of great value. But I can be eliminated at any time by a criminal or an idiot.

The second personal factor is Il Duce. His existence is also decisive.

If something happens to him, Italy's loyalty to the Alliance will no longer be certain. The basic attitude of the Italian Court is against the Duce. Above all, the Court sees in the expansion of the empire a burden. The Duce is the man with the strongest nerves in Italy.

The third factor favorable for us is Franco. We can ask only benevolent neutrality from Spain, but this depends on Franco's personality. He guarantees a certain uniformity and steadiness of the present system in Spain. We must take into account the fact that Spain does not as yet have a Fascist Party or our internal unity.

On the other side, a negative picture as far as decisive personalities are concerned: There is no outstanding personality in England or France.

For us, it is easy to make decisions. We have nothing to lose—we can only gain. Our economic situation is such, because of our restrictions, that we cannot hold out more than a few years. Göring can confirm this. We have no other choice; we must act. Our opponents risk much and can gain only a little. England's stake in a war is unimaginably great. Our enemies have men who are below average. No personalities, no masters, no men of action. Besides the personal factor, the political situation is favorable for us. In the Mediterranean, rivalry between Italy, France, and England. In the Orient, tension, which leads to the alarming of the Mohammedan world.

The English empire did not emerge from the last war strengthened. From a maritime point of view, nothing was achieved: conflict between England and Ireland, the South African Union became more independent, concessions had to be made to India, England is in great danger, unhealthy industries. A British statesman can look into the future only with concern.

France's position has also deteriorated, particularly in the Mediterranean.

Further favorable factors for us are these:

Since Albania, there is an equilibrium of power in the Balkans. Yugoslavia carries the germ of collapse because of her internal situation.

Romania did not grow stronger. She is liable to attack and vulnerable. She is threatened by Hungary and Bulgaria. Since Kemal's (Ataturk) death, Turkey has been ruled by small minds, unsteady weak men.

All these fortunate circumstances will no longer prevail in two or three years. No one knows how long I shall live. Therefore conflict is better now.

The creation of Greater Germany was a great achievement politically, but militarily it was questionable, since it was achieved through a bluff of the political leaders. It is necessary to test the military, if at all possible, not by general settlement, but by solving individual tasks.

The relation to Poland has become unbearable. My Polish policy hitherto was in contrast to the ideas of the people. My propositions to Poland, the Danzig corridor, were disturbed by England's intervention. Poland changed her tune towards us. The initiative cannot be allowed to pass to the others. This moment is more favorable than in two to three years. An attempt on my life or Mussolini's would change the situation to our disadvantage. One cannot eternally stand opposite one another with cocked rifle. A suggested compromise would have demanded that we change our convictions and make agreeable gestures. They talked to us again in the language of Versailles. There was danger of losing prestige. Now the probability is still great that the West will not interfere. We must accept the risk with reckless resolution. A politician must accept a risk as much as a military leader. We are facing the alternative

'The relation to Poland has become unbearable. My Polish policy hitherto was in contrast to the ideas of the people. My propositions to Poland, the Danzig corridor, were disturbed by England's intervention. Poland changed her tune towards us.'

to strike or be destroyed with certainty sooner or later.

Reference to previous risks:

I would have been stoned if I had not carried my point. The most dangerous step was the invasion of the neutral zone. Only a week before, I got a warning through France. I have always accepted a great risk in the conviction that it may succeed.

Now it is also a great risk. Iron nerves, iron resolution.

The following special reasons strengthen my idea. England and France are obligated, neither is in a position for it. There is no actual rearmament in England, just propaganda. It has done much damage that many reluctant Germans said and wrote to Englishmen after the solution of the Czech question: The Führer carried his point because you lost your nerve, because you capitulated too soon. This explains the present propaganda war. The English speak of a war of nerves. It is one element of this war of nerves to present the increase of armament. But how is the British rearmament in actual fact? The construction program of the Navy for 1938 has not yet been filled. Only mobilization of the reserve fleet...Purchase of fishing steamers.... Considerable strengthening of the Navy ... not before 1941 or 1942.

Little has been done on land. England will be able to send at most three divisions to the Continent. A little has been done for the Air Force, but it is only a beginning. 'AA' (anti-aircraft) defense is in its beginning stages. At the moment, England has only 150 AA guns. The new AA gun has been ordered. It will take a long time until enough have been produced. Fire directors are lacking. England is still vulnerable from the air. This can change in two or three years. At the moment the English air force has only 130,000 men, France 72,000 men, Poland 15,000 men. England does not want the conflict to break out for two or three years.

The following is characteristic of England. Poland wanted a loan from England for rearmament. England, however, only gave credit in order to make sure that Poland buys in England, although England cannot deliver. This means that England does not really want to support Poland. She does not risk eight million pounds in Poland, although she poured five hundred million into China. England's position in the world is very precarious. She will not take any risks.

France is short of men (decline in the birth rate). Little has been done for rearmament. The artillery is obsolete. France did not want to embark on this adventure. The West has only two possibilities for fighting against us:

I. Blockade: It will not be effective because of our autarchy and because we

'We will hold our position in the West until we have conquered Poland. We must bear in mind our great production capacity. It is much greater than in 1914–18.'

have sources of aid in the East

2. Attack in the West from the Maginot Line: I consider this impossible.

Another possibility would be the violation of Dutch, Belgian and Swiss neutrality. I have no doubt that all these states, as well as Scandinavia, will defend their neutrality with all available means. England and France will not violate the neutrality of these countries. Actually, England cannot help Poland. There still remains an attack on Italy. Military attack is out of the question. No one is counting on a long war. If Mr. von Brauchitsch had told me that I would need four years to conquer Poland, I would have replied: "Then it cannot be done." It is nonsense to say that England wants to wage a long war.

We will hold our position in the West until we have conquered Poland. We must bear in mind our great production capacity. It is much greater than in 1914–18.

The enemy had another hope, that Russia would become our enemy after the conquest of Poland. The enemy did not count on my great power of resolution. Our enemies are little worms. I saw them in Munich.

I was convinced that Stalin would never accept the English offer. Russia has no interest in maintaining Poland. Stalin knows that it would mean the end of his regime, no matter whether his soldiers emerged from a war victorious or beaten. Litvinow's replacement was decisive. I brought about the change toward Russia gradually. In connection with the commercial treaty, we got into political conversations.

Then came a general proposal from Russia. Four days ago, I took a special step, which brought it about that Russia answered yesterday that she was ready to sign.

The personal contact with Stalin is established. The day after tomorrow, von Ribbentrop will conclude the treaty. Now Poland is in the position in which I wanted her.

We need not be afraid of a blockade. The East will supply us with grain, cattle, coal, lead and zinc. It is a big aim, which demands great efforts. I am only afraid that at the last minute some schweinehund will make a proposal for mediation.

The political arm is set farther. A beginning has been made on the destruction of England's hegemony. The way will be open for the soldier, after I have made the political preparations.

Today's publication of the non-aggression pact with Russia hit like a shell. The consequences cannot be overlooked. Stalin also said that this course will benefit both countries. The effect on Poland will be tremendous.

Hermann Göring, the first Field Marshal of the Luftwaffe, allegedly responded to the speech 'with thanks to the Führer and the assurance that the Armed Forces will do their duty'. There is another version of the speech, however, which concludes: 'Göring jumped on a table, thanked blood-thirstily and made blood-thirsty promises. He danced like a wild man. The few that had misgivings remained quiet. ♪

This 'fourth' version of the Obersalzburg Speech was published in the Times of London under the title 'Nazi Germany's Road to War' on 24 November 1945. This highly exaggerated version was written by Louis P. Lochner, a former bureau chief of the Associated Press in Berlin, and published in his 1942 book 'What About Germany?' The speech had been leaked to Lochner by another anti-Hitler General named Ludwig Beck. Lochner's version of Hitler's speech had been introduced as evidence at the Nuremberg Tribunal the day before its London publication but was not accepted as evidence. Meticulous comparison of this version of Hitler's speech and the Nuremberg versions by several historians reveals that Lochner's was 'a strongly doctored version' designed to arouse a backlash against Hitler in Italy, Japan, Romania, Turkey and Armenia during the early years of the War.

Édouard Daladier

'The Nazis' Aim is Slavery'

Radio Broadcast (Paris, France), 29 January 1940

É douard Daladier (1876–1970) was the Prime Minister of France at the outbreak of World War II in 1939. Together with British Prime Minister Neville Chamberlain, Daladier signed the Munich Pact with Germany on 30 September 1938, all but abandoning Czechoslovakia to Nazi occupation, in the hope of avoiding another World War. Daladier was under no illusion as to the threat Germany now posed to his own homeland—as French War Minister he knew that his country was militarily, politically and socially unprepared for war—and he supported Britain's appeasement of Hitler rather than defending their Czech allies in an armed conflict with Germany.

A year later, Hitler's armies invaded Poland, Britain and France declared war against Germany and France itself was vulnerable to invasion. In January 1940, Daladier delivered the following radio address to the people of France in a belated recognition of Hitler's true intentions:

‘ A t the end of five months of war, one thing has become more and more clear. It is that Germany seeks to establish a domination over the world completely different from any known in history.

The domination at which the Nazis aim is not limited to the displacement of the balance of power and the imposition of supremacy of one nation. It seeks the systematic and total destruction of those conquered by Hitler and it does not treaty with the nations which he has subdued. He destroys them. He takes from them their whole political and economic existence and seeks even to deprive them of their history and their culture. He wishes to consider them only as vital space and a vacant territory over which he has every right.

The human beings who constitute these nations are for him only cattle.

He orders their massacre or their migration. He compels them to make room for their conquerors. He does not even take the trouble to impose any war tribute on them. He just takes all their wealth and, to prevent any revolt, he wipes out their leaders and scientifically seeks the physical and moral degradation of those whose independence he has taken away.

Under this domination, in thousands of towns and villages in Europe, there are millions of human beings now living in misery which, some months ago, they could never have imagined. Austria, Bohemia, Slovakia and Poland are only lands of despair. Their whole peoples have been deprived of the means of moral and material happiness. Subdued by treachery or brutal violence, they have no other recourse than to work for their executioners who grant them scarcely enough to assure the most miserable existence.

There is being created a world of masters and slaves in the image of Germany herself. For, while Germany is crushing beneath her tyranny the men of every race and language, she is herself being crushed beneath her own servitude and her domination mania. The German worker and peasant are the slaves of their Nazi masters while the worker and peasant of Bohemia and Poland have become in turn slaves of these slaves. Before this first realization of a mad dream, the whole world might shudder.

Nazi propaganda is entirely founded on the exploitation of the weakness of the human heart. It does not address itself to the strong or the heroic. It tells the rich they are going to lose their money. It tells the worker this is a rich man's war. It tells the intellectual and the artist that all he cherished is being destroyed by war. It tells the lover of good things that soon he will have none of them. It says to the Christian believer: "How can you accept this massacre?" It tells the adventurer: "A man like you should profit by the misfortunes of your country."

It is those who speak this way who have destroyed or confiscated all the wealth they could lay their hands on, who have reduced their workers to slavery, who have ruined all intellectual liberty, who have imposed terrible privations on millions of men and women and who have made murder their law. What do contradictions matter to them if they can lower the resistance of those who wish to bar the path of their ambitions to be masters of the world?

'The human beings who constitute these nations are for him only cattle. He orders their massacre or their migration. He compels them to make room for their conquerors. He does not even take the trouble to impose any war tribute on them. He just takes all their wealth...'

For us, there is more to do than merely win the war. We shall win it, but we must also win a victory far greater than that of arms. In this world of masters and slaves, which those madmen who rule at Berlin are seeking to forge, we must also save liberty and human dignity. ♪

In March 1940, Édouard Daladier resigned as Prime Minister when France failed to defend Finland from Russian invasion in the Winter War of December 1939 – March 1940.

When France fell in June of that year, Daladier was arrested by the Vichy puppet government and, following an aborted trial in 1942, he spent the remainder of the war under German guard in Austria. Two other failed French Prime Ministers, Paul Reynaud and Leon Blum, later joined him there.

Winston Churchill

'We Shall Fight on the Beaches'

British Parliament, London, 4 June 1940

When Winston Churchill (1874–1965) replaced Neville Chamberlain as British Prime Minister on 10 May 1940, his country was in a perilous position. In the first months of World War II, Norway had fallen, Germany's neighbours were under attack and France was poised for invasion. As he stated on 13 May, Churchill only had 'blood, toil, tears and sweat' to offer his people—a quote borrowed from a speech delivered by future US President Theodore Roosevelt in 1897—but he also had other qualities he would use to maximum effect...an affinity with the historic times in which he lived, a paternal and easily recognisable voice and the ability to inspire millions with his mastery of the English language.

On 4 June, in response to the remarkable evacuation of more than 331,000 British and French troops from the beaches of Dunkirk (France) after they had been cut off by the advancing German Army, Prime Minister Churchill delivered this rousing speech in the House of Commons.

Although France would soon fall, the escape of almost all the stranded troops on British destroyers, commercial vessels and small civilian boats raised hopes that all was not lost in the face of German military aggression. Churchill's anaphoric speech—often mimicked and more often misquoted—raised the morale of the British people as they now prepared for 'The Battle of Britain'.

6 I have, myself, full confidence that if all do their duty, if nothing is neglected and if the best arrangements are made, as they are being made, we shall prove ourselves once again able to defend our Island home, to ride out the storm of war and to outlive the menace of tyranny, if necessary for years, if necessary alone.

'We shall go on to the end, we shall fight in France, we shall fight on the seas and oceans...'

At any rate, that is what we are going to try to do. That is the resolve of His Majesty's Government—every man of them. That is the will of Parliament and the nation.

The British Empire and the French Republic, linked together in their cause and in their need, will defend to the death their native soil, aiding each other like good comrades to the utmost of their strength.

Even though large tracts of Europe and many old and famous States have fallen or may fall into the grip of the Gestapo and all the odious apparatus of Nazi rule, we shall not flag or fail.

We shall go on to the end, we shall fight in France, we shall fight on the seas and oceans, we shall fight with growing confidence and growing strength in the air, we shall defend our Island, whatever the cost may be, we shall fight on the beaches, we shall fight on the landing grounds, we shall fight in the fields and in the streets, we shall fight in the hills; we shall never surrender, and even if, which I do not for a moment believe, this Island or a large part of it were subjugated and starving, then our Empire beyond the seas, armed and guarded by the British Fleet, would carry on the struggle, until, in God's good time, the New World, with all its power and might, steps forth to the rescue and the liberation of the old. ♪

The Royal Air Force (RAF) maintained its air superiority over the Luftwaffe in the 'Battle of Britain' (July–October 1940) and put Germany's plans for an amphibious invasion on permanent hold. Winston Churchill worked tirelessly with allies France, the United States and later Russia, to bring a successful end to the war but, in the greatest blow of his political career, his Conservative government was voted out of office in July 1945—a month after Germany surrendered but before Japan could be defeated in the Pacific.

Winston Churchill spent the next six years as Opposition leader but in March 1946 he accepted an invitation from Westminster College, in Fulton, Missouri, to receive an honorary degree. There Churchill showed that he still had the power to influence world politics when he used the term 'Iron Curtain' in a speech entitled 'The Sinews of Peace'. Churchill had actually used the term for some decades and had included it in letters to US President Harry Truman, but ultimately it defined the way the Democratic West viewed the Communist East.

In 1951, Churchill's Conservative Party narrowly defeated the Labour Government and he was returned to power for a second time as Prime Minister. His four years in government, until his resignation in 1955 at age 80, saw him knighted in 1953 and receive the Nobel Prize for Literature (for his six-volume account, The Second World War) the same year. In 1963, two years before his death, the man once described as 'the greatest living Englishman' was granted honorary US citizenship by an Act of Congress.

Franklin D. Roosevelt

'A Day That Will Live In Infamy'

Washington DC, 8 December 1941

Franklin Delano Roosevelt (1882–1945) was the 32nd President of the United States of America. Born into great wealth to a prominent New York family, he married Eleanor Roosevelt—his father's fifth cousin and the niece of President Theodore Roosevelt—in 1905. Despite being stricken with polio in 1921 (which left him partially paralysed in the legs and necessitated the use of a wheelchair and a 'standing frame' to deliver public speeches), the former New York State Senator (1910–13) ran for President in 1928 and was elected governor of New York.

Popularly known as FDR, he was elected President in November 1932 at a time when America, and the world, had been paralysed by economic Depression for the past three years.

From his Inaugural Address in 1933, when he famously declared 'the only thing we have to fear is fear itself', Roosevelt outlined his plan for a 'New Deal' for the American public. But by the late 1930s, the United States faced an even greater hurdle—to retain its isolationist stance in face of increased fascism in Europe and Japanese nationalism. During the decade, Japan's foreign policy was inexorably linked to expansion, invasion and occupation in South East Asia.

When Britain and America froze oil imports to Japan, the United States—the dominant Pacific naval power at the time—was now seen as a severe threat to Japan's plans to extend its empire.

On 26 November 1941, a Japanese fleet of 33 warships and auxiliary craft under the control of Admiral Yamamoto sailed to the northern tip of Japan under strict radio silence before travelling westward 6500 km to Hawaii.

On 30 November 1941, US State Secretary Hull telephoned President Franklin D. Roosevelt at Warm Springs and prompted the US President to return to Washington DC because of the extreme acuteness of the diplomatic situation with Japan.

When Japan attacked the following Sunday morning, the US government was still negotiating for a diplomatic solution to the impasse with Japanese ambassadors in Washington.

In the early hours of 7 December, 183 planes armed with bombs and torpedos took off from six Japanese aircraft carriers 400 km north of Hawaii. During the previous night, five midget submarines with two-man crews were launched 15 km outside Pearl Harbour from larger 'mother' submarines. They were already inside the harbour when the first wave struck.

Japanese planes reached Pearl Harbour shortly before 8.00 am and completely surprised the US naval base because a long-range attack from the north was totally unsuspected. After the first wave arrived from the northwest, a second wave of Japanese planes attacked the Naval Air Station and Pearl Harbour at 8.40 am from the northeast.

American military losses were massive—12 battleships were sunk or beached (nine were damaged), 164 aircraft destroyed (159 damaged) with approximately 2400 lives lost. Most of the 1177 crew on the USS Arizona were killed when the ship was sunk by a 1760 lb armour piercing bomb that cut through the deck and ignited the ship's forward ammunition magazine. The ship sank in less than nine minutes.

The USS Oklahoma rolled over on its side after being hit by several torpedoes, with a loss of over 400 lives. The California, West Virginia, Utah and the Shaw were also sunk. The Nevada was beached after making a run for the open seas and the Maryland, Pennsylvania and Tennessee were severely damaged. Incredibly, three American aircraft carriers based at Pearl Harbour were outside on manoeuvres when the Japanese struck and survived the attack.

At about 5.00 pm that night in Washington DC, following meetings with his military advisers, President Roosevelt dictated to his secretary, Grace Tully, a request to Congress for a declaration of war. Roosevelt then revised the typed draft and made the most significant change in the opening sentence, which originally read 'a date which will live in world history.' On 8 December, at 12.30 pm, President Roosevelt addressed a joint session of Congress and the American people via radio.

‘Yesterday, December 7 1941—a date which will live in infamy—the United States of America was suddenly and deliberately attacked by naval and air forces of the Empire of Japan.

The United States was at peace with that Nation and, at the solicitation of Japan, was still in conversation with its Government and its Emperor looking toward the maintenance of peace in the Pacific. Indeed, one hour after Japanese air squadrons had commenced bombing in Oahu, the Japanese Ambassador to the United States and his colleague delivered to the Secretary of State a form reply to a recent American message. While this reply stated that it seemed useless to continue the existing diplomatic negotiations, it contained no threat or hint of war or armed attack.

It will be recorded that the distance of Hawaii from Japan makes it obvious that the attack was deliberately planned many days or even weeks ago. During the intervening time the Japanese Government had deliberately sought to deceive the United States by false statements and expressions of hope for continued peace.

The attack yesterday on the Hawaiian Islands has caused severe damage to American naval and military forces. Very many American lives have been lost. In addition, American ships have been reported torpedoed on the high seas between San Francisco and Honolulu.

Yesterday the Japanese Government also launched an attack against Malaya.

Last night Japanese forces attacked Hong Kong.

Last night Japanese forces attacked Guam.

Last night Japanese forces attacked the Philippine Islands.

Last night the Japanese attacked Midway Island.

Japan has, therefore, undertaken a surprise offensive extending throughout the Pacific area. The facts of yesterday speak for themselves. The people of the United States have already formed their opinions and well understand the implications to the very life and safety of our Nation.

As Commander-in-Chief of the Army and Navy, I have directed that all measures be taken for our defense.

Always will we remember the character of the onslaught against us.

No matter how long it may take us to overcome this premeditated invasion, the American people in their righteous might will win through to absolute victory.

I believe I interpret the will of the Congress and of the people when I assert that we will not only defend ourselves to the uttermost but will make very certain that this form of treachery shall never endanger us again.

Hostilities exist. There is no blinking at the fact that our people, our territory and our interests are in grave danger.

With confidence in our armed forces—with the unbounded determination of our people—we will gain the inevitable triumph—so help us God.

I ask that the Congress declare that since the unprovoked and dastardly attack by Japan on Sunday, December 7, a state of war has existed between the United States and the Japanese Empire. ♪

The US Senate responded with a unanimous vote in support of war (Montana pacifist Jeanette Rankin abstained from voting in the House of Representatives). At 4.00 pm that afternoon, President Roosevelt signed the declaration of war. Several days later, Germany and Italy declared war on the United States.

A new theatre had been opened in the Second World War—the Pacific. Franklin D. Roosevelt served an unprecedented four consecutive terms as President (1933–45)—a record no longer allowable due to a constitutional amendment—but died in office, aged 63, on 12 April 1945, before the war ended.

Harry S. Truman

'MacArthur and Korea'

Washington DC, 11 April 1951

Following the end of World War II in 1945, US President Harry S. Truman (1884–1972) proposed the 'Fair Deal' program but battled a 'do-nothing' Republican-dominated Congress which blocked most of his domestic reforms.

In March 1947, he committed America's economic, political and military support to countries threatened by 'outside pressures'—Communism. The Truman Doctrine, as it became known, hastened the advent of the Cold War and was directly responsible for portraying the United States as the democratic sheriff of the free world.

After winning a narrow victory over the Republican candidate, Thomas E. Dewey, in 1948 (newspapers actually reported that Dewey had won) Truman approved a post-war loan to Britain and sent US troops to South Korea for the police-action that eventually escalated into the Korean War (1950–53).

Under the command of General Douglas MacArthur, United Nations troops pushed the North Korean army back beyond the 38th Parallel in September 1950 and then pressed on to the northern capital, Pyongyang.

MacArthur was sure Russian and Chinese troops would not support the North Koreans, but he was wrong—many of the prisoners captured near the Yula River which bordered Manchuria were Chinese regulars. MacArthur bombed bridges on the Yula but this did not stop Chairman Mao sending 300,000 troops to support the North Koreans. United Nations forces, with MacArthur at the helm, were forced to retreat back below the 38th Parallel.

By early 1951, General MacArthur was openly critical of his President, his own military superiors and America's allies, for their lack of support in the face of Chinese aggression. When he made his intentions clear in the press—to blockade the Chinese mainland, use atomic weapons to suppress the enemy and invade both China and Korea with the help of Chiang Kai-shek's Chinese Nationalist forces—and then invited the Chinese Communist leadership to meet with him, Truman removed MacArthur from his command.

In this speech to the American people, relying heavily on the facts at hand, President Truman explained the reasons why he took this action:

'In the simplest terms, what we are doing in Korea is this: We are trying to prevent a third world war.

I think most people in this country recognized that fact last June. And they warmly supported the decision of the Government to help the Republic of Korea against the Communist aggressors. Now, many persons, even some who applauded our decision to defend Korea, have forgotten the basic reason for our action.

It is right for us to be in Korea. It was right last June. It is right today.

I want to remind you why this is true. The Communists in the Kremlin are engaged in a monstrous conspiracy to stamp out freedom all over the world. If they were to succeed, the United States would be numbered among their principal victims. It must be clear to everyone that the United States cannotand will not sit idly by and await foreign conquest.

The only question is: When is the best time to meet the threat and how?

The best time to meet the threat is in the beginning. It is easier to put out a fire in the beginning when it is small than after it has become a roaring blaze.

And the best way to meet the threat of aggression is for the peace-loving nations to act together. If they don't act together, they are likely to be picked off, one by one.

If they had followed the right policies in the 1930's—if the free countries had acted together, to crush the aggression of the dictators, and if they had acted in the beginning, when the aggression was small, there probably would have been no World War II.

If history has taught us anything, it is that aggression anywhere in the world is a threat to peace everywhere in the world. When that aggression is supported by cruel and selfish rulers of a powerful nation who are bent on conquest, it becomes a clear

'If history has taught us anything, it is that aggression anywhere in the world is a threat to peace everywhere in the world.'

and present danger to the security and independence of every free nation.

This is a lesson that most people in this country have learned thoroughly. This is the basic reason why we joined in creating the United Nations. And since the end of World War II, we have been putting that lesson into practice— we have been working with other free nations to check the aggressive designs of the Soviet Union before they can result in a third world war.

That is what we did in Greece, when that nation was threatened by the aggression of internationalCommunism. The attack against Greece could have led to general war. But this country came to the aid of Greece. The United Nations supported Greek resistance. With our help, the determination and efforts of the Greek people defeated the attack on the spot. Another big communist threat to peace was the Berlin blockade. That too could have led to war. But again it was settled because free men would not back down in an emergency. The aggression against Korea is the boldest and most dangerous move the communists have yet made. The attack on Korea was part of a greater plan for conquering all of Asia....

They want to control all Asia from the Kremlin....

The whole communist imperialism is back of the attack on peace in the Far East. It was the Soviet Union that trained and equipped the North Koreans for aggression. The Chinese communists massed 44 well-trained and well-equipped divisions on the Korean frontier. These were the troops they threw into battle when the North Korean Ccommunists were beaten....

So far, by fighting a limited war in Korea, we have prevented aggression from succeeding and bringing on a general war. And the ability of the whole free world to resist Communist aggression has been greatly improved.

We have taught the enemy a lesson. He has found out that aggression is not cheap or easy. Moreover, men all over the world who want to remain free have been given new courage and new hope. They know now that the champions of freedom can stand up and fight and that they will stand up and fight. Our resolute stand in Korea is helping the forces of freedom now fighting in Indochina and other countries in that part of the world. It has already slowed down the timetable of conquest....

But you may ask: Why can't we take other steps to punish the aggressor? Why don't we bomb Manchuria and China itself? Why don't we assist Chinese Nationalist troops to land on the mainland of China?

If we were to do these things, we would be running a very grave risk of starting a general war. If that were to happen, we would have brought about the exact situation we are trying to prevent.

If we were to do these things, we would become entangled in a vast conflict on the continent of Asia and our task would become immeasurably more difficult all over the world.

What would suit the ambitions of the Kremlin better than for our military forces to be committed to a full-scale war with Red China?

'The dangers are great. Make no mistake about it. Behind the North Koreans and Chinese Communists in the front lines stand additional millions of Chinese soldiers.'

It may well be that, in spite of our best efforts, the Communists may spread the war. But it would be wrong—tragically wrong—for us to take the initiative in extending the war.

The dangers are great. Make no mistake about it. Behind the North Koreans and Chinese Communists in the front lines stand additional millions of Chinese soldiers. And behind the Chinese stand the tanks, the planes, the submarines, the soldiers and the scheming rulers of the Soviet Union.

Our aim is to avoid the spread of the conflict.

The course we have been following is the one best calculated to avoid an all-out war. It is the course consistent with our obligation to do all we can to maintain international peace and security. Our experience in Greece and Berlin shows that it is the most effective course of action we can follow.

First of all, it is clear that our efforts in Korea can blunt the will of the Chinese Communists to continue the struggle. The United Nations forces have put up a tremendous fight in Korea and have inflicted very heavy casualties on the enemy. Our forces are stronger now than they have been before. These are plain facts which may discourage the Chinese Communists from continuing their attack.

Second, the free world as a whole is growing in military strength every day. In the United States, in Western Europe and throughout the world, free men are alert to the Soviet threat and are building their defenses. This may discourage the Communist rulers from continuing the war in Korea—and from undertaking new acts of aggression elsewhere.

If the Communist authorities realize that they cannot defeat us in Korea, if they realize it would be foolhardy to widen the hostilities beyond Korea, then they may recognize the folly of continuing their aggression.

A peaceful settlement may then be possible. The door is always open....

I believe that we must try to limit the war to Korea for these vital reasons: To make sure that the precious lives of our fighting men are not wasted; to see that the security of our country and the free world is not needlessly jeopardized; and to prevent a third world war.

A number of events have made it evident that General MacArthur did not agree with that policy. I have therefore considered it essential to relieve General MacArthur so that there would be no doubt or confusion as to the real purpose and aim of our policy.

It was with the deepest personal regret that I found myself compelled to take this action. General MacArthur is one of our greatest military commanders. But the cause of world peace is more important than any individual. ♪

United Nations troops eventually held under the biggest Communist offensive of the war and armistice negotiations commenced in July 1951. The terms: A full ceasefire, the retention of the 38th Parallel as a permanent border and the repatriation of prisoners—dragged the war on for another 15 months.

Harry Truman was defeated by Dwight D. Eisenhower in the 1952 Presidential election and Russian leader, Josef Stalin, died the following year. An armistice was signed in 1953 but no formal peace treaty has ever been signed to end the Korean War.

One hundred and eighty thousand United Nations troops were lost; the majority of them American (three million Korean military and civilian lost their lives).

In the years that have passed, Harry Truman's direct, plain-speaking rhetoric has made him something of a folk hero with the American public—but not until long after he left office in 1952 with one of the lowest approval ratings of any American president this century.

George H. Bush

'Operation Desert Storm'

Washington DC, 16 January 1991

On 2 August 1990, Saddam Hussein instructed Iraqi forces to invade the neighbouring oil rich nation of Kuwait. Within days, American troops were sent to Saudi Arabia to protect the country's oil fields from possible attack—an operation known as Desert Shield—and to act as a deterrent to the thousands of Iraqi troops already massing along the Saudi border. On 6 August, the United Nations Security Council imposed financial sanctions against Iraq and then authorised a naval blockade in the Persian

Gulf to use force, if necessary, to prevent any violation of the trade embargos.

In September, US President George H. Bush addressed Congress and stated America, and the world, could not allow Iraqi dictator, Saddam Hussein, to seize control of vital oil resources in the Middle East. While Iraq remained silent to world condemnation, Bush doubled the size of Allied forces to 430,000 soldiers. On 29 November, the UN Security Council authorised member nations to use 'all necessary means' to expel Iraqi troops from Kuwait if they did not withdraw by 15 January 1991.

President Bush then ordered more troops to the Gulf to pressure Saddam Hussein into withdrawing from Kuwait. On 12 January 1991, as the deadline approached and diplomatic discussions with Iraq faltered, the US House of Representatives voted 250–183 (and the US Senate 52–47) supporting the use of military force. When the 15 January deadline passed, there were 539,000 American troops and 270,000 Allied troops in the Gulf—the largest deployment of troops since World War II.

The following day Desert Shield became Desert Storm as US and Allied jets launched their attack on Iraqi air defences, communications systems and chemical weapons facilities in and around the capital, Baghdad.

In a sign of the times, and something never before been seen by a generation of Vietnam War baby boomer protesters and their Generation X offspring, the war was broadcast live to a global audience by CNN correspondents reporting from inside the Iraqi capital.

This is the televised speech President Bush gave shortly after the attack commenced at 6.45 pm US Eastern Standard Time (2.45 am January 17, Baghdad time):

'Just two hours ago, allied air forces began an attack on military targets in Iraq and Kuwait. These attacks continue as I speak. Ground forces are not engaged.

This conflict started on August 2 when the dictator of Iraq invaded a small and helpless neighbor. Kuwait—a member of the Arab League and a member of the United Nations—was crushed; its people, brutalized. Five months ago, Saddam Hussein started this cruel war against Kuwait. Tonight, the battle has been joined.

This military action, taken in accord with United Nations resolutions and with the consent of the United States Congress, follows months of constant and virtually endless diplomatic activity on the part of the United Nations, the United States and many, many other countries. Arab leaders sought what became known as an Arab solution, only to conclude that Saddam Hussein was unwilling to leave Kuwait. Others traveled to Baghdad in a variety of efforts to restore peace and justice. Our Secretary of State, James Baker, held an historic meeting in Geneva, only to be totally rebuffed. This past weekend, in a lastditch effort, the Secretary-General of the United Nations went to the Middle East with peace in his heart—his second such mission. And he came back from Baghdad with no progress at all in getting Saddam Hussein to withdraw from Kuwait.

Now the 28 countries with forces in the Gulf area have exhausted all reasonable efforts to reach a peaceful resolution—they have no choice but to drive Saddam from Kuwait by force. We will not fail.

'Now the 28 countries with forces in the Gulf area have exhausted all reasonable efforts to reach a peaceful resolution—they have no choice but to drive Saddam from Kuwait by force. We will not fail.'

As I report to you, air attacks are under way against military targets in Iraq. We are determined to knock out Saddam Hussein's nuclear bomb potential. We will also destroy his chemical weapons facilities. Much of Saddam's artillery and tanks will be destroyed. Our operations are designed to best protect the lives of all the coalition forces by targeting Saddam's vast military arsenal. Initial reports from General Schwarzkopf are that our operations are proceeding according to plan.

Our objectives are clear: Saddam Hussein's forces will leave Kuwait. The legitimate government of Kuwait will be restored to its rightful place and Kuwait will once again be free. Iraq will eventually comply with all relevant United Nations resolutions, and then, when peace is restored, it is our hope that Iraq will live as a peaceful and cooperative member of the family of nations, thus enhancing the security and stability of the Gulf.

Some may ask: Why act now? Why not wait? The answer is clear: The world could wait no longer. Sanctions, though having some effect, showed no signs of accomplishing their objective. Sanctions were tried for well over five months and we and our allies concluded that sanctions alone would not force Saddam from Kuwait.

While the world waited, Saddam Hussein systematically raped, pillaged and plundered a tiny nation, no threat to his own. He subjected the people of Kuwait to unspeakable atrocities—and among those maimed and murdered innocent children.

While the world waited, Saddam sought to add to the chemical weapons arsenal he now possesses, an infinitely more dangerous weapon of mass destruction—a nuclear weapon. And while the world waited, while the world talked peace and withdrawal, Saddam Hussein dug in and moved massive forces into Kuwait.

While the world waited, while Saddam stalled, more damage was being done to the fragile economies of the Third World, the emerging democracies of Eastern Europe, to the entire world, including to our own economy.

The United States, together with the United Nations, exhausted every means at our disposal to bring this crisis to a peaceful end. However, Saddam clearly felt that by stalling and threatening and defying the United Nations, he could weaken the forces arrayed against him.

While the world waited, Saddam Hussein met every overture of peace with open contempt. While the world prayed for peace,

'While the world waited, Saddam Hussein met every overture of peace with open contempt. While the world prayed for peace, Saddam prepared for war.'

Saddam prepared for war.

I had hoped that when the United States Congress, in historic debate, took its resolute action, Saddam would realize he could not prevail and would move out of Kuwait in accord with the United Nation resolutions. He did not do that. Instead, he remained intransigent, certain that time was on his side.

Saddam was warned over and over again to comply with the will of the United Nations: Leave Kuwait, or be driven out. Saddam has arrogantly rejected all warnings. Instead, he tried to make this a dispute between Iraq and the United States of America.

Well, he failed. Tonight, 28 nations—countries from five continents, Europe and Asia, Africa and the Arab League—have forces in the Gulf area standing shoulder to shoulder against Saddam Hussein. These countries had hoped the use of force could be avoided. Regrettably, we now believe that only force will make him leave.

Prior to ordering our forces into battle, I instructed our military commanders to take every necessary step to prevail as quickly as possible, and with the greatest degree of protection possible for American and allied service men and women. I've told the American people before that this will not be another Vietnam and I repeat this here tonight. Our troops will have the best possible support in the entire world and they will not be asked to fight with one hand tied behind their back. I'm hopeful that this fighting will not go on for long and that casualties will be held to an absolute minimum.

This is an historic moment. We have in this past year made great progress in ending the long era of conflict and cold war. We have before us the opportunity to forge for ourselves and for future generations a new world order—a world where the rule of law, not the law of the jungle, governs the conduct of nations. When we are successful—and we will be—we have a real chance at this new world order, an order in which a credible United Nations can use its peacekeeping role to fulfill the promise and vision of the UN's founders.

'It is my hope that somehow the Iraqi people can, even now, convince their dictator that he must lay down his arms, leave Kuwait, and let Iraq itself rejoin the family of peace-loving nations.'

We have no argument with the people of Iraq. Indeed, for the innocents caught in this conflict, I pray for their safety. Our goal is not the conquest of Iraq. It is the liberation of Kuwait. It is my hope that somehow the Iraqi people can, even now, convince their dictator that he must lay down his arms, leave Kuwait, and let Iraq itself rejoin the family of peace-loving nations.

Thomas Paine wrote many years ago: "These are the times that try men's souls." Those well-known words are so very true today. But even as planes of the multinational forces attack Iraq, I prefer to think of peace, not war. I am convinced not only that we will prevail but that out of the horror of combat will come the recognition that no nation can stand against a world united, no nation will be permitted to brutally assault its neighbor.

No President can easily commit our sons and daughters to war. They are the Nation's finest. Ours is an all-volunteer force, magnificently trained, highly motivated. The troops know why they're there. And listen to what they say, for they've said it better than any president or prime minister ever could.

Listen to Hollywood Huddleston, Marine Lance Corporal. He says, "Let's free these people, so we can go home and be free again." And he's right. The terrible crimes and tortures committed by Saddam's henchmen against the innocent people of Kuwait are an affront to mankind and a challenge to the freedom of all.

Listen to one of our great officers out there, Marine Lieutenant General Walter Boomer. He said: "There are things worth fighting for. A world in which brutality and lawlessness are allowed to go unchecked isn't the kind of world we're going to want to live in."

Listen to Master Sergeant J.P. Kendall of the 82nd Airborne: "We're here for more than just the price of a gallon of gas. What we're doing is going to chart the future of the world for the next 100 years. It's better to deal with this guy now than five years from now."

And finally, we should all sit up and listen to Jackie Jones, an Army Lieutenant, when she says: "If we let him get away with this, who knows what's going to be next?"

I have called upon Hollywood and Walter and JP and Jackie and all their courageous comrades-in-arms to do what must be done. Tonight, America and the world are deeply grateful to them and to their families. And let me say to everyone listening or watching tonight: When the troops we've sent in finish their work, I am determined to bring them home as soon as possible.

Tonight, as our forces fight, they and their families are in our prayers. May God bless each and every one of them and the coalition forces at our side in the Gulf and may He continue to bless our nation, the United States of America. ♪

George Herbert Bush, the son of a Wall Street banker, was born in Massachusetts in 1924. Enlisting in the air force as soon as he turned 18, Bush flew over 50 missions in the Pacific theatre of the Second World War (and was even shot down once), before resuming his studies at Yale and becoming a West Texas oilman.

A grass roots supporter of the local Republican Party in Houston, Bush later served two terms in Congress and was Ronald Reagan's running mate in the 1980 Presidential elections. After serving two terms as Reagan's Vice-President, George H. Bush became the 41st President of the United States in January 1989.

Operation Desert Storm, which lasted for only six weeks against demoralised Iraqi forces, was an unqualified success—even if troops did not venture onto Baghdad after entering Iraq and rid the world of Saddam Hussein as many Americans wanted—and the undoubted high point of his Presidency. Despite Bush's international success (and the collapse of the Soviet Union later that year), a domestic recession, raised taxes and the perception that he was out of touch with ordinary Americans saw him defeated by Democratic candidate Bill Clinton in the 1992 Presidential race.

Bush's re-election campaign was obviously hurt by a competitive third candidate—billionaire Ross Perot, who polled 19 per cent of the vote. But despite leaving the White House after only one term in office, George H. Bush did so with a 56 per cent job approval rating.

George W. Bush

'Pre-Invasion of Iraq Speech'

The White House, Washington DC, 7 October, 2002

After the liberation of Afghanistan in 2002, the United States of America looked towards Iraq as the new focus for regime change. President George W. Bush argued the need for an invasion of Iraq before the American people in October of that year. Many people, however, remained unconvinced of Bush's motives for connecting the previous year's September 11 attack and the terrorist threat posed by Al-Qaeda to the need to overthrow Iraqi dictator Saddam Hussein (his 27 September 2002 quote: 'After all this is the guy who tried to kill my dad', was equally unconvincing). While the United Nations was unmoved, President Bush's conviction that Iraq was producing 'weapons of mass destruction' became the false premise on which the invasion was ultimately based.

'Good evening.

Tonight I want to take a few minutes to discuss a grave threat to peace and America's determination to lead the world in confronting that threat.

The threat comes from Iraq. It arises directly from the Iraqi regime's own actions—its history of aggression and its drive toward an arsenal of terror.

Eleven years ago, as a condition for ending the Persian Gulf War, the Iraqi regime was required to destroy its weapons of mass destruction, to cease all development of such weapons and to stop all support for terrorist groups. The Iraqi regime has violated all of those obligations. It possesses and produces chemical and biological weapons. It is seeking nuclear weapons. It has given shelter and support to terrorism and practices terror against its own people. The entire world has witnessed Iraq's eleven-year history of defiance, deception and bad faith.

We also must never forget the most vivid events of recent history.

On September 11 2001, America felt its vulnerability—even to threats that gather on the other side of the earth. We resolved then, and we are resolved today, to confront every threat, from any source, that could bring sudden terror and suffering to America.

Members of the Congress of both political parties and members of the United Nations Security Council agree that Saddam Hussein is a threat to peace and must disarm. We agree that the Iraqi dictator must not be permitted to threaten America and the world with horrible poisons and diseases and gases and atomic weapons. Since we all agree on this goal, the issue is: "How can we best achieve it?"

Many Americans have raised legitimate questions: About the nature of the threat. About the urgency of action—and why be concerned now? About the link between Iraq developing weapons of terror and the wider war on terror. These are all issues we have discussed broadly and fully within my Administration. And tonight, I want to share those discussions with you.

First, some ask why Iraq is different from other countries or regimes that also have terrible weapons. While there are many dangers in the world, the threat from Iraq stands alone—because it gathers the most serious dangers of our age in one place. Iraq's weapons of mass destruction are controlled by a murderous tyrant, who has already used chemical weapons to kill thousands of people. This same tyrant has tried to dominate the Middle East, has invaded and brutally occupied a small neighbor, has struck other nations without warning and holds an unrelenting hostility towards the United States.

By its past and present actions, by its technological capabilities, by the merciless nature of its regime, Iraq is unique. As a former chief weapons inspector for the UN has said: "The fundamental problem with Iraq remains the nature of the regime itself. Saddam Hussein is a homicidal dictator who is addicted to weapons of mass destruction."

'If we know Saddam Hussein has dangerous weapons today—and we do—does it make any sense for the world to wait to confront him as he grows even stronger and develops even more dangerous weapons?'

Some ask how urgent this danger is to America and the world. The danger is already significant and it only grows worse with time. If we know Saddam Hussein has dangerous weapons today—and we do—does it make any sense for the world to wait to confront him as he grows even stronger and develops even more dangerous weapons?

In 1995, after several years of deceit by the Iraqi regime, the head of Iraq's military

Nobel prize winner and Prime Minister of Britain through World War II, Winston Churchill was the pinnacle of hope and leadership to the United Kingdom. Here, Winston Churchill gives a speech at London's County Hall in 1941.

The notorious Austrian-born politician and German chancellor, Adolph Hitler, transformed the history of Europe. Pictured above, Hitler addresses a rally during World War II (circa 1936).

First lady of the United States from 1933-1945, Eleanor Roosevelt speaks in the 1950s.

Committed to civil rights and anti-war, American politician Robert Kennedy announces his decision to challenge Lyndon Baines Johnson for the presidential nomination of the Democratic Party, 18 March 1968.

During a speech in Cincinnati in October 2002, the 43rd United States President George W. Bush issues a warning to Sadaam Husein's generals should they act unlawfully against American soldiers during the War on Terror.

King George V, who shed the Royal family's German ancestry by adopting the surname 'Windsor', inspects a troop of honour during his trip, with Queen Mary, to Ireland to open the Northern Parliament in 1921.

Former South African President Nelson Mandela addresses a crowd of residents from the Phola Park squatter camp during his tour of townships in September 1990, the year of his release from a 27 year prison sentence.

The youngest person and first woman to become Prime Minister, Benazir Bhutto revolutionised Pakistani politics. Benazir Bhutto sits on a stage during a public meeting in Peshawar, 26 December 2007, two days before her assassination.

Newly elected Australian Prime Minister Kevin Rudd apologises to the indigenous
people of Australia for past treatment on 13 February 2008.

Through his time as president, Boris Yeltsin revolutionized modern-day Russia, praised by many Russians as a saviour. A year before the dissolution of the Soviet Union, Boris Yeltsin gives a passionate speech to the people of Russia in 1990.

industries defected. It was then that the regime was forced to admit that it had produced more than 30,000 liters of anthrax and other deadly biological agents. The inspectors, however, concluded that Iraq had likely produced two to four times that amount. This is a massive stockpile of biological weapons that has never been accounted for and is capable of killing millions. We know that the regime has produced thousands of tons of chemical agents, including mustard gas, sarin nerve gas, and VX nerve gas. Saddam Hussein also has experience in using chemical weapons. He has ordered chemical attacks on Iran, and on more than forty villages in his own country. These actions killed or injured at least 20,000 people, more than six times the number of people who died in the attacks of September 11. And surveillance photos reveal that the regime is rebuilding facilities that it has used to produce chemical and biological weapons.

Every chemical and biological weapon that Iraq has or makes is a direct violation of the truce that ended the Persian Gulf War in 1991. Yet Saddam Hussein has chosen to build and keep these weapons, despite international sanctions, UN demands and isolation from the civilized world.

Iraq possesses ballistic missiles with a likely range of hundreds of miles—far enough to strike Saudi Arabia, Israel, Turkey and other nations—in a region where more than 135,000 American civilians and service members live and work. We have also discovered through intelligence that Iraq has a growing fleet of manned and unmanned aerial vehicles that could be used to disperse chemical or biological weapons across broad areas. We are concerned that Iraq is exploring ways of using UAVs (unmanned aerial vehicles) for missions targeting the United States. And of course, sophisticated delivery systems are not required for a chemical or biological attack—all that might be required is a small container and one terrorist or Iraqi intelligence operative to deliver it.

And that is the source of our urgent concern about Saddam Hussein's links to international terrorist groups. Over the years, Iraq has provided safe haven to terrorists such as Abu Nidal, whose terror organization carried out more than ninety terrorist attacks in twenty countries that killed or injured nearly 900 people, including 12 Americans. Iraq has also provided safe haven to Abu Abbas, who was responsible for seizing the Achille Lauro and killing an American passenger. And we know that Iraq is continuing to finance terror and gives assistance to groups that use terrorism to undermine Middle East peace.

We know that Iraq and the al-Qaida terrorist network share a common enemy—the United States of America. We know that Iraq and al-Qaida have

> **'Some have argued that confronting the threat from Iraq could detract from the war against terror. To the contrary, confronting the threat posed by Iraq is crucial to winning the war on terror.'**

had high-level contacts that go back a decade. Some al-Qaida leaders who fled Afghanistan went to Iraq.

These include one very senior al-Qaida leader who received medical treatment in Baghdad this year and who has been associated with planning for chemical and biological attacks. We have learned that Iraq has trained al-Qaida members in bomb making, poisons and deadly gases. And we know that after September 11, Saddam Hussein's regime gleefully celebrated the terrorist attacks on America.

Iraq could decide on any given day to provide a biological or chemical weapon to a terrorist group or individual terrorists. Alliances with terrorists could allow the Iraqi regime to attack America without leaving any fingerprints.

Some have argued that confronting the threat from Iraq could detract from the war against terror. To the contrary, confronting the threat posed by Iraq is crucial to winning the war on terror. When I spoke to the Congress more than a year ago, I said that those who harbor terrorists are as guilty as the terrorists themselves. Saddam Hussein is harboring terrorists and the instruments of terror, the instruments of mass death and destruction. And he cannot be trusted. The risk is simply too great that he will use them, or provide them to a terror network.

Terror cells and outlaw regimes building weapons of mass destruction are different faces of the same evil. Our security requires that we confront both. And the United States military is capable of confronting both.

Many people have asked how close Saddam Hussein is to developing a nuclear weapon. We don't know exactly, and that is the problem. Before the Gulf War, the best intelligence indicated that Iraq was eight to ten years away from developing a nuclear weapon; after the war, international inspectors learned that the regime had been much closer. The regime in Iraq would likely have possessed a nuclear weapon no later than 1993. The inspectors discovered that Iraq had an advanced nuclear weapons development program, had a design for a workable nuclear weapon and was pursuing several different methods of enriching uranium for a bomb.

Before being barred from Iraq in 1998, the International Atomic Energy Agency dismantled extensive nuclear weapons-related facilities, including three uranium-enrichment sites. That same year, information from a high-ranking Iraqi nuclear engineer who had defected, revealed that despite his public promises, Saddam Hussein had ordered his nuclear program to continue.

The evidence indicates that Iraq is reconstituting its nuclear weapons program. Saddam Hussein has held numerous meetings with Iraqi nuclear scientists, a group he calls his "nuclear mujahedeen"—his nuclear holy warriors. Satellite photographs reveal that

'We have experienced the horror of September 11. We have seen that those who hate America are willing to crash airplanes into buildings full of innocent people.'

Iraq is rebuilding facilities at sites that have been part of its nuclear program in the past. Iraq has attempted to purchase high-strength aluminum tubes and other equipment needed for gas centrifuges, which are used to enrich uranium for nuclear weapons.

If the Iraqi regime is able to produce, buy or steal an amount of highly enriched uranium a little larger than a single softball, it could have a nuclear weapon in less than a year. And if we allow that to happen, a terrible line would be crossed. Saddam Hussein would be in a position to blackmail anyone who opposes his aggression. He would be in a position to dominate the Middle East. He would be in a position to threaten America. And Saddam Hussein would be in a position to pass nuclear technology to terrorists.

Some citizens wonder: After eleven years of living with this problem, why do we need to confront it now? There is a reason. We have experienced the horror of September 11. We have seen that those who hate America are willing to crash airplanes into buildings full of innocent people. Our enemies would be no less willing—in fact they would be eager—to use a biological or chemical weapon, or, when they have one, a nuclear weapon.

Knowing these realities, America must not ignore the threat gathering against us. Facing clear evidence of peril, we cannot wait for the final proof—the smoking gun—that could come in the form of a mushroom cloud. As President Kennedy said in October of 1962: "Neither the United States of America nor the world community of nations can tolerate deliberate deception and offensive threats on the part of any nation, large or small. We no longer live in a world," he said, "where only the actual firing of weapons represents a sufficient challenge to a nation's security to constitute maximum peril."

Understanding the threats of our time, knowing the designs and deceptions of the Iraqi regime, we have every reason to assume the worst, and we have an urgent duty to prevent the worst from occurring.

Some believe we can address this danger by simply resuming the old approach to inspections and applying diplomatic and economic pressure.

Yet this is precisely what the world has tried to do since 1991. The UN inspections program was met with systematic deception. The Iraqi regime bugged hotel rooms and offices of inspectors to find where they were going next. They forged documents, destroyed evidence and developed mobile weapons facilities to keep a step ahead of inspectors. Eight so-called presidential palaces were declared off-limits to unfettered inspections. These sites actually encompass twelve square miles, with hundreds of structures, both above and below the ground, where sensitive materials could be hidden.

The world has also tried economic sanctions and watched Iraq use billions of dollars in illegal oil revenues to fund more weapons purchases, rather than providing for the needs of the Iraqi people.

The world has tried limited military strikes to destroy Iraq's weapons of mass destruction capabilities, only to see them openly rebuilt, while the regime again denies they even exist.

The world has tried no-fly zones to keep Saddam from terrorizing his own people, and in the last year alone, the Iraqi military has fired upon American and British pilots more than 750 times.

After eleven years during which we have tried containment, sanctions, inspections, even selected military action, the end result is that Saddam Hussein still has chemical and biological weapons and is increasing his capabilities to make more. And he is moving ever closer to developing a nuclear weapon.

Clearly, to actually work, any new inspections, sanctions, or enforcement mechanisms will have to be very different. America wants the UN to be an effective organization that helps to keep the peace. That is why we are urging the Security Council to adopt a new resolution setting out tough, immediate requirements. Among those requirements, the Iraqi regime must reveal and destroy, under UN supervision, all existing weapons of mass destruction. To ensure that we learn the truth, the regime must allow witnesses to its illegal activities to be interviewed outside of the country. And these witnesses must be free to bring their families with them, so they are all beyond the reach of Saddam Hussein's terror and murder. And inspectors must have access to any site, at any time, without pre-clearance, without delay, without exceptions.

> 'After eleven years during which we have tried containment, sanctions, inspections, even selected military action, the end result is that Saddam Hussein still has chemical and biological weapons and is increasing his capabilities to make more. And he is moving ever closer to developing a nuclear weapon.'

The time for denying, deceiving and delaying has come to an end. Saddam Hussein must disarm himself—or, for the sake of peace, we will lead a coalition to disarm him.

Many nations are joining us in insisting that Saddam Hussein's regime be held accountable. They are committed to defending the international security that protects the lives of both our citizens and theirs. And that is why America is challenging all nations to take the resolutions of the UN Security Council seriously. Those resolutions are very clear. In addition to declaring and destroying all of its weapons of mass destruction, Iraq must end its support for terrorism. It must cease the persecution of its civilian population. It must stop all illicit trade outside the oil-for-food program. And it must release or account for all Gulf War personnel, including an American pilot, whose fate is still unknown.

By taking these steps, and only by taking these steps, the Iraqi regime has an opportunity to avoid conflict. These steps would also change the nature of the Iraqi regime itself.

America hopes the regime will make that choice.

Unfortunately, at least so far, we have little reason to expect it. This is why two administrations—mine and President Clinton's—have stated that regime change in Iraq is the only certain means of removing a great danger to our nation.

I hope this will not require military action, but it may. And military conflict could be difficult. An Iraqi regime faced with its own demise may attempt cruel and desperate measures. If Saddam Hussein orders such measures, his generals would be well advised to refuse those orders. If they do not refuse, they must understand that all war criminals will be pursued and punished. If we have to act, we will take every precaution that is possible. We will plan carefully, we will act with the full power of the United States military, we will act with allies at our side and we will prevail.

There is no easy or risk-free course of action. Some have argued we should wait—and that is an option. In my view, it is the riskiest of all options—because the longer we wait, the stronger and bolder Saddam Hussein will become. We could wait and hope that Saddam does not give weapons to terrorists, or develop a nuclear weapon to

'As Americans, we want peace—we work and sacrifice for peace—and there can be no peace if our security depends on the will and whims of a ruthless and aggressive dictator. I am not willing to stake one American life on trusting Saddam Hussein.'

blackmail the world. But I am convinced that is a hope against all evidence. As Americans, we want peace—we work and sacrifice for peace—and there can be no peace if our security depends on the will and whims of a ruthless and aggressive dictator. I am not willing to stake one American life on trusting Saddam Hussein.

Failure to act would embolden other tyrants; allow terrorists access to new weapons and new resources; and make blackmail a permanent feature of world events. The United Nations would betray the purpose of its founding, and prove irrelevant to the problems of our time. And through its inaction, the United States would resign itself to a future of fear.

That is not the America I know. That is not the America I serve. We refuse to live in fear. This nation—in world war and in Cold War—has never permitted the brutal and lawless to set history's course. Now, as before, we will secure our nation, protect our freedom and help others to find freedom of their own.

Some worry that a change of leadership in Iraq could create instability and make the situation worse. The situation could hardly get worse, for world security and for the people of Iraq.

The lives of Iraqi citizens would improve dramatically if Saddam Hussein were no longer in power, just as the lives of Afghanistan's citizens improved after the Taliban. The dictator of Iraq is a student of Stalin, using murder as a tool of terror and control—within his own cabinet, within his own army and even within his own family. On Saddam Hussein's orders, opponents have been decapitated, wives and mothers of political opponents have been systematically raped as a method of intimidation and political prisoners have been forced to watch their own children being tortured.

America believes that all people are entitled to hope and human rights—to the non-negotiable demands of human dignity. People everywhere prefer freedom to slavery; prosperity to squalor; self-government to the rule of terror and torture. America is a friend to the people of Iraq. Our demands are directed only at the regime that enslaves them and threatens us. When these demands are met, the first and greatest benefit will come to Iraqi men, women and children. The oppression of Kurds, Assyrians, Turkomans, Shiites, Sunnis, and others will be lifted. The long captivity of Iraq will end and an era of new hope will begin. Iraq is a land rich in culture, resources and talent. Freed from the

'America is a friend to the people of Iraq. Our demands are directed only at the regime that enslaves them and threatens us.'

weight of oppression, Iraq's people will be able to share in the progress and prosperity of our time.

If military action is necessary, the United States and our allies will help the Iraqi people rebuild their economy and create the institutions of liberty in a unified Iraq at peace with its neighbors.

Later this week, the United States Congress will vote on this matter. I have asked Congress to authorize the use of America's military, if it proves necessary, to enforce UN Security Council demands. Approving this resolution does not mean that military action is imminent or unavoidable. The resolution will tell the United Nations, and all nations, that America speaks with one voice and is determined to make the demands of the civilized world mean something. Congress will also be sending a message to the dictator in Iraq that his only choice is full compliance—and the time remaining for that choice is limited.

Members of Congress are nearing an historic vote and I am confident they will fully consider the facts and their duties.

The attacks of September 11 showed our country that vast oceans no longer protect us from danger. Before that tragic date, we had only hints of al-Qaida's plans and designs. Today in Iraq, we see a threat whose outlines are far more clearly defined—and whose consequences could be far more deadly. Saddam Hussein's actions have put us on notice...and there is no refuge from our responsibilities.

We did not ask for this present challenge, but we accept it. Like other generations of Americans, we will meet the responsibility of defending human liberty against violence and aggression. By our resolve, we will give strength to others. By our courage, we will give hope to others. By our actions, we will secure the peace and lead the world to a better day.

Thank you, and good night.

The Iraq War, also known as Operation Iraqi Freedom began on 20 March 2003. The US-led invasion by a multinational coalition force that included British, and to a lesser degree, Australian, Danish and Polish troops, captured Baghdad on 9 April. By 1 May, President Bush had famously announced 'Mission Accomplished' on the aircraft carrier, USS Abraham Lincoln.

Saddam Hussein was captured in December 2003, tried and later executed in 2006 by the newly installed Iraqi government. Largely on the quick successes of the invasions of Afghanistan and Iraq,

President George W. Bush was elected to a second term in office in November 2004.

But more than five years after the invasion commenced, the United States is still in Iraq—supported now by a United Nations force but with coalition support wavering—as it tries to stop the country from further sliding into civil war and anarchy. In March 2008, US forces suffered their four thousandth fatality—97 per cent of whom died after President Bush's 'Mission Accomplished' proclamation—while Iraqi civilian casualties of the war have been conservatively estimated at a million people.

In 2008, it was determined by investigative journalists that President Bush and seven of his top aides publicly made 935 false statements between the 9/11 attacks and the invasion of Iraq in March 2003—in speeches, briefings, interviews, testimony and such—most regarding Iraq's possession of weapons of mass destruction and having links to Al Qaeda.

The truth is, Iraq did not.

Great Women

Helen Keller

'Against the War'

Carnegie Hall, New York City, 5 January 1916

With the rest of the world engulfed in a catastrophic war in Europe, there was a concerted push within the United States of America for the elected government to reverse its isolationist stance and enter the conflict. One of the many voices calling out against American involvement in World War I (1914–1918)—and conscription of its troops—was that of author and lecturer Helen Keller (1880–1968).

After losing her sight and hearing when she contracted meningitis as an infant, Keller had been taught to speak, read and write by teacher Anne Sullivan.

Keller, who obtained her degree in 1904, had already published her autobiography, The Story of My Life, and had since established a career as a respected lecturer and author.

On 5 January 1916, Helen Keller addressed a gathering under the auspices of the Women's Peace Party and the Labor Forum at Carnegie Hall, New York City.

'To begin with, I have a word to say to my good friends, the editors, and others who are moved to pity me. Some people are grieved because they imagine I am in the hands of unscrupulous persons who lead me astray and persuade me to espouse unpopular causes and make me the mouthpiece of their propaganda.

Now, let it be understood once and for all that I do not want their pity;

I would not change places with one of them. I know what I am talking about. My sources of information are as good and reliable as anybody else's. I have papers and magazines from England, France, Germany and Austria that I can read myself. Not all the editors I have met can do that. Quite a number of them have to take their French and German second hand. No, I will not disparage the editors. They are an overworked, misunderstood class. Let them remember, though, that if I cannot see the fire at the end of their cigarettes, neither can they thread a needle in the dark. All I ask, gentlemen, is a fair field and no favor. I have entered the fight against preparedness and against the economic system under which we live. It is to be a fight to the finish and I ask no quarter.

The future of the world rests in the hands of America. The future of America rests on the backs of 80 million working men and women and their children. We are facing a grave crisis in our national life. The few who profit from the labor of the masses want to organize the workers into an army which will protect the interests of the capitalists. You are urged to add to the heavy burdens you already bear, the burden of a larger army and many additional warships. It is in your power to refuse to carry the artillery and the dreadnoughts and to shake off some of the burdens, too, such as limousines, steam yachts and country estates. You do not need to make a great noise about it. With the silence and dignity of creators you can end wars and the system of selfishness and exploitation that causes wars. All you need to do to bring about this stupendous revolution is to straighten up and fold your arms.

We are not preparing to defend our country. Even if we were as helpless as Congressman Gardner says we are, we have no enemies foolhardy enough to attempt to invade the United States. The talk about attack from Germany and Japan is absurd. Germany has its hands full and will be busy with its own affairs for some generations after the European war is over.

With full control of the Atlantic Ocean and the Mediterranean Sea, the allies failed to land enough men to defeat the Turks at Gallipoli; and then they failed again to land an army at Salonica in time to check the Bulgarian invasion of Serbia. The conquest of America by water is a nightmare confined exclusively to ignorant persons and members of the Navy League.

Yet, everywhere, we hear fear advanced as argument for armament. It reminds me of a fable I read. A certain man found a horseshoe. His neighbor began to weep and wail because, as he justly pointed out, the man who found the horseshoe might some day find a horse. Having found the shoe, he might shoe him. The neighbor's child might some day go so near the horse's heels as to be kicked, and die.

'We are not preparing to defend our country. Even if we were as helpless as Congressman Gardner says we are, we have no enemies foolhardy enough to attempt to invade the United States.'

Undoubtedly the two families would quarrel and fight and several valuable lives would be lost through the finding of the horseshoe.

You know, the last war we had we quite accidentally picked up some islands in the Pacific Ocean which may some day be the cause of a quarrel between ourselves and Japan. I'd rather drop those islands right now and forget about them than go to war to keep them. Wouldn't you?

Congress is not preparing to defend the people of the United States. It is planning to protect the capital of American speculators and investors in Mexico, South America, China and the Philippine Islands. Incidentally, this preparation will benefit the manufacturers of munitions and war machines.

Until recently there were uses in the United States for the money taken from the workers. But American labor is exploited almost to the limit now and our national resources have all been appropriated. Still the profits keep piling up new capital. Our flourishing industry in implements of murder is filling the vaults of New York's banks with gold. And a dollar that is not being used to make a slave of some human being is not fulfilling its purpose in the capitalistic scheme. That dollar must be invested in South America, Mexico, China or the Philippines...

Every modern war has had its root in exploitation. The Civil War was fought to decide whether the slave holders of the South or the capitalists of the North should exploit the West. The Spanish-American War decided that the United States should exploit Cuba and the Philippines. The South African War decided that the British should exploit the diamond mines. The Russo-Japanese War decided that Japan should exploit Korea. The present war is to decide who shall exploit the Balkans, Turkey, Persia, Egypt, India, China, Africa. And we are whetting our sword to scare the victors into sharing the spoils with us. Now, the workers are not interested in the spoils; they will not get any of them anyway.

The preparedness propagandists have still another object, and a very important one. They want to give the people something to think about besides their own unhappy condition. They know the cost of living is high, wages are low, employment is uncertain and will be much more so when the European call for munitions stops. No matter how hard and incessantly the people work, they often cannot afford the comforts of life; many cannot obtain the necessities.

Every few days we are given a new war scare to lend realism to their propaganda. They have had us on the verge of war over the Lusitania, the Gulflight, the Ancona, and now they want the working men to become excited over the sinking of the Persia. The working man has no interest in any of these ships. The Germans might sink every vessel on the Atlantic Ocean and the Mediterranean Sea and kill Americans with every one—the American working man would still have no reason to go to war.

All the machinery of the system has been set in motion. Above the complaint and din of the protest from the workers is heard the voice of authority.

"Friends," it says, "fellow workmen, patriots; your country is in danger! There are foes on all sides of us. There is nothing between us and our enemies except the Pacific Ocean and the Atlantic Ocean. Look at what has happened to Belgium. Consider the fate of Serbia. Will you murmur about low wages when your country—your very liberties—are in jeopardy? What are the miseries you endure compared to the humiliation of having a victorious German army sail up the East River? Quit your whining, get busy and prepare to defend your firesides and your flag. Get an army, get a navy; be ready to meet the invaders like the loyal-hearted free men you are."

Will the workers walk into this trap? Will they be fooled again? I am afraid so. The people have always been amenable to oratory of this sort.

The workers know they have no enemies except their masters. They know that their citizenship papers are no warrant for the safety of themselves or their wives and children. They know that honest sweat, persistent toil and years of struggle bring them nothing worth holding on to, worth fighting for. Yet, deep down in their foolish hearts they believe they have a country. Oh blind vanity of slaves!

The clever ones, up in the high places, know how childish and silly the workers are. They know that if the government dresses them up in khaki and gives them a rifle and starts them off with a brass band and waving banners, they will go forth to fight valiantly for their own enemies. They are taught that brave men die for their country's honor. What a price to pay for an abstraction—the lives of millions of young men; other millions crippled and blinded for life; existence made hideous for still more millions of human beings; the achievement and inheritance of generations swept away in a moment-and nobody better off for all the misery!

This terrible sacrifice would be comprehensible if the thing you die for and call country fed, clothed, housed and warmed you, educated and cherished your children. I think the workers are the most unselfish of the children of men; they toil and live and die for other people's country, other people's sentiments, other people's liberties and other people's happiness! The workers have no liberties of their own; they are not free when they are compelled to work twelve

> **'There has never existed a truly free and democratic nation in the world. From time immemorial, men have followed with blind loyalty the strong men who had the power of money and of armies.'**

or ten or eight hours a day. They are not free when they are ill-paid for their exhausting toil. They are not free when their children must labor in mines, mills and factories or starve and when their women may be driven by poverty to lives of shame. They are not free when they are clubbed and imprisoned because they go on strike for a raise of wages and for the elemental justice that is their right as human beings.

We are not free unless the men who frame and execute the laws represent the interests of the lives of the people and no other interest. The ballot does not make a free man out of a wage slave. There has never existed a truly free and democratic nation in the world. From time immemorial, men have followed with blind loyalty the strong men who had the power of money and of armies. Even while battlefields were piled high with their own dead, they have tilled the lands of the rulers and have been robbed of the fruits of their labor. They have built palaces and pyramids, temples and cathedrals that held no real shrine of liberty.

As civilization has grown more complex, the workers have become more and more enslaved, until today they are little more than parts of the machines they operate. Daily they face the dangers of railroad, bridge, skyscraper, freight train, stokehold, stockyard, lumber raft and mine. Panting and straining at the docks, on the railroads and underground and on the seas, they move the traffic and pass from land to land the precious commodities that make it possible for us to live. And what is their reward? A scanty wage, often poverty, rents, taxes, tributes and war indemnities.

The kind of preparedness the workers want is reorganization and reconstruction of their whole life, such as has never been attempted by statesmen or governments. The Germans found out years ago that they could not raise good soldiers in the slums, so they abolished the slums. They saw to it that all the people had at least a few of the essentials of civilization—decent lodging, clean streets, wholesome if scanty food, proper medical care and proper safeguards for the workers in their occupations. That is only a small part of what should be done, but what wonders that one step toward the right sort of preparedness has wrought for Germany! For eighteen months it has kept itself free from invasion while carrying on an extended war of conquest and its armies are still pressing on with unabated vigor. It is your business to force these reforms on the administration. Let there be no more talk about what a government can or cannot do. All these things have been done by all the belligerent nations in the hurly-burly of war. Every fundamental industry has been managed better by the governments than by private corporations.

It is your duty to insist upon still more radical measures. It is your business to see that no child is employed in an industrial establishment or mine or store and that no worker is needlessly exposed to accident or disease. It is your business to make them give you clean cities, free from smoke, dirt and congestion. It is your business to make them pay you a living wage. It is your business to see that this kind of preparedness is carried into every department of the nation, until everyone has a chance to be well born, well nourished, rightly educated, intelligent and serviceable to the country at all times.

Strike against all ordinances and laws and institutions that continue the slaughter of peace and the butcheries of war. Strike against war, for without you no battles can be fought. Strike against manufacturing shrapnel and gas bombs and all other tools of murder. Strike against preparedness that means death and misery to millions of human being. Be not dumb, obedient slaves in an army of destruction. Be heroes in an army of construction. ♪

Helen Keller's remarkable story was later immortalised in William Gibson's stage play, The Miracle Worker. The film version, which was released in 1962, won Academy Awards for Anne Bancroft (as Anne Sullivan) and teenager Patty Duke, as Helen Keller, who both reprised their Broadway roles.

Carrie Chapman Catt

'The Crisis'

Atlantic City, New Jersey, 1916

Carrie Chapman Catt (1859–1947) had been involved in the National American Women's Suffrage Association since 1890. Ten years later, she became President of the Association and served a second term from 1915 until her death 32 years later. Catt, who was educated at Iowa State College, reformed the Women's Suffrage organisation and her work directly brought about securing the vote for women in 1920.

In 1916, at the height of World War I and with American involvement in the conflict teetering on the brink, Catt addressed a meeting in Atlantic City, New Jersey, and frankly set out the battle that still lay ahead.

' I have taken for my subject, "The Crisis," because I believe that a crisis has come in our movement which, if recognized and the opportunity seized with vigor, enthusiasm and will, means the final victory of our great cause in the very near future. I am aware that some suffragists do not share this belief; they see no signs nor symptoms today which were not present yesterday; no manifestations in the year 1916 which differ significantly from those in the year 1910. To them, the movement has been a steady, normal growth from the beginning and must so continue until the end. I can only defend my claim with the plea that it is better to imagine a crisis where none exists than to fail to recognize one when it comes; for a crisis is a culmination of events which calls for new considerations and new decisions. A failure to answer the call may mean an opportunity lost, a possible victory postponed....

Therefore, fellow suffragists, I invite your attention to the signs which point to a crisis and your consideration of plans for turning the crisis into victory...

"The Woman's Hour has struck." It has struck for the women of Europe and for those of all the world. The significance of the changed status of European women has not been lost upon the men and women of our land; our own people are not so unlearned in history, nor so lacking in National pride that they will allow the Republic to lag long behind the Empire, presided over by the descendant of George III. If they possess the patriotism and the sense of nationality which should be the inheritance of an American, they will not wait until the war is ended, but will boldly lead in the inevitable march of democracy, our own American specialty. Sisters, let me repeat, the Woman's Hour has struck!

...The four cornerstones of the foundations were laid long years ago. We read upon the first: "We demand for women education, for not a high school or college is open to her"; upon the second, "We demand for women religious liberty for in few churches is she permitted to pray or speak"; upon the third, "We demand for women the right to own property and an opportunity to earn an honest living. Only six, poorly-paid occupations are open to her, and if she is married, the wages she earns are not hers"; upon the fourth, "We demand political freedom and its symbol, the vote."

The stones in the foundation have long been overgrown with the moss and mould of time, and some there are who never knew they were laid. Of late, four capstones at the top have been set to match those in the base and we read upon the first: "The number of women who are graduated from high schools, colleges and universities is legion"; upon the second, "The Christian Endeavor, that mighty, undenominational church militant, asks the vote for women and the Methodist Episcopal Church, and many another, joins that appeal"; upon the third, "Billions of dollars worth of property are earned [and] owned by women; more than eight millions of women are wage-earners. Every occupation is open to them"; upon the fourth: "Women vote in twelve States; they share in the determination of 91 electoral votes."

After the capstones and cornice comes the roof. Across the empty spaces, the rooftree has been flung and fastened well in place. It is not made of stone but of two planks—planks in the platform of the two majority parties, and these are well supported by planks in the platforms of all minority parties.

'Our cause has won the endorsement of all political parties. Every candidate for the Presidency is a suffragist. It has won the endorsement of most churches; it has won the hearty approval of all great organizations of women.'

And we who are the builders of 1916, do we see a crisis? Standing upon these planks which are stretched across the top-most peak of this edifice of woman's liberty, what shall we do? Over our heads, up there in the clouds, but tantalizing [sic] near, hangs the roof of our edifice—the vote.

What is our duty? Shall we spend time in admiring the capstones and cornice? Shall we lament the tragedies which accompanied the laying of the cornerstones? Or, shall we, like the builders of old, chant: "Ho! all hands, all hands, heave to! All hands, heave to!" and while we chant, grasp the overhanging roof and with a long pull, a strong pull and a pull together, fix it in place forever more? Is the crisis real or imaginary? If it be real, it calls for action, bold, immediate and decisive.

Let us then take measure of our strength. Our cause has won the endorsement of all political parties. Every candidate for the Presidency is a suffragist. It has won the endorsement of most churches; it has won the hearty approval of all great organizations of women. It was won the support of all reform movements; it has won the progressives of every variety. The majority of the press in most States is with us. Great men in every political party, church and movement are with us. The names of the greatest men and women of art, science, literature and philosophy, reform, religion and politics are on our lists. We have not won the reactionaries of any party, church or society and we never will. From the beginning of things, there have been Antis. The Antis drove Moses out of Egypt; they crucified Christ who said, "Love thy neighbor as thyself" [Matt. 19:19, 22:39]; they have persecuted Jews in all parts of the world; they poisoned Socrates, the great philosopher; they cruelly persecuted Copernicus and Galileo, the first great scientists; they burned Giordano Bruno at the stake because he believed the world was round; they burned Savonarola who warred upon church corruption; they burned Eufame McIlyane [sic] because she used an anaesthetic; they burned Joan d'Arc for a heretic; they have sent great men and women to Siberia to eat their hearts out in isolation; they burned in effigy William Lloyd Garrison; they egged Abbie Kelley and Lucy Stone and mobbed Susan B. Anthony. Yet, in proportion to the enlightenment of their respective ages, these Antis were persons of intelligence and honest purpose. They were merely deaf to the call of Progress and were enraged because the world insisted upon moving on. Antis, male and female, there still are and will be to the end of time. Give to them a prayer of forgiveness for they know not what they do; and prepare for the forward march.

We have not won the ignorant and illiterate and we never can. They are too undeveloped mentally to understand that the institutions of today are not those of yesterday nor will be those of tomorrow.

We have not won the forces of evil and we never will. Evil has ever been timorous and suspicious of all change. It is an instinctive act of self-preservation which makes it fear and consequently oppose votes for women. As the Hon. Champ Clark said the other day: "Some good and intelligent people are opposed to women's suffrage; but all the ignorant and evil-minded are against it."

These three forces are the enemies of our cause.

Before the vote is won, there must and will be a gigantic final conflict between the forces of progress, righteousness and democracy and the forces of ignorance, evil and reaction. That struggle may be postponed, but it cannot be evaded or avoided. There is no question as to which side will be the victor.

Shall we play the coward, then, and leave the hard knocks for our daughters, or shall we throw ourselves into the fray, bare our own shoulders to the blows and thus bequeath to them a politically liberated womanhood? We have taken note of our gains and of our resources and they are all we could wish.

Before the final struggle, we must take cognizance of our weaknesses. Are we prepared to grasp the victory? Alas, no! Our movement is like a great Niagara with a vast volume of water tumbling over its ledge but turning no wheel. Our organized machinery is set for the propagandist stage and not for the seizure of victory. Our supporters are spreading the argument for our cause; they feel no sense of responsibility for the realization of our hopes. Our movement lacks cohesion, organization, unity and consequent momentum.

Behind us, in front of us, everywhere about us are suffragists—millions of them—but inactive and silent. They have been "agitated and educated" and are with us in belief. There are thousands of women who have at one time or another been members of our organization but they have dropped out because, to them, the movement seemed negative and pointless. Many have taken up other work whose results were more immediate. Philanthropy, charity, work for corrective laws of various kinds, temperance, relief for working women and numberless similar public services have called them. Others have turned to the pleasanter avenues of clubwork, art or literature.

There are thousands of other women who have never learned of the earlier struggles of our movement. They found doors of opportunity open to them on every side. They found well-paid posts awaiting the qualified woman and they have availed themselves of all these blessings.

Almost without exception, they believe in the vote but they feel neither gratitude to those who opened the doors through which they have entered to economic liberty nor any sense of obligation to open other doors for those who come after.

There are still others who, timorously looking over their shoulders to see if any listeners be near, will tell us they hope we will win and win soon but they are too frightened of Mother Grundy to help. There are others too occupied with the small things of life to help. They say they could find time to vote but not to work for the vote. There are men, too, millions of them, waiting to be called. These men and women are our reserves. They are largely unorganized and untrained soldiers with little responsibility toward our movement. Yet these reserves must be mobilized. The final struggle needs their numbers and the momentum those numbers will bring. Were never another convert made, there are suffragists enough in this country, if combined, to make so irresistible a driving force that victory might be seized at once.

How can it be done? By a simple change of mental attitude. If we are to seize the victory, that change must take place in this hall, here and now!

The old belief, which has sustained suffragists in many an hour of discouragement, "women's suffrage is bound to come," must give way to the new, "The Woman's Hour has struck." The long drawn out struggle, the cruel hostility which, for years, was arrayed against our cause, have accustomed suffragists to the idea of indefinite postponement, but eventual victory.

The slogan of a movement sets its pace. The old one counseled patience. It said, there is plenty of time. It pardoned sloth and half-hearted effort. It set the pace of an educational campaign. The "Woman's Hour has struck" sets the pace of a crusade which will have its way. It says: "Awake, arise, my sisters, let your hearts be filled with joy—the time of victory is here. Onward March."

If you believe with me that a crisis has come to our movement—if you believe that the time for final action is now if you catch the rosy tints of the coming day—what does it mean to you? Does it not give you a thrill of exaltation? Does the blood not course more quickly through your veins? Does it not bring a new sense of freedom, of joy and of determination? Is it not true that you who wanted a little time ago to lay down the work because you were weary with long service, now, under the compelling influence of a changed mental attitude, are ready to go on until the vote is won?

The change is one of spirit! Aye, and the spiritual effect upon you will come to others.

'Then let us sound a bugle call here and now to the women of the Nation: "The Woman's Hour has struck."'

Let me borrow an expression from Hon. John Finlay: What our great movement needs now is a "mobilization of spirit"—the jubilant, glad spirit of victory.

Then let us sound a bugle call here and now to the women of the Nation: "The Woman's Hour has struck." Let the bugle sound from the suffrage headquarters of every State at the inauguration of a State campaign. Let the call

'The veins of American women are not filled with milk and water. They are neither cowards nor slackers. They will come. They only await the bugle call to learn that the final battle is on.'

go forth again and again and yet again. Let it be repeated in every article written, in every speech made, in every conversation held. Let the bugle blow again and yet again. The political emancipation of our sex call[s] you, women of America, arise! Are you content that others shall pay the price of your liberty? Women in schools and counting houses, in shops and on the farm, women in the home with babes at their breasts and women engaged in public careers, will hear. The veins of American women are not filled with milk and water. They are neither cowards nor slackers. They will come. They only await the bugle call to learn that the final battle is on.

In 1920, the 19th Amendment to the US Constitution was passed giving women the right to vote. Carrie Chapman Catt helped to establish the League of Women Voters in 1919 and devoted the remainder of her life to campaigning for world peace.

Eleanor Roosevelt

'The Struggle for Human Rights'

Paris, France, 28 September 1948

E leanor Roosevelt (1884–1962) was the niece of President Theodore Roosevelt (1901–09) and the wife of her distant cousin, Franklin D. Roosevelt, the 32nd President of the United States. Eleanor Roosevelt provided the moral and emotional strength to her husband's political career (especially after he contracted polio in 1921) and was a close adviser to him on social and civil issues during World War II. Forthright in her views and unshakable in her beliefs, her husband's preoccupation with the war effort during the early 1940s put a strain on the Roosevelts' relationship.

After her husband's death in office in 1945, Eleanor Roosevelt expanded her social activism as delegate to the United Nations (1946), US representative to the General Assembly (1946–52) and chair of the UN Human Rights Commission.

In September 1948, she addressed a gathering in Paris regarding the struggle for human rights after the cataclysmic events of World War II. In this speech she spoke of the political, social and philosophical differences between America and the USSR and the common purpose of recognising the dignity of the human being.

' I have come this evening to talk with you on one of the greatest issues of our time—that is the preservation of human freedom. I have chosen to discuss it here in France, at the Sorbonne, because here in this soil the roots of human freedom have long ago struck deep and here they have been richly nourished. It was here the Declaration of the Rights of Man was proclaimed and the great slogans of the French Revolution—liberty, equality, fraternity—fired the imagination of men. I have chosen to discuss this issue in Europe because this has been the scene of the greatest historic battles between freedom and tyranny. I have chosen to discuss it in the early days of the General Assembly because the issue of human liberty is decisive for the settlement of outstanding political differences and for the future of the United Nations.

The decisive importance of this issue was fully recognized by the founders of the United Nations at San Francisco. Concern for the preservation and promotion of human rights and fundamental freedoms stands at the heart of the United Nations. Its Charter is distinguished by its preoccupation with the rights and welfare of individual men and women. The United Nations has made it clear that it intends to uphold human rights and to protect the dignity of the human personality. In the preamble to the Charter, the keynote is set when it declares: "We the people of the United Nations determined...to reaffirm faith in fundamental human rights, in the dignity and worth of the human person, in the equal rights of men and women and of nations large and small, and...to promote social progress and better standards of life in larger freedom." This reflects the basic premise of the Charter that the peace and security of mankind are dependent on mutual respect for the rights and freedoms of all.

One of the purposes of the United Nations is declared in Article 1 to be: "To achieve international cooperation in solving international problems of an economic, social, cultural or humanitarian character, and in promoting and encouraging respect for human rights and for fundamental freedoms for all without distinction as to race, sex, language or religion."

This thought is repeated at several points and notably in Articles 55 and 56 the Members pledge themselves to take joint and separate action in cooperation with the United Nations for the promotion of "universal respect for, and observance of, human rights and fundamental freedoms for all without distinction as to race, sex, language or religion."

The Human Rights Commission was given as its first and most important task the preparation of an International Bill of Rights. The General Assembly, which opened its third session here in Paris a few days ago, will have before it the first fruit of the Commission's labors in this task; that is the International Declaration of Human Rights.

The Declaration was finally completed after much work during the last session of the Human Rights Commission in New York in the spring of 1948. The Economic and Social Council has sent it without recommendation to the General Assembly, together with other documents transmitted by the Human Rights Commission.

It was decided in our Commission that a Bill of Rights should contain two parts:

1. A Declaration which could be approved through action of the Member States of the United Nations in the General Assembly. This declaration would have great moral force and would say to the peoples of the world "this is what we hope human rights may mean to all people in the years to come." We have put down here the rights that we consider basic for individual human beings the world over to have. Without them, we feel that the full development of individual personality is impossible.

2. The second part of the bill, which the Human Rights Commission has not yet completed because of the lack of time, is a covenant which would be in the form of a treaty to be presented to the nations of the world. Each nation, as it is prepared to do so, would ratify this covenant and the covenant would then become binding on the nations which adhere to it. Each nation ratifying would then be obligated to change its laws wherever they did not conform to the points contained in the covenant.

This covenant, of course, would have to be a simpler document. It could not state aspirations, which we feel to be permissible in the Declaration. It could only state rights which could be assured by law and it must contain methods of implementation and no state ratifying the covenant could be allowed to disregard it. The methods of implementation have not yet been agreed upon, nor have they been given adequate consideration by the Commission at any of its meetings. There certainly should be discussion on the entire question of this world Bill of Human Rights and there may be acceptance by this Assembly of the Declaration if they come to agreement on it. The acceptance of the Declaration, I think, should encourage every nation in the coming months to discuss its meaning with its people so that they will be better prepared to accept the covenant with a deeper understanding of the problems involved when that is presented, we hope, a year from now and, we hope, accepted.

The Declaration has come from the Human Rights Commission with unanimous acceptance except for four abstentions—the USSR, Yugoslavia, Ukraine, and Byelorussia. The reason for this is a fundamental difference in the conception of human rights as they exist in these states and in certain other Member States in the United Nations.

In the discussion before the Assembly, I think it should be made crystal clear what these differences are and tonight I want to spend a little time making them clear to you. It seems to me there is a valid reason for taking the time today to think carefully and clearly on the subject of human rights, because in the acceptance and observance of these rights lies the root, I believe, of our chance of peace in the future, and for the strengthening of the United Nations organization to the point where it can maintain peace in the future.

> *'Democracy, freedom, human rights have come to have a definite meaning to the people of the world which we must not allow any nation to so change that they are made synonymous with suppression and dictatorship.'*

We must not be confused about what freedom is. Basic human rights are simple and easily understood: Freedom of speech and a free press; freedom of religion and worship; freedom of assembly and the right of petition; the right of men to be secure in their homes and free from unreasonable search and seizure and from arbitrary arrest and punishment.

We must not be deluded by the efforts of the forces of reaction to prostitute the great words of our free tradition and thereby to confuse the struggle. Democracy, freedom, human rights have come to have a definite meaning to the people of the world which we must not allow any nation to so change that they are made synonymous with suppression and dictatorship.

There are basic differences that show up even in the use of words between a democratic and a totalitarian country. For instance "democracy" means one thing to the USSR and another in the USA and, I know, in France. I have served, since the first meeting of the nuclear commission on the Human Rights Commission, and I think this point stands out clearly.

The USSR representatives assert that they already have achieved many things which we, in what they call the "bourgeois democracies", cannot achieve because their government controls the accomplishment of these things.

Our government seems powerless to them because, in the last analysis, it is controlled by the people. They would not put it that way—they would say that the people in the USSR control their government by allowing their government to have certain absolute rights. We, on the other hand, feel that certain rights can never be granted to the government, but must be kept in the hands of the people.

For instance, the USSR will assert that their press is free because the state makes it free by providing the machinery, the paper and even the money for salaries for the people who work on the paper. They state that there is no control over what is printed in the various papers that they subsidize in this manner, such, for instance, as a trade union paper. But what would happen if a paper were to print ideas which were critical of the basic policies and beliefs of

> **'...what would happen if a paper were to print ideas which were critical of the basic policies and beliefs of the Communist government? I am sure some good reason would be found for abolishing the paper.'**

the Communist government? I am sure some good reason would be found for abolishing the paper.

It is true that there have been many cases where newspapers in the USSR have criticized officials and their actions and have been responsible for the removal of those officials, but in doing so, they did not criticize anything which was fundamental to Communist beliefs. They simply criticized methods of doing things, so one must differentiate between things which are permissible, such as criticism of any individual or of the manner of doing things, and the criticism of a belief which would be considered vital to the acceptance of Communism.

What are the differences, for instance, between trade unions in the totalitarian states and in the democracies? In the totalitarian state a trade union is an instrument used by the government to enforce duties, not to assert rights. Propaganda material which the government desires the workers to have is furnished by the trade unions to be circulated to their members.

Our trade unions, on the other hand, are solely the instrument of the workers themselves. They represent the workers in their relations with the government and with management and they are free to develop their own opinions without government help or interference. The concepts of our trade unions and those in totalitarian countries are drastically different. There is little mutual understanding.

I think the best example one can give of this basic difference of the use of terms is "the right to work." The Soviet Union insists that this is a basic right which it alone can guarantee because it alone provides full employment by the government. But the right to work in the Soviet Union means the assignment of workers to do whatever task is given to them by the government without an opportunity for the people to participate in the decision that the government should do this. A society in which everyone works is not necessarily a free society and may indeed be a slave society. On the other hand, a society in which there is widespread economic insecurity can turn freedom into a barren and vapid right for millions of people.

We in the United States have come to realize it means freedom to choose one's job, to work or not to work as one desires. We in the United States have come to realize, however, that people have a right to demand that their government will not allow them to starve because as individuals they cannot find work of the kind they are accustomed to doing. This is a decision brought about by public opinion which came as a result of the great Depression in which many people were out of work. But we would not consider in the United States that we had gained any freedom if we were compelled to follow a dictatorial assignment to work where and when we were told. The right of choice would seem to us an important, fundamental freedom.

'We are fighting this battle again today as it was fought at the time of the French Revolution and at the time of the American Revolution.'

I have great sympathy with the Russian people. They love their country and have always defended it valiantly against invaders. They have been through a period of revolution, as a result of which they were for a time cut off from outside contact. They have not lost their resulting suspicion of other countries and the great difficulty is today that their government encourages this suspicion and seems to believe that force alone will bring them respect.

We in the democracies believe in a kind of international respect and action which is reciprocal. We do not think others should treat us differently from the way they wish to be treated. It is interference in other countries that especially stirs up antagonism against the Soviet Government. If it wishes to feel secure in developing its economic and political theories within its territory, then it should grant to others that same security. We believe in the freedom of people to make their own mistakes. We do not interfere with them and they should not interfere with others.

The basic problem confronting the world today, as I said in the beginning, is the preservation of human freedom for the individual and consequently for the society of which he is a part. We are fighting this battle again today as it was fought at the time of the French Revolution and at the time of the American Revolution. The issue of human liberty is as decisive now as it was then. I want to give you my conception of what is meant in my country by freedom of the individual.

Long ago in London during a discussion with Mr. Vyshinsky, he told me there was no such thing as freedom for the individual in the world. All freedom of the individual was conditioned by the rights of other individuals. That, of course, I granted. I said: "We approach the question from a different point of view; we here in the United Nations are trying to develop ideals which will be broader in outlook, which will consider first the rights of man, which will consider what makes man more free; not governments, but man." The totalitarian state typically places the will of the people second to decrees

> **'Through normal democratic processes, we are coming to understand our needs and how we can attain full equality for all our people. Free discussion on the subject is permitted.'**

promulgated by a few men at the top.

Naturally, there must always be consideration of the rights of others; but in a democracy this is not a restriction. Indeed, in our democracies we make our freedoms secure because each of us is expected to respect the rights of others and we are free to make our own laws. Freedom for our peoples is not only a right, but also a tool. Freedom of speech, freedom of the press, freedom of information, freedom of assembly-these are not just abstract ideals to us; they are tools with which we create a way of life, a way of life in which we can enjoy freedom.

Sometimes the processes of democracy are slow, and I have known some of our leaders to say that a benevolent dictatorship would accomplish the ends desired in a much shorter time than it takes to go through the democratic processes of discussion and the slow formation of public opinion. But there is no way of ensuring that a dictatorship will remain benevolent or that power once in the hands of a few will be returned to the people without struggle or revolution. This we have learned by experience and we accept the slow processes of democracy because we know that shortcuts compromise principles on which no compromise is possible.

The final expression of the opinion of the people with us is through free and honest elections, with valid choices on basic issues and candidates. The secret ballot is essential to free elections, but you must have a choice before you. I have heard my husband say many times that a people need never lose their freedom if they kept their right to a secret ballot and if they used that secret ballot to the full. Basic decisions of our society are made through the expressed will of the people. That is why when we see these liberties threatened, instead of falling apart, our nation becomes unified and our democracies come together as a unified group in spite of our varied backgrounds and many racial strains.

In the United States we have a capitalistic economy. That is because public opinion favors that type of economy under the conditions in which we live. But we have imposed certain restraints. For instance, we have antitrust laws. These are the legal evidence of the determination of the American people to maintain an economy of free competition and not to allow monopolies to take away the people's freedom.

Our trade unions grow stronger because the people come to believe that this is the proper way to guarantee the rights of the workers and that the right to organize and to bargain collectively keeps the balance between the actual producer, the investor of money and the manager in industry who watches over the man who works with his hands and who produces the materials which are our tangible wealth.

In the United States, we are old enough not to claim perfection. We recognize that we have some problems of discrimination but we find steady progress being made in the solution of these problems. Through normal democratic processes, we are coming to understand our needs and how we can attain full equality for all our people. Free discussion on the subject is permitted. Our Supreme Court has recently rendered decisions to clarify a number of our laws to guarantee the rights of all.

The USSR claims it has reached a point where all races within her borders are officially considered equal and have equal rights and they insist that they have no discrimination where minorities are concerned.

This is a laudable objective, but there are other aspects of the development of freedom for the individual which are essential before the mere absence of discrimination is worth much; and these are lacking in the Soviet Union. Unless they are being denied freedoms which they want and which they see other people have, people do not usually complain of discrimination. It is these other freedoms—the basic freedoms of speech, of the press, of religion and conscience, of assembly, of fair trial and freedom from arbitrary arrest and punishment, which a totalitarian government cannot safely give its people and which give meaning to freedom from discrimination.

It is my belief, and I am sure it is also yours, that the struggle for democracy and freedom is a critical struggle, for their preservation is essential to the great objective of the United Nations to maintain international peace and security. Among free men the end cannot justify the means. We know the patterns of totalitarianism—the single political party, the control of schools, press, radio, the arts, the sciences and the church to support autocratic authority. These are the age-old patterns against which men have struggled for three thousand years. These are the signs of reaction, retreat, and retrogression. The United Nations must hold fast to the heritage of freedom won by the struggle of its people; it must help us to pass it on to generations to come.

'It is my belief, and I am sure it is also yours, that the struggle for democracy and freedom is a critical struggle, for their preservation is essential to the great objective of the United Nations to maintain international peace and security.'

The development of the ideal of freedom and its translation into the every day life of the people in great areas of the earth is the product of the efforts of many peoples. It is the fruit of a long tradition of vigorous thinking and courageous action. No one race and no one people can claim to have done all the work to achieve greater dignity for human beings and great freedom to develop human personality. In each generation and in each country there must be a continuation of the struggle and new steps forward must be taken since this is pre-eminently a field in which to stand still is to retreat.

The field of human rights is not one in which compromise on fundamental principles is possible. The work of the Commission on Human Rights is illustrative. The Declaration of Human Rights provides: "Everyone has the right to leave any country, including his own." The Soviet representative said he would agree to this right if a single phrase was added to it—"in accordance with the procedure laid down in the laws of that country." It is obvious that to accept this would be not only to compromise but to nullify the right stated. This case forcefully illustrates the importance of the proposition that we must ever be alert not to compromise fundamental human rights merely for the sake of reaching unanimity and thus lose them.

As I see it, it is not going to be easy to attain unanimity with respect to our different concepts of government and human rights. The struggle is bound to be difficult and one in which we must be firm but patient. If we adhere faithfully to our principles, I think it is possible for us to maintain freedom and to do so peacefully and without recourse to force.

The future must see the broadening of human rights throughout the world. People who have glimpsed freedom will never be content until they have secured it for themselves. In a truest sense, human rights are a fundamental object of law and government in a just society. Human rights exist to the degree that they are respected by people in relations with each other and by governments in relations with their citizens.

The world at large is aware of the tragic consequences for human beings ruled by totalitarian systems. If we examine Hitler's rise to power, we see how the chains are forged which keep the individual a slave and we can see many similarities in the way things are accomplished in other countries. Politically, men must be free to discuss and to arrive at as many facts as possible and there must be at least a two-party system in a country because when there is only one political party, too many things can be subordinated to the interests of that one party and it becomes a tyrant and not an instrument of democratic government.

The propaganda we have witnessed in the recent past, like that we perceive in these days, seeks to impugn, to undermine and to destroy the liberty and independence of peoples. Such propaganda poses to all peoples the issue whether to doubt their heritage of rights and therefore to compromise the principles by which they live, or try to accept the challenge, redouble their vigilance, and stand steadfast in the struggle to maintain and enlarge human freedoms... ♪

The year that she delivered this speech Eleanor Roosevelt was considered as a Vice-Presidential running mate to Harry S. Truman— decades before Geraldine Ferraro (1984) and 60 years before Hillary Rodham Clinton's failed run for the Presidency (2008).

Mrs Roosevelt declined all approaches, however, and continued her diplomatic work for the fledgling United Nations, her promotion of the status of working women and completed her seven volume autobiography (which was published in 1961). She continued her political support for the Democratic Party from her home in Hyde Park, New York, where she died on 7 November 1962, aged 78.

Barbara Jordan

'Articles of Impeachment of the President'

Washington DC, 25 June 1974

Barbara Charline Jordan (1936–96) overcame her humble beginnings in Houston's Fifth Ward to become the first African American woman elected to the US House of Representatives from a Southern State (Texas, 1972). Jordan rose to national prominence in June 1974 when she delivered what many consider to be the most powerful speech of the House Judiciary Committee hearings into the Watergate scandal which had engulfed Richard Nixon's Presidency.

In the early hours of 17 June 1972, five men wearing business suits were caught breaking into the offices of the Democratic National Committee in the Watergate Building in Washington DC. When the men were bailed later that Saturday morning, one of the burglars' address books contained the phone number of White House consultant, Howard Hunt. Two Washington Post reporters, Carl Bernstein and Bob Woodward, later traced a $25,000 cheque deposited into one of the burglars' bank accounts to a donation for President Nixon's re-election campaign fund. This was the first link tying the burglary to a dirty tricks slush fund run by the White House.

Although Nixon was re-elected in a landslide in November 1972, the Watergate scandal would not go away. White House aides, H.R. Haldeman and John Ehrlichman, as well as new Attorney General Richard Kleindienst, resigned over the Watergate scandal. White House counsel, John Dean, was fired when he refused to take the blame for the White House cover-up of the burglary and informed President Nixon that he was duty-bound to inform any investigation that a cover-up had indeed been discussed.

For the remainder of 1973, President Nixon steadfastly refused to hand over tape recordings of his Oval Office meetings to the special prosecutor assigned to the Senate Watergate Committee. When he finally relented and turned over the tapes in December that year, there was an 18-minute gap on one of the tapes.

In February 1974, the special Watergate prosecution team obtained guilty pleas from seven White House aides, while former Attorney-General John Mitchell, Haldeman and Ehrlichman faced charges of obstruction of justice and perjury.

In June 1974, Texas Congresswoman Barbara Jordan was selected to present the Opening Statement to the House Judiciary Committee as it began its momentous task of outlining the case for the Impeachment of President Richard Nixon on charges that he covered up the Watergate scandal:

‘Mr. Chairman,
I join my colleague Mr. Rangel [Charles Rangel, Democrat Congressman from New York] in thanking you for giving the junior members of this committee the glorious opportunity of sharing the pain of this inquiry. Mr. Chairman, you are a strong man. It has not been easy, but we have tried as best we can to give you as much assistance as possible.

Earlier today, we heard the beginning of the Preamble to the Constitution of the United States: "We, the people." It's a very eloquent beginning. But when that document was completed on the seventeenth of September in 1787, I was not included in that "We, the people." I felt somehow for many years that George Washington and Alexander Hamilton just left me out by mistake. But through the process of amendment, interpretation and court decision, I have finally been included in "We, the people."

Today I am an inquisitor. A hyperbole would not be fictional and would not overstate the solemness that I feel right now. My faith in the Constitution is whole; it is complete; it is total. And I am not going to sit here and be an idle spectator to the diminution, the subversion, the destruction of the Constitution.

"Who can so properly be the inquisitors for the nation as the representatives of the nation themselves? The subjects of its jurisdiction are those offenses which proceed from the misconduct of public men."

And that's what we're talking about. In other words, [the jurisdiction comes] from the abuse or violation of some public trust.

'...it is a misreading of the Constitution for any member here to assert that for a member to vote for an article of impeachment means that that member must be convinced that the President should be removed from office.'

It is wrong, I suggest, it is a misreading of the Constitution for any member here to assert that for a member to vote for an article of impeachment means that that member must be convinced that the President should be removed from office. The Constitution doesn't say that. The powers relating to impeachment are an essential check in the hands of the body of the legislature against and upon the encroachments of the executive.

In the division between the two branches of the legislature, the House and the Senate, assigning to the one the right to accuse and to the other the right to judge, the framers of this Constitution were very astute. They did not make the accusers and the judgers—and the judges—the same person.

We know the nature of impeachment. We've been talking about it a while now. It is chiefly designed for the President and his high ministers to somehow be called into account. It is designed to "bridle" the executive if he engages in excesses. "It is designed as a method of national inquest into the conduct of public men."? The framers confided in the Congress the power if need be, to remove the President in order to strike a delicate balance between a President swollen with power and grown tyrannical and preservation of the independence of the executive.

The nature of impeachment: A narrowly channeled exception to the separation-of-powers maxim. The Federal Convention of 1787 said that. It limited impeachment to high crimes and misdemeanors and discounted and opposed the term "maladministration."

"It is to be used only for great misdemeanors," so it was said in the North Carolina ratification convention. And in the Virginia ratification convention: "We do not trust our liberty to a particular branch. We need one branch to check the other."

'The nature of impeachment: A narrowly channeled exception to the separation-of-powers maxim. The Federal Convention of 1787 said that.'

"No one need be afraid"—the North Carolina ratification convention—"No one need be afraid that officers who commit oppression will pass with immunity."

"Prosecutions of impeachments will seldom fail to agitate the passions of the whole community," said Hamilton in the

Federalist Papers, number 65. "We divide into parties more or less friendly or inimical to the accused." I do not mean political parties in that sense.

The drawing of political lines goes to the motivation behind impeachment; but impeachment must proceed within the confines of the constitutional term "high crime[s] and misdemeanors." Of the impeachment process, it was Woodrow Wilson who said that "nothing short of the grossest offenses against the plain law of the land will suffice to give them speed and effectiveness. Indignation so great as to overgrow party interest may secure a conviction; but nothing else can."

Common sense would be revolted if we engaged upon this process for petty reasons. Congress has a lot to do: Appropriations, Tax Reform, Health Insurance, Campaign Finance Reform, Housing, Environmental Protection, Energy Sufficiency, Mass Transportation. Pettiness cannot be allowed to stand in the face of such overwhelming problems. So today we are not being petty. We are trying to be big, because the task we have before us is a big one.

This morning, in a discussion of the evidence, we were told that the evidence which purports to support the allegations of misuse of the CIA by the President is thin. We're told that that evidence is insufficient. What that recital of the evidence this morning did not include is what the President did know on June 23, 1972.

The President did know that it was Republican money, that it was money from the Committee for the Re-Election of the President, which was found in the possession of one of the burglars arrested on June 17. What the President did know on the 23 June was the prior activities of E. Howard Hunt, which included his participation in the break-in of Daniel Ellsberg's psychiatrist, which included Howard Hunt's participation in the Dita Beard ITT affair, which included Howard Hunt's fabrication of cables designed to discredit the Kennedy Administration.

We were further cautioned today that perhaps these proceedings ought to be delayed because certainly there would be new evidence forthcoming from the President of the United States. There has not even been an obfuscated indication that this committee would receive any additional materials from the President. The committee subpoena is outstanding, and if the President wants to supply that material, the committee sits here. The fact is that yesterday, the American people waited with great anxiety for eight hours, not knowing whether their President would obey an order of the Supreme Court of the United States.

> *'The Carolina ratification convention impeachment criteria: Those are impeachable "who behave amiss or betray their public trust."'*

At this point, I would like to juxtapose a few of the impeachment criteria with some of the actions the President has engaged in. Impeachment criteria: James Madison, from the Virginia ratification convention. "If the President be connected in any suspicious manner with any person and there be grounds to believe that he will shelter him, he may be impeached."

We have heard time and time again that the evidence reflects the payment to defendants of money. The President had knowledge that these funds were being paid and these were funds collected for the 1972 Presidential campaign. We know that the President met with Mr. Henry Petersen twenty-seven times to discuss matters related to Watergate, and immediately thereafter met with the very persons who were implicated in the information Mr. Petersen was receiving. The words are: "If the President is connected in any suspicious manner with any person and there be grounds to believe that he will shelter that person, he may be impeached."

Justice Story: "Impeachment is attended—"is intended for occasional and extraordinary cases where a superior power acting for the whole people is put into operation to protect their rights and rescue their liberties from violations."

We know about the Houston plan. We know about the break-in of the psychiatrist's office. We know that there was absolute complete direction on September 3 when the President indicated that a surreptitious entry had been made in Dr Fielding's office, after having met with Mr. Ehrlichman and Mr. Young. "Protect their rights. Rescue their liberties from violation."

The Carolina ratification convention impeachment criteria: Those are impeachable "who behave amiss or betray their public trust."

Beginning shortly after the Watergate break-in and continuing to the present time, the President has engaged in a series of public statements and actions designed to thwart the lawful investigation by government prosecutors. Moreover, the President has made public announcements and assertions bearing on the Watergate case, which the evidence will show he knew to be false. These assertions, false assertions, impeachable, those who misbehave. Those who "behave amiss or betray the public trust."

James Madison again at the Constitutional Convention: "A President is impeachable if he attempts to subvert the Constitution." The Constitution charges the President with the task of taking care that the laws be faithfully executed, and yet the President has counseled his aides to commit perjury, willfully disregard the secrecy of grand jury proceedings, conceal surreptitious entry, attempt to compromise a federal judge, while publicly displaying his cooperation with the processes of criminal justice.

"A President is impeachable if he attempts to subvert the Constitution."

If the impeachment provision in the Constitution of the United States will not reach the offenses charged here, then perhaps that 18th century Constitution should be abandoned to a 20th century paper shredder.

Has the President committed offenses and planned and directed and acquiesced in a course of conduct which the Constitution will not tolerate? That's the question. We know that. We know the question. We should now forthwith proceed to answer the question. It is reason, and not passion, which must guide our deliberations, guide our debate, and guide our decision.)

On 27 July 1974 the House Judiciary Committee voted 27–11 to recommend the first article of impeachment against the President (Obstruction of Justice). The second (Abuse of Power) and third (Contempt of Congress) articles were passed on 29 July and 30 July respectively.

Finally, on 9 August 1974, in order to avoid impeachment, Richard Nixon became the first person to resign the US Presidency.

Margaret Thatcher

'Speech to the Foreign Policy Association'

New York, 18 December 1979

Britain's first female Prime Minister, Margaret Thatcher—the so called Iron Lady of world politics during the 1980s—was born Margaret Hilda Roberts in Grantham, Lincolnshire in 1925. In May 1979, the Conservative Party was swept to power. In this speech at the end of that year, Thatcher outlined her government's approach to foreign policy—a decidedly right wing platform that would polarise both Britain and the world.

'As I speak today, 1979—and with it the 1970s—has less than two weeks to run. I myself will have some reason to remember both the year and the decade with affection. But in general, few, I suspect, will regret the passing of either.

The last ten years have not been a happy period for the Western democracies, domestically or internationally. Self-questioning is essential to the health of any society. But we have perhaps carried it too far and carried to extremes, of course, it causes paralysis. The time has come when the West—above all Europe and the United States—must begin to substitute action for introspection.

We face a new decade—I have called it the dangerous decade—in which the challenges to our security and to our way of life may, if anything, be more acute than in the 1970s. The response of Western nations and their leaders will need to be firm, calm and

> 'The response of Western nations and their leaders will need to be firm, calm and concerted. Neither weakness nor anger nor despair will serve us. The problems are daunting, but there is, in my view, ample reason for optimism.'

concerted. Neither weakness nor anger nor despair will serve us. The problems are daunting, but there is, in my view, ample reason for optimism.

Few international problems today lend themselves to simple solutions. One reason is that few such problems can any longer be treated in isolation. Increasingly they interact, one with the other. Thanks to a still-accelerating technological revolution, we become daily more aware that the earth and its resources are finite and, in most respects, shrinking.

The fact of global interdependence—I apologise for the jargon—is nothing new. Four hundred years ago, South American gold and silver helped to cause inflation in Europe—an early example of the evils of excess money supply. Two hundred years ago, men fought in India and along the Great Lakes here in America in order that, as Macaulay put it, the King of Prussia might rob a neighbour whom he had promised to defend.

But the popular perception of interdependence lagged far behind the fact. When I was in my teens, a British Prime Minister could still refer to Czechoslovakia as "a faraway country" of whose quarrels the British people knew nothing; and an American President could still experience difficulty in persuading his people of the need to concern themselves with a European war.

Today it is painfully obvious that no man—and no nation—is an island. What President Cleveland once described as "foreign broils" are brought into every home. The price of oil in Saudi Arabia and Nigeria, the size of the grain harvest in Kansas and the Ukraine—these are of immediate concern to people all over the world. The Middle East and the middle West have become neighbours and will remain so, uncomfortable though they may on occasion find it. The bell tolls for us all.

This has been tragically underlined in recent weeks. The world has watched with anger and dismay the events of Tehran. We have all felt involved with the fate of the hostages. Nothing can excuse the treatment they have received. For hundreds of years the principle of the immunity of the messenger and the diplomat has been respected. Now this principle, central to the civilised conduct of relations between states, is being systematically flouted.

We in Britain have respected and supported the calmness and resolution with which President Carter has handled an appalling situation. With our partners in Europe we have given full public and private support to his efforts to secure the unconditional release of the hostages. We will continue to support and to help in any way we can. Above all we have admired the forbearance with which the American people have responded to the indignities inflicted upon their fellow citizens. That restraint has undoubtedly been in the best interests of the captives.

'...I am convinced that there is little force left in the original Marxist stimulus to revolution. Its impetus is petering out as the practical failure of the doctrine becomes daily more obvious.'

The Iranian crisis epitomises the problems which we face in trying to co-exist in a shrinking world where political, economic and social upheavals are endemic. Some would add religious upheavals to that list. But I do not believe we should judge Islam by events in Iran. Least of all should we judge it by the taking of hostages. There is a tide of self-confidence and self-awareness in the Muslim world which preceded the Iranian Revolution and will outlast its present excesses. The West should recognise this with respect, not hostility. The Middle East is an area where we have much at stake. It is in our own interests, as well as in the interests of the people of that region, that they build on their own deep religious traditions. We do not wish to see them succumb to the fraudulent appeal of imported Marxism.

Because, to look beyond the Middle East, I am convinced that there is little force left in the original Marxist stimulus to revolution. Its impetus is petering out as the practical failure of the doctrine becomes daily more obvious. It has failed to take root in the advanced democracies. In those countries where it has taken root—countries backward or, by tradition, authoritarian—it has failed to provide sustained economic or social development. What is left is a technique of subversion and a collection of catch-phrases. The former, the technique of subversion, is still dangerous. Like terrorism, it is a menace that needs to be fought wherever it occurs—and British Prime Ministers have had reason to speak with some passion about terrorism in recent years. As for the catch-phrases of Marxism, they still have a certain drawing power. But they have none in the countries which are ruled by the principles of Marx. Communist regimes can no longer conceal the gulf that separates their slogans from reality.

'The immediate threat from the Soviet Union is military rather than ideological. The threat is not only to our security in Europe and North America but also, both directly and by proxy, in the third world.'

The immediate threat from the Soviet Union is military rather than ideological. The threat is not only to our security in Europe and North America but also, both directly and by proxy, in the third world. I have often spoken about the military challenge which the West faces today. I have sometimes been deliberately misunderstood, especially by my enemies who have labelled me the "Iron Lady." They are quite right—I am. Let me, therefore, restate a few simple propositions.

The Soviet Union continues to proclaim the ideological struggle.

It asserts that the demise of the Western political system is inevitable. It neglects the fact that few indeed who live in Western democracies show any sign of wanting to exchange their system for that operated by the Russians. In 1919, Lenin said:

"World imperialism cannot live side by side with a victorious Soviet revolution—the one or the other will be victorious in the end."

The Soviet government has not repudiated this threatening prediction. Indeed they broadcast their ambitions wholesale. They should not be surprised if we listen and take note.

Meanwhile, they expand their armed forces on land, sea and air. They continually improve the quality of their armaments. They and their allies outnumber us in Europe. Their men, their ships and their aircraft appear ever more regularly in parts of the world where they have never been seen before. Their Cuban and East German proxies likewise.

We can argue about Soviet motives. But the fact is that the Russians have the weapons and are getting more of them. It is simple prudence for the West to respond. We in Britain intend to do that to the best of our ability and at every level, including the strategic. President Carter has shown that he intends to do likewise. And the Alliance last week decided to modernise its long-range theatre nuclear weapons. This in due course will help to balance the new and sophisticated weapons the Russians already have targeted on Europe. The strategic power of the USA in the Western Alliance remains paramount. But I would underline the contribution of the European members of NATO -a contribution which is never overlooked by the Russians.

Modern weapons are totally destructive and immensely expensive. It is in nobody's interest that they should be piled up indefinitely. It makes good sense for both sides to seek agreements on arms control which preserve the essential security of each. We in Britain have therefore supported the talks on Strategic Arms Limitation and on Mutual and Balanced Force Reductions. The British Government hopes that the SALT II agreement can be ratified.

I have been attacked by the Soviet Government for arguing that the West should put itself in a position to negotiate from strength. But in saying this, I have done no more than echo the constant ambition of the Soviet Government itself. I am not talking about negotiations from a position of superiority. What I am seeking is a negotiation in which we and they start from

'The immediate prospects are sombre. Inflation will be difficult to eradicate. Growth has fallen sharply from its earlier levels. There is a constant threat of disorder in the world oil market.'

the position of balance, and if both sides can negotiate, genuinely, to maintain that balance at lower levels, I shall be well content. It is in that spirit that I approach the proposals which have recently been made by President Brezhnev and others.

The East/West conflict permeates most global issues. But other equally pressing problems have arisen. These affect above all the world economy and the relationship between the developed Western world and the newly emerging countries of Latin America, Africa and Asia.

No country can today escape economic involvement with the economies of others. In the UK external trade has always been of central importance to our economy. In the USA this has been less so. But recently you have become much more dependent on overseas countries. Ten years ago you imported five per cent of your oil. Now it is fifty per cent. But it is not just oil—this has obvious consequences for your foreign policy. So, rich and poor, Communist and non-Communist, oil-producers and oil-consumers—our economic welfare is increasingly affected by the operation of the market. Increasingly affected by the growing demand of complex industries for scarce materials and by the pressure on the world's finite resources of fossil fuels.

All of this has coincided with a prolonged period of uneasiness in the world's economy. The immediate prospects are sombre. Inflation will be difficult to eradicate. Growth has fallen sharply from its earlier levels. There is a constant threat of disorder in the world oil market. News of recent price rises can only have added to the general uncertainty which is one of the most damaging consequences of the present oil situation. The task of economic management, both nationally and internationally, is becoming more and more difficult. The precarious balance of the world economy could at any time be shaken by political upheavals in one or more countries over which the rest of us might have very little influence.

In these circumstances, we all have a direct practical interest in the orderly settlement of political disputes.

These were some considerations which, in addition to the obvious ones, persuaded the new British Government of the need for a decisive effort to secure a settlement in Zimbabwe-Rhodesia. As you know, after months of strenuous negotiation, overall agreement was finally reached yesterday on the new Constitution, arrangements for free and fair elections and a ceasefire. The agreement secured in London showed that even the most intractable problem will yield to the necessary combination of resolve and imagination. Concessions were made by all sides. Many difficult decisions were involved—not least for the British Government, which found itself acquiring a new colony, albeit for a short period. We are grateful for the forceful and timely support we received throughout the negotiations from the United States Government and from President Carter personally, especially in the final stages.

We have no illusion about the practical problems of implementing this agreement on the ground, against a background of years of bitter conflict. But now is a time for reconciliation and for restoring normal relations between all the states in the area. The Lancaster House agreement could prove a major step toward peaceful evolution and away from violent revolution in Southern Africa. We are encouraged to persevere with the Five Power Initiative to achieve an all-party settlement in Namibia.

In this context, I want to say a particular word about South Africa. There is now a real prospect that the conflicts on South Africa's borders, in Rhodesia and Namibia, will shortly be ended. This, combined with welcome initiatives in South African domestic policies, offers a chance to defuse a regional crisis which was potentially of the utmost gravity and to make progress toward an ending of the isolation of South Africa in world affairs.

We must not regard these problems as insoluble. The West has immense material and moral assets. To those assets must be added the clarity to see where our strengths should be used; the will and confidence to use them with precision; and the stamina to see things through.

Let us never forget that despite the difficulties to which I have referred, the Western democracies remain overwhelmingly strong in economic terms. We are, it is true, more vulnerable than before. Vulnerable because of our reliance on raw materials; vulnerable because of the specialisation and complexity of our societies. It is vital, therefore, that we keep a steady nerve and that we concert our policies. We already agree on the basic requirements—on the need to defeat inflation; to avoid protectionism: to use our limited energy resources better. And as we deal with the problems, our inherent vitality will reassert itself. There is, after all, no discernible challenge to the role of the Western democracies as the driving force of the world economy.

The political strength and stability of the West is equally striking. Preoccupied by passing political dramas, we often overlook the real sturdiness of our political institutions. They are not seriously challenged from within. They meet the aspirations of ordinary people. They attract the envy of those who do not have them. In the thirty-five years since the last war, they have shown themselves remarkably resistant to subversive influences.

Our democratic systems have made it possible to organise our relationships with one another on a healthy basis. The North Atlantic Alliance and the European Community are—and remain—free associations of free peoples. Policies are frankly debated. Of course the debates are often lively and occasionally heated. But those debates are a sign of strength just as the regimented agreements of the Communist alliances are a mark of weakness.

The argument now going on in the European Community is a case in point. The Community is used to debate, often difficult and prolonged. We are seeing at present something more serious than many of the disputes which have taken place in the past. But the interests that unite the members of the Community are stronger than those which divide them—particularly when viewed in the light of other international problems. I believe that these common interests will assert themselves. I am confident that an acceptable solution will be found and that the European Community will emerge fortified from the debate. And a strong Europe is the best partner for the United States. It is on the strength of that partnership that the strength of the free world depends.

The last asset I want to mention today is the West's relationship with the countries of the Third World. Neither recent events; nor past injustices; nor the outdated rhetoric of anti-colonialism can disguise the real convergence of interest between the Third World and the West.

It is we in the West who have the experience and contacts the Third World needs. We supply most of the markets for their goods and their raw materials. We supply most of the technology they require. We provide them with private investment as well as government aid.

We do this not only for our own sake but also because we support the efforts of the countries of the Third World to develop their own economies.

I have only been able to touch on a few current international issues. There are many I have not mentioned. Nor would I wish anyone to think that I underestimate the difficulties, particularly on the domestic economic front, faced by Britain and our Western partners, including the United States. But these difficulties can and will be overcome provided we do not undervalue ourselves nor decry our strength. We shall need self-confidence to tackle the dangerous decade.

It is a time for action, action for the eighties.

The cynics among you will say that none of this is new. Quite right. It isn't. But there are no new magic formulae. We know what we have to do. Our problems will only yield to sustained effort. That is the challenge of political leadership.

Enduring success never comes easily to an individual or to a country. To quote Walt Whitman: "It takes struggles in life to make strength; it takes fight for principles to make fortitude; it takes crisis to give courage and singleness of purpose to reach an objective."

Let us go down in history as the generation which not only understood what needed to be done but a generation which had the strength, the self-discipline and the resolve to see it through. That is our generation. That is our task for the 80s. ♪

Under Margaret Thatcher's Conservative Party, her strong-willed style and economics saw the privatisation of nationalised industries and institutions and the marketisation of education, health care and local government services. Despite presiding over the worst unemployment figures since the Depression, Thatcher's government was re-elected with an increased majority in 1983. The reasons for this were twofold: the lack of an organised opposition party and public support for Thatcher after the Falklands War (1982).

Ann Richards

'We Can Do Better'

Atlanta, Georgia, 19 July 1988

D orothy Ann Willis was born on 1 September 1933 in Lakeview, Texas. Marrying her high school boyfriend, David Richards, she won a debate scholarship to Baylor University and obtained a Bachelor's Degree.

Ann Richards taught history at Fulmore Junior High School and raised a family of four children. A committed equal rights campaigner who was instrumental in establishing The Women's History Museum in Dallas, she was elected to Travis County, Texas Commissioner Court in 1976.

Despite a bitter campaign in which much was made of the fact that she was a recovering alcoholic, Richards became the first woman in more than 50 years to be elected State Treasurer in 1982. Four years later, she was re-elected to the position unopposed. At the Democratic National Convention in 1988, Ann Richards became only the second woman in the history of the party to deliver the Keynote Address.

The day after Vice-Presidential nominee Jesse Jackson addressed the convention in Atlanta, Georgia, Ann Richards took the stage. What Jackson's speech lacked in humility, Richards more than made up for with old-fashioned common sense and a dose of good humour.

' T hank you. Thank you. Thank you very much.

Good evening, ladies and gentlemen. Buenas noches, mis amigos.

I'm delighted to be here with you this evening, because after listening to George Bush all these years, I figured you needed to know what a real Texas accent sounds like.

Twelve years ago, Barbara Jordan, another Texas woman, Barbara made the keynote address to this convention, and two women in a hundred and sixty years is about par for the course.

But, if you give us a chance, we can perform. After all, Ginger Rogers did everything that Fred Astaire did. She just did it backwards and in high heels.

I want to announce to this nation that in a little more than 100 days, the Reagan-Meese-Deaver-Nofziger-Poindexter-North-Weinberger-Watt-Gorsuch-Lavelle-Stockman-Haig-Bork-Noriega-George Bush [era] will be over!

You know, tonight I feel a little like I did when I played basketball in the 8th grade. I thought I looked real cute in my uniform. And then I heard a boy yell from the bleachers, "Make that basket, Birdlegs!"

And my greatest fear is that same guy is somewhere out there in the audience tonight and he's going to cut me down to size. Because where I grew up, there really wasn't much tolerance for self-importance, people who put on airs.

I was born during the Depression in a little community just outside Waco and I grew up listening to Franklin Roosevelt on the radio. Well, it was back then that I came to understand the small truths and the hardships that bind neighbors together. Those were real people with real problems and they had real dreams about getting out of the Depression. I can remember summer nights when we'd put down what we called the Baptist pallet and we listened to the grown-ups talk. I can still hear the sound of the dominoes clicking on the marble slab my daddy had found for a tabletop. I can still hear the laughter of the man telling jokes you weren't supposed to hear—talkin' about how big that old buck deer was, laughin' about mama puttin' Clorox in the well when the frog fell in.

They talked about war and Washington and what this country needed. They talked the straight talk. And it came from people who were living their lives as best they could. And that's what we're going to do tonight. We're going to tell how the cow ate the cabbage.

I got a letter last week from a young mother in Lorena, Texas, and I wanna read part of it to you. She writes,

"Our worries go from pay day to pay day, just like millions of others. And we have two fairly decent incomes, but I worry how I'm going to pay the rising car insurance and food. I pray my kids don't have a growth spurt from August to December, so I don't have to buy new jeans. We buy clothes at the budget stores and we have them fray and fade and stretch in the first wash. We ponder and try to figure out how we're gonna pay for college and braces and tennis shoes. We don't take vacations and we don't go out to eat. Please don't think me ungrateful. We have jobs and a nice place to live, and we're healthy. We're the people you see every day in the grocery stores, and we obey the

> *'This Republican Administration treats us as if we were pieces of a puzzle that can't fit together. They've tried to put us into compartments and separate us from each other. Their political theory is "divide and conquer."'*

laws and pay our taxes. We fly our flags on holidays and we plod along trying to make it better for ourselves and our children and our parents. We aren't vocal any more. I think maybe we're too tired. I believe that people like us are forgotten in America."

Well, of course you believe you're forgotten, because you have been.

This Republican Administration treats us as if we were pieces of a puzzle that can't fit together. They've tried to put us into compartments and separate us from each other. Their political theory is "divide and conquer." They've suggested time and time again that what is of interest to one group of Americans is not of interest to any one else. We've been isolated. We've been lumped into that sad phraseology called "special interests." They've told farmers that they were selfish, that they would drive up food prices if they asked the government to intervene on behalf of the family farm and we watched farms go on the auction block while we bought food from foreign countries. Well, that's wrong!

They told working mothers it's all their fault—their families are falling apart because they had to go to work to keep their kids in jeans and tennis shoes and college. And they're wrong!

They told American labor they were trying to ruin free enterprise by asking for 60 days' notice of plant closings, and that's wrong. And they told the auto industry and the steel industry and the timber industry and the oil industry, companies being threatened by foreign products flooding this country, that you're protectionist if you think the government should enforce our trade laws. And that is wrong!

When they belittle us for demanding clean air and clean water, for trying to save the oceans and the ozone layer, that's wrong!

No wonder we feel isolated and confused. We want answers and their answer is that "something is wrong with you." Well nothing's wrong with you. Nothing's wrong with you that you can't fix in November!

We've been told—we've been told that the interests of the South and the Southwest are not the same interests as the North and the Northeast. They pit one group against the other. They've divided this country and in our isolation we think government isn't gonna help us and we're alone in our feelings. We feel forgotten. Well, the fact is that we are not an isolated piece of their puzzle.

We are one nation. We are the United States of America.

Now, we Democrats believe that America is still the country of fair play; that we can come out of a small town or a poor neighborhood and have the same chance as anyone else and it doesn't matter whether we are black or Hispanic or disabled or a women [sic]. We believe that America is a country where small business owners must succeed, because they are the bedrock, backbone of our economy.

We believe that our kids deserve good day care and public schools. We believe our kids deserve public schools where students can learn and teachers can teach. And we wanna believe that our parents will have a good retirement and that we will too. We Democrats believe that social security is a pact that cannot be broken.

We wanna believe that we can live out our lives without the terrible fear that an illness is going to bankrupt us and our children. We Democrats believe that America can overcome any problem, including the dreaded disease called AIDS. We believe that America is still a country where there is more to life than just a constant struggle for money. And we believe that America must have leaders who show us that our struggles amount to something and contribute to something larger, leaders who want us to be all that we can be. We want leaders like Jesse Jackson.

Jesse Jackson is a leader and a teacher who can open our hearts and open our minds and stir our very souls. And he has taught us that we are as good as our capacity for caring, caring about the drug problem, caring about crime, caring about education and caring about each other.

Now, in contrast, the greatest nation of the free world has had a leader for eight straight years that has pretended that he cannot hear our questions over the noise of the helicopters. And we know he doesn't wanna answer. But we have a lot of questions. And when we get our questions asked, or there is a leak, or an investigation the only answer we get is: "I don't know," or "I forgot."

But you wouldn't accept that answer from your children. I wouldn't. Don't tell me "you don't know" or "you forgot." We're not going to have the America that we want until we elect leaders who are gonna tell the truth; not most days but every day; leaders who don't forget what they don't want to remember. And for eight straight years George Bush hasn't displayed the slightest interest in

> *'...they tell us that they're fighting a war against terrorists. And then we find out that the White House is selling arms to the Ayatollah.'*

anything we care about. And now that he's after a job he can't get appointed to, he's like Columbus discovering America. He's found child care. He's found education. Poor George. He can't help it. He was born with a silver foot in his mouth.

Well, no wonder, no wonder we can't figure it out. Because the leadership of this nation is telling us one thing on TV and doing something entirely different. They tell us, they tell us that they're fighting a war against terrorists. And then we find out that the White House is selling arms to the Ayatollah. They tell us that they're fighting a war on drugs and then people come on TV and testify that the CIA and the DEA and the FBI knew they were flying drugs into America all along. And they're negotiating with a dictator who is shoveling cocaine into this country like crazy. I guess that's their Central American strategy.

Now, they tell us that employment rates are great, and that they're for equal opportunity. But we know it takes two pay-checks to make ends meet today, when it used to take one. And the opportunity they're so proud of is low-wage, dead-end jobs. And there is no major city in America where you cannot see homeless men sitting in parking lots holding signs that say "I will work for food."

Now, my friends, we really are at a crucial point in American history. Under this Administration we have devoted our resources into making this country a military colossus. But we've let our economic lines of defense fall into disrepair. The debt of this nation is greater than it has ever been in our history. We fought a world war on less debt than the Republicans have built up in the last eight years. You know, it's kind of like that brother-in-law who drives a flashy new car but he's always borrowin' money from you to make the payments.

But let's take what they are most proud of. That is their stand on defense. We Democrats are committed to a strong America, and, quite frankly, when our leaders say to us: "We need a new weapons system," our inclination is to say: "Well, they must be right."

But when we pay billions for planes that won't fly, billions for tanks that won't fire and billions for systems that won't work, that old dog won't hunt. And you don't have to be from Waco to know that when the Pentagon makes crooks rich and doesn't make America strong, that it's a bum deal.

Now I'm going to tell you I'm really glad that our young people missed the Depression and missed the great big war. But I do regret that they missed the leaders that I knew, leaders who told us when things were tough and that we'd have to sacrifice and that these difficulties might last for a while. They didn't tell us things were hard for us because we were different, or isolated, or special interests. They brought us together and they gave us a sense of national purpose.

They gave us Social Security and they told us they were setting up a system where we could pay our own money in, and when the time came for our retirement we could take the money out. People in the rural areas were told that we deserved to have electric lights and they were gonna harness the energy that was necessary to give us electricity so my grandmama didn't have to carry that old coal oil lamp around.

And they told us that they were going to guarantee when we put our money in the bank, that the money was going to be there and it was going to be insured. They did not lie to us.

And I think one of the saving graces of Democrats is that we are candid. We talk straight talk. We tell people what we think. And that tradition and those values live today in Michael Dukakis from Massachusetts.

Michael Dukakis knows that this country is on the edge of a great new era, that we're not afraid of change, that we're for thoughtful, truthful, strong leadership. Behind his calm, there's an impatience to unify this country and to get on with the future. His instincts are deeply American. They're tough and they're generous. And personally, I have to tell you that I have never met a man who had a more remarkable sense about what is really important in life.

And then there's my friend and my teacher for many years, Senator Lloyd Bentsen. And I couldn't be prouder, both as a Texan and as a Democrat, because Lloyd Bentsen understands America. From the barrio to the boardroom, he knows how to bring us together, by regions, by economics and by example. And he's already beaten George Bush once. So, when it comes right down to it, this election is a contest between those who are satisfied with what they have and those who know we can do better. That's what this election is really all about. It's about the American dream—those who want to keep it for the few and those who know it must be nurtured and passed along.

I'm a grandmother now. And I have one nearly perfect granddaughter named Lily. And when I hold that grandbaby, I feel the continuity of life that unites us, that binds generation to generation, that ties us to each other. And sometimes I spread that Baptist pallet out on the floor and Lily and I roll a ball back and forth. And I think of all the families like mine, like the one in Lorena, Texas, like the ones that nurture children all across America. And as I look at

Lily, I know that it is within families that we learn both the need to respect individual human dignity and to work together for our common good. Within our families, within our nation, it is the same.

And as I sit there, I wonder if she'll ever grasp the changes I've seen in my life—if she'll ever believe that there was a time when blacks could not drink from public water fountains, when Hispanic children were punished for speaking Spanish in the public schools and women couldn't vote.

I think of all the political fights I've fought and all the compromises I've had to accept as part payment. And I think of all the small victories that have added up to national triumphs; and all the things that would never have happened and all the people who would've been left behind if we had not reasoned and fought and won those battles together. And I will tell Lily that those triumphs were Democratic Party triumphs. I want so much to tell Lily how far we've come, you and I. And as the ball rolls back and forth, I want to tell her how very lucky she is that for all our difference, we are still the greatest nation on this good earth. And our strength lies in the men and women who go to work every day, who struggle to balance their family and their jobs, and who should never, ever be forgotten.

I just hope that like her grandparents and her great-grandparents before that, Lily goes on to raise her kids with the promise that echoes in homes all across America: That we can do better. And that's what this election is all about.

Thank you very much. ♪

Ann Richards' speech placed her in the national spotlight and in November 1990, she was elected Governor of Texas. A popular Governor, it was said that she 'appointed more women, African Americans and Hispanics to government positions than any of her predecessors', but she was defeated after just one term by White House-bound George W. Bush.

After her defeat, Richards continued to advocate healthier lifestyle choices for women. She was diagnosed with osteoporosis in 1996 and championed women's issues in the remaining decade of her life.

Benazir Bhutto

'Address to the US Congress'

Washington DC, 7 June 1989

Benazir Bhutto (1953–2007) was the eldest daughter of former Pakistani leader, Zulfikar Ali Bhutto, and the first woman leader of a Muslim country in modern history.

Her father served as the President of Pakistan from 1971 to 1973 and Prime Minister from 1973 to 1977.

In November 1977, General Mohammed Zia-ul-Haq seized power in a military coup and Zulfikar Bhutto was arrested, tried and executed on the trumped-up charge of having ordered a political assassination in the early 1970s.

Having suffered a series of arrests following her father's political downfall, Benazir Bhutto fled to England in 1984 where she became head of her father's political party, the Pakistan People's Party (PPP).

In 1988, after President Zia and the American Ambassador to Pakistan were killed in a plane crash, Benazir Bhutto returned to Pakistan and launched a vigorous campaign for democratic elections. On 16 November 1988, Pakistani citizens voted in their first open election in more than a decade and Bhutto's PPP won a majority in the National Assembly.

On 1 December, 1988, Benazir Bhutto took office as Prime Minister of Pakistan.

The following year, the 35-year-old Prime Minister was invited to the United States where, in a speech before both Houses of Congress and President George H. Bush, she urged America to press for a broad-based political settlement to the Soviet invasion of Afghanistan. It was reported that Ms. Bhutto, a member of Radcliffe College (Harvard) Class of 1973, 'captivated Congress with a speech portraying herself as the embodiment of democracy, a spokesman for women, youth and those in the Islamic mainstream, a fighter for freedom in Afghanistan and a political descendant of John F. Kennedy.'

Mr. President, distinguished Members of the Congress, As Salaam-o-Alaikum. Peace be with you.

We gather together, friends and partners, who have fought, side by side, in the cause of liberty.

We gather together to celebrate freedom, to celebrate democracy, to celebrate the three most beautiful words in the English language: 'We the People.'

I stand here conscious of the honor you bestow on my country and on me.

I am not new to America. I recall fondly my four years I spent here as a student at Harvard.

America is a land of great technology. America is a land of economic power.

Your products are sent all over the world, a tribute to the creativity and productivity of your people.

But your greatest export is not material. Your greatest export is not a product. Your greatest export is an idea.

America's greatest contribution to the world is its concept of democracy, its concept of freedom, freedom of action, freedom of speech and freedom of thought.

President Bush, in his inaugural address, spoke of a new breeze across America. In fact, this new breeze is sweeping the whole world.

In Afghanistan, the people have freed their country of foreign occupation.

In South America, the generals are returning to their barracks and the people to the halls of government.

In the Orient, the old order is changing and the demands growing.

Glasnost and Perestroika are shaking the East bloc… the ultimate tribute to the strength of freedom, to the desire of people wherever they live to control their own destiny.

And it is the words of Lincoln that are quoted… "a government of the people, by the people, for the people."

For many of us, the root of all this progress, the foundation of democracy, lies on this continent, 200 years ago, in your covenant of freedom, in words penned by Madison… "We the People."

'For many of us, the root of all this progress, the foundation of democracy, lies on this continent, 200 years ago, in your covenant of freedom…'

My presence before you is a testament to the force of freedom and democracy in Pakistan.

Throughout 1988, the call for democratic change in Pakistan grew louder.

After a decade of repression, the wave of freedom surged in Pakistan.

On November 16, the people of Pakistan participated in the first party-based elections in eleven years.

The Pakistan People's Party won a convincing victory, showing wide national support all across the four provinces of our great country. Democracy had at last returned to Pakistan.

We the people had spoken.

We the people had prevailed.

In its first days, our new government released political prisoners, legalized labor and student unions and restored press freedoms.

We signaled our right of recognition to the role of the opposition in a democratic society, giving them free and regular access to the state media for the first time in our history.

We set as our focus reconciliation, not retribution.

Some claimed to fear revenge, revenge against the murderers and torturers, revenge against those who subverted constitutional law.

But, ladies and gentlemen, there was no revenge.

For them, and for dictators across the world... democracy is the greatest revenge.

For us, the election was the end to an unspeakable ordeal.

A democratic government was overthrown in a military coup and for eleven years dictatorship ruled our nation.

Political parties were banned.

Political expression prohibited.

There was no freedom of the press.

The Constitution was suspended and amended into virtual non-existence.

Women were subjugated and laws written specifically to discriminate against them.

Political opponents were imprisoned, tortured and hanged. It was the luckier ones who went into exile.

Our struggle was driven by faith...faith in our people's ability to resist—faith in our religion, Islam, which teaches us that 'tyranny cannot endure.'

It is this same faith which has fuelled the battle for freedom next door in Afghanistan.

Both our countries have stood alongside the Afghans in their struggle for more than a decade.

For ten long years the people of Pakistan have provided sanctuary to our Afghan brothers and sisters.

We have nurtured and sustained their families.

More than three million refugees are on our soil. Still more are coming, fleeing the bloodshed.

And we have welcomed them, housed them and fed them.

And for ten long years, the United States, in a united bipartisan effort of three Administrations and six Congresses, has stood side by side with Pakistan and the brave Mujahidin.

We both deserve to be proud of that effort.

But that effort did not come without a price. Our villages were strafed, our people killed.

Our peaceful country has changed. The war has brought the curse of drug addiction to Pakistan—over one million heroin addicts—to a land that never before knew it.

Our forests and natural resources have been depleted.

Yet our commitment to pay the price for freedom has not been shaken.

And now, despite the Soviet withdrawal, peace has not returned to Afghanistan.

Even now, the Soviet Government is giving full backing to the Kabul regime's efforts to cling to power.

It has left in its possession vast quantities of lethal weapons—weapons supplemented by a regular supply of hardware including Scud missiles, some of which have already hit Pakistan territory.

More threats have been received, threats to supply new weapons never before seen in the region.

The Soviets have gone. But the force of foreign arms continues to deny Afghanistan the ultimate fruit of victory…self-determination.

Those responsible for a decade of death and destruction now blame us for the continuing bloodshed.

They accuse us of interfering in Afghanistan. Nothing is farther from the truth and nothing is more unjust.

Our concerns are for a stable, independent and neutral Afghanistan, an Afghanistan where the people can choose their own system, their own government in free and fair elections.

We in Pakistan would like to see the refugees return to their homes in peace and dignity.

Unfortunately, the conflict is not over. It has entered its closing stage, a stage often the most complex and difficult.

Distinguished friends, Pakistan and the United States have traveled a long road with the Afghans in their quest for self-determination.

Let us not at this stage, out of impatience or fatigue, become indifferent. We cannot, we must not, abandon their cause.

The world community must rise to the challenge which lies ahead. The challenge of achieving a broad-based, political settlement to the war, of rebuilding a shattered country, of helping the victims of war, of developing the Afghan economy.

Mr. Speaker, now Pakistan and the United States enter a new phase of an enduring relationship. Our shared interests and common international goals have not disappeared. If anything, they have been strengthened.

Our partnership is not a friendship of convenience. For decades we have been tied together by mutual international goals and by shared interests.

But something new has entered into the equation of bilateral relations—democracy.

We are now moral as well as political partners. Two elected governments bonded together in a common respect for constitutional government, accountability and a commitment to freedom.

Because of the intensity of our struggle for freedom, we will never take it for granted in Pakistan.

Our democratic institutions are still new and need careful tending.

Democracy's doubters have never believed that it could successfully address the problems of developing countries. But democracy in Pakistan must succeed to signal nations in political transition all over the world that freedom is on the rise.

This is the time in Pakistan when democracy's friends must come forward. We need the time and the resources to build a truly strong constitutional government. If we succeed, all democracies share in that success.

Today we are on the threshold of a new democratic partnership between our two countries, addressing new priorities. A partnership which addresses both our security concerns and our social and economic needs. A partnership which will carry us into the twenty-first century—strong in mutual trust, close in common interest, constant to the values we share; working in association with democratic governments all across the world to promote the values of freedom. This is the partnership, the new democratic Pakistan we hope to build with your continuing help.

The time is right, my friends, to make miracles in Pakistan. The dictatorship of the past has given way to the forces of the future. The years of social and economic neglect beg for redress. So I come to this land of freedom to talk about the future. The future of my country and the future of freedom

> **'I come before you to declare that we cannot choose between development and democracy. We must work for both. Partners in democracy must now focus attention on urgent problems which affect mankind as a whole.'**

everywhere. The future of our children—my child—and yours.

I come before you to declare that we cannot choose between development and democracy. We must work for both. Partners in democracy must now focus attention on urgent problems which affect mankind as a whole.

The widening gap between rich and poor countries; environmental pollution; drug abuse and trafficking; the pressure of population on world resources; and full economic participation for women everywhere.

We must join together to find remedies and solutions for these problems before they overcome us.

Of all the crises facing us, my government is giving the highest priority to the problem of drug abuse.

We are determined to eradicate this plague from our country. To that end we have established a new Ministry for Narcotics Control.

We are taking vigorous action against drug offenders.

Our close cooperation—and that of other nations—must be strengthened if we are to turn back the tide of drugs sweeping your nation and mine.

So, too, must we work together, as partners, to avert the catastrophe of a nuclear arms race.

Speaking for Pakistan, I can declare that we do not possess nor do we intend to make a nuclear device.

That is our policy.

We are committed to a regional approach to the nuclear problem and we remain ready to accept any safeguards, inspections and verifications that are applied on a non-discriminatory regional basis.

Pakistan has long advocated the creation of a nuclear-weapon-free zone in the region.

A first step in that direction could be a nuclear test ban agreement between Pakistan and its neighbors in South Asia.

We are prepared for any negotiation to prevent the proliferation of nuclear weapons in our region.

We will not provoke a nuclear arms race in the subcontinent.

The United States has long held a commitment to peace in South Asia.

It is a commitment which Pakistan shares.

It is in this spirit of peace, of regional cooperation and bilateral partnership, that I come before you today.

This then must be our agenda, democracy and development, security and international cooperation.

The people of Pakistan appreciate the assistance you have given us, the assistance which you continue to give us.

Your military assistance has helped maintain a relative balance in the region. It has contributed to Pakistan's sense of security. It has strengthened the peace and stability of the South Asian region.

Mr. Speaker, everywhere the sun is setting on the day of the dictator.

In Pakistan when the moment came, the transition was peaceful.

The whole nation, farmers, workers, the soldiers and civilians, men and women, together heralded the return of democracy.

The people have taken power in their hands.

But our work has just begun.

My friends, freedom is not an end. Freedom is a beginning.

And in Pakistan, at long last, we are ready to begin.

Our two countries stood together in the last decade to support the fight of the Afghan people for freedom.

Let us stand together now as the people of Pakistan strive to give meaning to their newfound freedom.

Come with us toward a tomorrow, better than all the yesterdays we knew.

History, the rush of events, perhaps even destiny has brought me here today.

I am proud to be the elected Prime Minister of Pakistan in this critical time.

It is an awesome obligation.

But in the words of John Fitzgerald Kennedy…"I do not shrink from this responsibility—I welcome it."

As a representative of the young, let me be viewed as one of a new generation of leaders unshackled by the constraints and irrational hatreds of the past.

As a representative of women, let my message be to them, "Yes you can!"

As a believer of Islam in this august Chamber, let my message be about a compassionate and tolerant religion, teaching hard work and family values under a merciful God, for that is the Islam which we must all come to understand.

For me and the people of Pakistan, the last eleven years have encompassed a painful odyssey.

My countrymen and I did not see our loved ones killed, or tortured, or lashed, or languishing in solitary confinement, deprived of basic human rights and freedom, in order that others might again suffer such indignities.

We sacrificed a part of our lives and bore the pain of confronting tyranny to build a just society.

We believed in ourselves, in our cause, in our people and in our country.

And when you believe, then there is no mountain too high to scale.

That is my message to the youth of America, to its women, and to its people.

Thank you distinguished Members. ♪

Benazir Bhutto remained a staunch supporter of the pro-Taliban guerrillas in Afghanistan—a position enthusiastically embraced by many American politicians at the time—but this stance changed considerably on both sides of the Pacific in the 1990s.

Bhutto, however, faced more pressing domestic issues almost from the start. Her government fell in 1990, largely because of corruption charges, but she again served as Pakistani leader from 1993 to 1996.

Attempts to modernise Pakistan had made her many enemies and, in 1996, she was once again dismissed from office on charges of corruption. When Pakistan Army Chief, Pervez Musharraf, came to power after a military coup in 1999, Bhutto and her family were living in exile in Dubai and fighting charges of international money laundering.

Despite being banned by President Musharraf from serving a third term as Prime Minister, Benazir Bhutto vowed to return to her homeland. After entering into power-sharing discussions with the President—a move which alienated her from many of her supporters—Bhutto returned to Pakistan under amnesty from her corruption charges to campaign for the 2008 elections.

On her first day back in Pakistan, on 18 October 2007, 136 people were killed in an explosion near her political rally. Just two months later, after being released from house arrest during the country's state of emergency, Benazir Bhutto was assassinated on 27 December while campaigning in Rawalpindi, Punjab province.

Al-Qaeda operatives based in Afghanistan later claimed responsibility for the assassination.

Aung San Suu Kyi

'Freedom of Thought'

American University, Washington DC, 26 January 1997

Aung San Suu Kyi was born in Burma on January 1945, the daughter of national hero, General Aung San, who founded the modern Burmese Army which liberated the country from Japanese occupation during World War II. When Aung was two years old, her father, who headed the shadow Burmese government under British rule, was assassinated by a political rival. Her mother, Khin Kyi, was later appointed Burmese ambassador to India. Aung studied politics at New Delhi University and later gained her BA at St Hugh's College, Oxford.

In 1962, democratic rule in Burma ended with a military coup headed by General Ne Win. For the next 26 years, the military enforced the 'Burmese Way to Socialism' which led to the establishment of one party rule under the Burma Socialist Programme Party (BSPP) in 1974.

In 1988, Aung San Suu Kyi, who had married British scholar Michael Aris and had given birth to two sons, returned to Burma to care for her ailing mother. This coincided with a bloody military response to peaceful student demonstrations against one party rule and the resignation of General Ne Win as head of the BSPP.

On 26 August, in Rangoon, Aung San Suu Kyi stood under a large poster of her slain father and addressed a large gathering of democratic supporters and proposed the establishment of a People's Consultative Committee to help resolve the crisis.

In October, the democratic movement was brutally crushed by another military coup headed by General Saw Maung and Burma's second struggle for independence began.

Although she had lived overseas for most of her life, Aung San Suu Kyi could not 'remain indifferent' to Burma's struggle. She became the leader of the National League of Democracy and was first placed under house arrest in Rangoon in July 1989.

Under martial law, this meant that she could be detained for three years without trial. Her husband and sons visited her for what would be the last time as a family in September 1989. The following year, the military government attempted to cut her contact with the outside world.

Separated from her family and denied her personal liberty and freedom of speech, Aung continued to speak out against Burma's military rule—a stance which saw her win the 1990 Sakharov Prize for Freedom of Thought (awarded by the European Parliament), the 1991 Nobel Peace Prize and the 1992 Nehru Peace Prize.

Although she was released from house detention in 1995 and was briefly reunited with her husband, she refused to leave Burma because she knew she would not have been allowed to re-enter her own country. As a result, all of Aung San Suu Kyi's most famous speeches have been delivered by third parties, by video or in essay form.

The commencement address at the American University, Washington DC, on 26 January, 1997, was delivered on her behalf by her husband, Dr. Michael Aris, upon her receiving an Honorary Doctor of Laws degree.

‘It is an honour to receive an honorary Doctor of Laws degree from a university known for its liberal values and international outlook. It is a privilege to deliver the commencement speech at this assembly. However, what would have been the greatest joy, that of seeing the faces of the graduating students, has been denied to me. There is little that can compare with the light of hope and anticipation that shines from those who have satisfactorily completed one phase of their lives and are about to embark on another more complete, more challenging phase.

No educational institutional can fully prepare its pupils to cope with all that they will have to face during the course of their lives. However, such values as intellectual freedom, humanitarian ideals and public service, fostered by the American University, should go a long way towards equipping young men and young women to make the best of any environment in which they may find themselves.

Beginning a new life is a challenge that will put to the test our mental, intellectual, emotional and spiritual resources. Some are destined to lead tranquil lives, safe in the security of a society that guarantees fundamental rights. Others may find themselves in situations where they have to strive incessantly for the most basic of rights, the right to life itself.

'Beginning a new life is a challenge that will put to the test our mental, intellectual, emotional and spiritual resources.'

It is no simple matter to decide who are the more fortunate, those to whom life gives all or those who have to give all to life. A fulfilled life is not necessarily one constructed strictly in accordance with one's own blueprint, it can be a glorious collage of materials that have come unexpectedly to hand.

How wonderful it is that we do not know what tomorrow will bring.

Of course we all hope that our tomorrow will be happy. But happiness takes on many forms. Political prisoners have known the most sublime moments of perfect communion with their highest ideals during periods when they were incarcerated in isolation, cut off from contact with all that was familiar and dear to them. From where do those resources spring, if not from an innate strength at our core, a spiritual strength that transcends material bounds? My colleagues who spent years in the harsh conditions of Burmese prisons, and I myself, have had to draw on such inner resources on many occasions.

Nobody can take away from us the essential and ultimate freedom of choosing our priorities in life.

We may not be able to control the external factors that affect our existence, but we can decide how we wish to conduct our inner lives. We may live in a society that does not grant freedom of expression, but we can decide how much value we wish to put on the duty to speak out for our rights. We may not be able to pursue our beliefs without bringing down on us the full vengeance of a cruel state mechanism, but we can decide how much we are prepared to sacrifice for our beliefs.

Those of us who decided to work for democracy in Burma made our choice in the conviction that the danger of standing up for basic human rights in a repressive society was preferable to the safety of a quiescent life in servitude. Ours is a non-violent movement that depends on faith in the human predilection for fair play and compassion. Some would insist that man is primarily an economic animal interested only in his material well being. This is too narrow a view of a species which has produced numberless brave men and women who are prepared to undergo relentless persecution for the sake of upholding deeply held beliefs and principles. It is my pride and inspiration

> **'We may not be able to pursue our beliefs without bringing down on us the full vengeance of a cruel state mechanism, but we can decide how much we are prepared to sacrifice for our beliefs.'**

that such men and women exist in my country today.

In Burma, it is accepted as a political tradition that revolutionary changes are brought about through the active participation of students. The independence movement of our country was carried out to a successful conclusion by young leaders, including my own father, General Aung San, who began their political careers at Rangoon University. An institution with such an outstanding reputation for spirited opposition to established authority is naturally a prime target for any authoritarian government. The military regime which assumed state power in 1962 blasted the Rangoon University Students' Union building out of existence within a few months of their rule and made it illegal for students to form a union.

In 1988, the people of Burma rose up against the rule of the Burma Socialist Programme Party, the civilian cloak of a military dictatorship. At the vanguard of the nationwide demonstrations were students who demanded, among other basic rights, the right to form a union. The response of the military junta was to shoot them down. More than eight years and much repression on, the students of Burma have still not relinquished their quest for an association which would promote their interests and articulate their aspirations and grievances.

As recently as last month, there were student demonstrations where the call for the right to form a union was reiterated. The security forces used violence to disperse the demonstrators and a number of young people from my party, the National League for Democracy, were arrested on the grounds that they had been involved in the organization of the demonstrations. I was accused o f having held meetings with students and holding discussion with them. Things have indeed come to a sorry pass in a country if meetings between politicians and students are seen as acts of subversion.

My party has never made a secret of our sympathy for the aspirations of students. We work to forge close links between the different generations that a continuity of purpose and endeavour might be threaded into the fabric of our nation.

When we are struggling against overwhelming odds, when we are pitting ourselves against the combined might of the state apparatus and military power, we are sometimes subject to doubts, usually the doubts of those whose belief in the permanence of an existing order is absolute. It is amazing how many people still remain convinced that it is only wisdom to accept the status quo. We have faith in the power to change what needs to be changed, but we are under no illusion that the transition from dictatorship to liberal democracy will be easy, or that democratic government will mean the end of all our problems.

We know that our greatest challenges lie ahead of us and that our struggle to establish a stable, democratic society will continue beyond our own lifespan. We are aware that much will be demanded of us and that there will be times when we are discouraged and disappointed. But we know that we are not alone.

The cause of liberty and justice finds sympathetic responses in far reaches of the globe. Thinking and feeling people everywhere, regardless of colour or creed, understand the deeply rooted human need for a meaningful existence that goes beyond the mere gratification of material desires. Those fortunate enough to live in societies where they are entitled to full political rights can reach out to help their less fortunate brethren in other parts of our troubled planet. Young women and young men setting forth to leave their mark on the world might wish to cast their eyes beyond their own frontiers towards the shadowlands of lost rights. You who are gathered here to celebrate the opening of the doors of hope and opportunity might wish to assist our fight for a Burma where young people can know the joys of hope and opportunity.

Part of our struggle is to make the international community understand that we are a poor country, not because there is an insufficiency of resources and investment, but because we are deprived of the basic institutions and practices that make for good government. There are multinational business concerns which have no inhibitions about dealing with repressive regimes. Their justification for economic involvement in Burma is that their presence will actually assist the process of democratization.

Investment that only goes to enrich an already wealthy elite bent on monopolizing both economic and political power cannot contribute towards legality and justice, the foundation stones for a sound democracy. I would therefore like to call upon those who have an interest in expanding their capacity for promoting intellectual freedom and humanitarian ideals to take a principled stand against companies which are doing business with the military regime of Burma. Please use your liberty to promote ours.

This honorary degree that you have conferred on me today constitutes a recognition of our struggle. I would like to conclude by expressing my sincere thanks to the American University and its Board of Trustees for thus supporting the cause of democracy and human rights in Burma.

Thank you.

Although Michael Aris was stricken with prostate cancer, the Burmese government (which was renamed the Union of Myanmar by the military government in 1989) would not allow him to visit his wife.

When he passed away in 1999, Aung San Suu Kyi regarded the separation as 'one of the sacrifices she had had to make in order to work for a free Burma.' Aung was placed under house arrest again in September 2000, but although she was freed after nineteen months, she was later held in 'secret detention' for three months before being returned to house arrest.

In 2007, it was anticipated that protests from Buddhist monks in Burma and growing international pressure would lead to her release after twelve years, but despite solidarity protests held in twelve cities around the world, Aung remains still under house arrest.

Aung is often called 'Daw' Aung San Suu Kyi in her homeland, which is a maternal title of affection meaning a favourite aunt.

The name Aung San Suu Kyi itself means 'a bright collection of small victories'.

Elizabeth Glaser

'AIDS: A Personal Story'

Democratic National Convention, New York, 14 July 1992

E lizabeth Glaser (nee Meyer) was the wife of television actor/ director Paul Michael Glaser, of 1970s Starsky and Hutch fame. During the birth of their daughter, Ariel, in 1981, Elizabeth received a blood transfusion which contained the HIV/AIDS virus. Not a lot was known of the disease in the early 1980s; how it was transmitted or the implications for screening blood donations. Before she could be diagnosed, she had passed the disease onto her daughter and another child, a son Jake. However, while scientists slowly unlocked the secrets to containing and eradicating the disease, federal government support for research was minimal and the media's portrayal of HIV/AIDS as a gay lifestyle disease did little to inform the public of the insidious nature of the problem at hand.

It took the death of several high profile celebrities—actor Rock Hudson (1985), rock musician Freddy Mercury (1991), singer-songwriter Peter Allen (1992), tennis player Arthur Ashe (1993) and ballet star Rudolph Nureyev (1993) among them—and the courageous public stance of ordinary citizens such as young Ryan White, presidential aide Mary Davis Fisher and mother, Elizabeth Glaser, to shock the public and the United States government out of its complacency.

The Glasers knew first hand the ignorance surrounding the disease and the growing social stigma HIV victims—both young and old—were experiencing. When the Glaser family was diagnosed in 1986, they were advised not to go public with the details because society was not ready to handle the news. It was only when a tabloid newspaper threatened to reveal the cause of their daughter's death in 1988 that the Glasers granted an interview to the LA Times.

The publicity generated from their brave fight enabled Elizabeth and Paul Michael Glaser to convince President Ronald Reagan to film the following public service message. The commercial was directed by Paul Michael Glaser.

We all grow old and learn in our lives, and I've learned that all kinds of people can get AIDS. Even children. But it's the disease that's frightening, not the people who have it. Maybe it's time we learned something new.

However, in the four years of George H. Bush's presidency, funding for HIV/AIDS research did not kept pace with the growth of the disease.

In 1992, Elizabeth Glaser addressed the Democratic National Convention and spoke of her personal journey.

'I'm Elizabeth Glaser. Eleven years ago, while giving birth to my first child, I hemorrhaged and was transfused with seven pints of blood. Four years later, I found out that I had been infected with the AIDS virus and had unknowingly passed it on to my daughter, Ariel, through my breast milk, and my son, Jake, in utero.

Twenty years ago I wanted to be at the Democratic Convention because it was a way to participate in our country.

Today I am here because it's a matter of life and death.

Exactly four years ago, my daughter died of AIDs—she did not survive the Reagan administration. I am here because my son and I may not survive four more years of leaders who say they care, but do nothing. I am in a race with the clock. This is not about being a Republican or an Independent or a Democrat—it's about the future... for each and every one of us.

I started out just a mom—fighting for the life of her child. But along the way I learned how unfair America can be. Not just for the people who have HIV, but for many, many people—gay people, people of color, children. A strange spokesperson for such a group—a well-to-do white woman—but I have learned my lessons the hard way and I know that America has lost her path and is at risk of losing her soul. America wake up—we are all in a struggle between life and death.

I understand the sense of frustration and despair in our country, because I know first hand about screaming for help and getting no answer. I went to Washington to tell Presidents Reagan and Bush we needed to do much, much more for AIDS research and care and that children couldn't be forgotten.

The first time, when nothing happened, I thought: Oh, they just didn't hear. The second time, when nothing happened, I thought: Maybe I didn't shout loud enough. But now I realize that they don't hear because they don't want to listen. When you cry for help and no one listens, you start to lose hope.

I began to lose faith in America. I felt my own country was letting me down—and it was.

This is not the America I was raised to be proud of. I was raised to believe that others' problems were my problems as well. But when I tell most people about HIV, hoping they will care and try to help, I see the look in their eyes— its not my problem they're thinking—well, it's everyone's problem and we need a leader who will tell us that.

We need a visionary to guide us—to say it wasn't all right for Ryan White to be banned from school because he had HIV, or a man or woman denied a job because they were infected with this virus. We need a leader who is truly committed to educating us.

I believe in America—but not with a leadership of selfishness and greed where the wealthy get health care and insurance and the poor don't. Do you know how much my AIDS care costs? More than $40,000 a year. Someone without insurance can't afford this. Even the drugs that I hope will keep me alive are out of reach for others. Is their life any less valuable? Of course not.

This is not the America I was raised to be proud of—where the rich people get care and drugs that poor people can't. We need health care for all. We need a leader to say this and do something about it.

I believe in America—but not with a leadership that talks about problems but is incapable of solving them. Two HIV commission reports with recommendations about what to do to solve this crisis are sitting on shelves, gathering dust. We need a leader who will not only listen to these recommendations, but will implement them.

I believe in America—but not with a leadership that doesn't hold government accountable. I go to Washington to the National Institutes of Health and say: "Show me what you're doing on HIV." They hate it when I come because I try to tell them how to do it better. But that's why I love being a taxpayer— because it's my money and they must become accountable.

I believe in an America where our leaders talk straight. When anyone tells President Bush that the battle against AIDS is seriously underfunded, he juggles the numbers to mislead the public into thinking we're spending twice as much as we really are. While they play games with numbers, people are dying.

I believe in America—but an America where there is light in every home. One thousand points of light just weren't enough—my house has been dark for too long.

'Once every generation, history brings us to an important crossroads. Sometimes in life there is that moment when it's possible to make a change for the better. This is one of those moments.'

Once every generation, history brings us to an important crossroads. Sometimes in life there is that moment when it's possible to make a change for the better. This is one of those moments.

For me, this is not politics. It's a crisis of caring.

In this hall is the future: Women, men of all colors saying, "Take America back."

We are just real people wanting a more hopeful life. But words and ideas are not enough. Good thoughts won't save my family. What's the point of caring if we don't do something about it? We must have ACTION:

A President and a Congress who can work together so we can get out of this gridlock and move ahead. Because I don't win my war if the Congress cares and the President doesn't—or if the President cares and the Congress doesn't support his ideas.

The people in this hall—this week, the Democratic Party—all of us can begin to deliver that partnership and in November we can all bring it home.

My daughter lived seven years and in her last year, when she couldn't walk or talk, her wisdom shone through. She taught me to help others, when all I wanted to do was hate. She taught me to help others, when all I wanted to do was help myself. She taught me to be brave, when all I felt was fear.

My daughter and I loved each other with simplicity. America, we can do the same. This was the country that offered hope. This was the place where dreams could come true. Not just economic dreams, but dreams of freedom, justice and equality. We all need to hope that our dreams can come true. I challenge you to make it happen, because all our lives, not just mine, depend on it.

Elizabeth and Paul Michael Glaser founded the Elizabeth Glaser Pediatric AIDS Foundation, lobbied congressmen to fund research into the cause and prevention of the disease and spoke to doctors, patients and children about living with HIV/AIDS.

In her own way, Elizabeth Glaser educated millions of people about the need to embrace victims and not to act out of ignorance.

Elizabeth Glaser passed away on 3 December 1994 at the age of 47. In 2005, the Glasers' son, Jake, celebrated his 21st birthday—a living testimony to his parents' perseverance in giving all HIV sufferers hope.

Hillary Clinton

'On Women's Rights'

UN World Conference on Women, Beijing, China, 5 September 1995

On the inauguration of husband Bill Clinton to the US Presidency in 1993, Hillary Rodham Clinton (b. 1948) became equally well-known as America's First Lady.

Hillary Rodham had previously worked for the Children's Defense Fund and was a member of a House of Representatives Committee preparing to impeach President Nixon in 1974. She joined Bill Clinton on the faculty of the University of Arkansas Law School and the pair married in 1976.

Politically savvy, with a strong sense of justice and morality, Hillary Rodham Clinton was at her husband's side in 1991 when the Democratic nominee for the US presidency confirmed to 60 Minutes that his dalliances with other women had 'caused pain' in their marriage. Her steadfast belief in her husband was crucial to Clinton's subsequent success and she became one of his most important advisers during his presidency—to the point of taking an office in the West Wing of the White House.

In September 1995, during the first term of her husband's presidency (1993-2001), Hillary Clinton was invited to address the Fourth Annual United Nations Conference on Women, which was held in Beijing, China.

The following speech drew widespread applause from the delegates of 180 countries for its confronting and remarkably frank addressing of issues, but also took on a special resonance because it was delivered in China, where many violations of human rights against women still occur.

‘This is truly a celebration—a celebration of the contributions women make in every aspect of life: in the home, on the job, in their communities, as mothers, wives, sisters, daughters, learners, workers, citizens and leaders.

It is also a coming together, much the way women come together every day in every country. We come together in fields and in factories. In village markets and supermarkets. In living rooms and board rooms.

Whether it is while playing with our children in the park, or washing clothes in a river, or taking a break at the office water cooler, we come together and talk about our aspirations and concerns. And time and again, our talk turns to our children and our families.

However different we may be, there is far more that unites us than divides us. We share a common future. And we are here to find common ground so that we may help bring new dignity and respect to women and girls all over the world—and in so doing, bring new strength and stability to families as well.

By gathering in Beijing, we are focusing world attention on issues that matter most in the lives of women and their families: access to education, health care, jobs, and credit, the chance to enjoy basic legal and human rights and participate fully in the political life of their countries.

There are some who question the reason for this conference. Let them listen to the voices of women in their homes, neighborhoods and workplaces.

There are some who wonder whether the lives of women and girls matter to economic and political progress around the globe. Let them look at the women gathered here and at Huairou—the homemakers, nurses, teachers, lawyers, policy makers and women who run their own businesses.

It is conferences like this that compel governments and peoples everywhere to listen, look and face the world's most pressing problems.

Wasn't it after the women's conference in Nairobi ten years ago that the world focused for the first time on the crisis of domestic violence?

Earlier today, I participated in a World Health Organization forum, where government officials, NGOs and individual citizens are working on ways to address the health problems of women and girls.

Tomorrow, I will attend a gathering of the United Nations Development Fund for Women. There, the discussion will focus on local—and highly successful—programs that give hard-working women access to credit so they can improve their lives and the lives of their families.

What we are learning around the world is that if women are healthy and educated, their families will flourish. If women are free from violence, their families will flourish. If women have a chance to work and earn as full and equal partners in society, their families will flourish.

And when families flourish, communities and nations will flourish.

That is why every woman, every man, every child, every family and every nation on our planet has a stake in the discussion that takes place here.

Over the past 25 years, I have worked persistently on issues relating to women, children and families. Over the past two and a half years, I have had the opportunity to learn more about the challenges facing women in my country and around the world. I have met new mothers in Jogjakarta, Indonesia, who come together regularly in their village to discuss nutrition, family planning and baby care. I have met working parents in Denmark who talk about the comfort they feel in knowing that their children can be cared for in creative, safe and nurturing after-school centers. I have met women in South Africa who helped lead the struggle to end apartheid and are now helping build a new democracy. I have met with the leading women of the western hemisphere who are working every day to promote literacy and better health care for the children of their countries. I have met women in India and Bangladesh who are taking out small loans to buy milk cows, rickshaws, thread and other materials to create a livelihood for themselves and their families. I have met doctors and nurses in Belarus and Ukraine who are trying to keep children alive in the aftermath of Chernobyl.

The great challenge of this conference is to give voice to women everywhere whose experiences go unnoticed, whose words go unheard.

Women comprise more than half the world's population. Women are 70 per cent of the world's poor and two-thirds of those who are not taught to read and write. Women are the primary caretakers for most of the world's children and elderly. Yet much of the work we do is not valued—not by economists, not by historians, not by popular culture and not by government leaders.

At this very moment, as we sit here, women around the world are giving birth, raising children, cooking meals, washing clothes, cleaning houses, planting crops, working on assembly lines, running companies and running countries.

Women are also dying from diseases that should have been prevented or treated. They are watching their children succumb to malnutrition caused by poverty and economic deprivation. They are being denied the right to go to school by their own fathers and brothers. They are being forced into prostitution and they are being barred from the ballot box and the bank lending office.

Those of us with the opportunity to be here have the responsibility to speak for those who could not.

As an American, I want to speak up for women in my own country—women who are raising children on the minimum wage, women who can't afford health care or child care, women whose lives are threatened by violence, including violence in their own homes.

I want to speak up for mothers who are fighting for good schools, safe neighborhoods, clean air and clean airwaves; for older women, some of them widows, who have raised their families and now find that their skills and life experiences are not valued in the workplace; for women who are working all night as nurses, hotel clerks and fast food chefs so that they can be at home during the day with their kids; and for women everywhere who simply don't have enough time to do everything they are called upon to do each day.

Speaking to you today, I speak for them, just as each of us speaks for women around the world who are denied the chance to go to school, or see a doctor, or own property, or have a say about the direction of their lives, simply because they are women.

The truth is that most women around the world work both inside and outside the home, usually by necessity.

We need to understand that there is no formula for how women should lead their lives. That is why we must respect the choices that each woman makes for herself and her family. Every woman deserves the chance to realize her God-given potential. We must also recognize that women will never gain full dignity until their human rights are respected and protected.

Our goals for this conference, to strengthen families and societies by empowering women to take greater control over their own destinies, cannot be fully achieved unless all governments—here and around the world—accept their responsibility to protect and promote internationally recognized human rights.

The international community has long acknowledged, and recently affirmed at Vienna, that both women and men are entitled to a range of protections and personal freedoms, from the right of personal security to the right to determine freely the number and spacing of the children they bear.

No one should be forced to remain silent for fear of religious or political persecution, arrest, abuse or torture.

Tragically, women are most often the ones whose human rights are violated. Even in the late twentieth century, the rape of women continues to be used as an instrument of armed conflict. Women and children make up a large majority of the world's refugees. And when women are excluded from the political process, they become even more vulnerable to abuse.

I believe that, on the eve of a new millennium, it is time to break our silence. It is time for us to say here in Beijing, and for the world to hear, that it is no longer acceptable to discuss women's rights as separate from human rights. These abuses have continued because, for too long, the history of women has been a history of silence.

Even today, there are those who are trying to silence our words. The voices of this conference and of the women at Huairou must be heard loud and clear. It is a violation of human rights when women and girls are sold into the slavery of prostitution.

It is a violation of human rights when women are doused with gasoline, set on fire and burned to death because their marriage dowries are deemed too small.

It is a violation of human rights when individual women are raped in their own communities and when thousands of women are subjected to rape as a tactic or prize of war. It is a violation of human rights when a leading cause of death worldwide among women aged fourteen to 44 is the violence they are subjected to in their own homes.

It is a violation of human rights when young girls are brutalized by the painful and degrading practice of genital mutilation.

It is a violation of human rights when women are denied the right to plan their own families and that includes being forced to have abortions or being sterilized against their will.

If there is one message that echoes forth from this conference, it is that human rights are women's rights, and women's rights are human rights. Let us not forget that among those rights are the right to speak freely and the right to be heard.

Women must enjoy the right to participate fully in the social and political lives of their countries if we want freedom and democracy to thrive and endure.

It is indefensible that many women in non-governmental organizations who wished to participate in this conference have not been able to attend—or have been prohibited from fully taking part.

Let me be clear. Freedom means the right of people to assemble, organize and debate openly. It means respecting the views of those who may disagree with the views of their governments. It means not taking citizens away from their loved ones and jailing them, mistreating them, or denying them their freedom or dignity because of the peaceful expression of their ideas and opinions.

In my country, we recently celebrated the 75th anniversary of women's suffrage. It took 150 years after the signing of our Declaration of Independence for women to win the right to vote. It took 72 years of organized struggle on the part of many courageous women and men. It was one of America's most divisive philosophical wars. But it was also a bloodless war. Suffrage was achieved without a shot fired.

We have also have been reminded, in VJ Day observances last weekend, of the good that comes when men and women join together to combat the forces of tyranny and build a better world.

We have seen peace prevail in most places for a half century. We have avoided another world war. But we have not solved older, deeply rooted problems that continue to diminish the potential of half the world's population.

Now it is time to act on behalf of women everywhere.

If we take bold steps to better the lives of women, we will be taking bold steps to better the lives of children and families too. Families rely on mothers and wives for emotional support and care; families rely on women for labor in the home; and increasingly, families rely on women for income needed to raise healthy children and care for other relatives. As long as discrimination and inequities remain so commonplace around the world—as long as girls and women are valued less, fed less, fed last, overworked, underpaid, not schooled and subjected to violence in and out of their homes—the potential of the human family to create a peaceful, prosperous world will not be realized.

Let this conference be ours, and the world's call to action.

And let us heed the call so that we can create a world in which every woman is treated with respect and dignity, every boy and girl is loved and cared for equally and every family has the hope of a strong and stable future.

Thank you very much. ♪

The Clintons' eight years in the White House were controversial, productive and ultimately shook their marriage to its very foundation.

Hillary Rodham Clinton's sponsorship of a scheme to reform health care was a spectacular failure when brought before Congress in 1993, but her support of her husband as the Lewinsky Affair destroyed the last year of his presidency, portrayed her as strong, loyal and forgiving.

In 2000, she was elected Democratic Senator for New York but despite a tenacious struggle to the very end, she faltered in her bid to be the first woman to sit in the White House when beaten by Barack Obama in the race for the Democratic nomination in 2008.

Change

Fidel Castro

'History Will Absolve Me'

Santiago, Cuba, 16 October 1953

Fidel Castro (b. 1926) was a Cuban lawyer and revolutionary leader opposed to the Batista government which had come to power after a military coup in 1952. The following year, on 26 July, Castro was captured after a failed attack on the government garrison, the Moncada Barracks, outside Santiago. Although there is some conjecture whether Castro took part in the attack, he and his brother Raúl were fortunate not to have been executed on the spot following their capture. Instead, they stood trial on charges of treason at the end of the year. An unrepentant Fidel Castro warned those now in power who were judging him that this was not the end of his struggle… history would not only absolve him but also prove him right.

The right of rebellion against tyranny, Honorable Judges, has been recognized from the most ancient times to the present day by men of all creeds, ideas and doctrines.

It was so in the theocratic monarchies of remote antiquity. In China, it was almost a constitutional principle that when a king governed rudely and despotically he should be deposed and replaced by a virtuous prince.

The philosophers of ancient India upheld the principle of active resistance to arbitrary authority. They justified revolution and very often put their theories into practice. One of their spiritual leaders used to say that "an opinion held by the majority is stronger than the king himself. A rope woven of many strands is strong enough to hold a lion."

'The right of rebellion against tyranny, Honorable Judges, has been recognized from the most ancient times to the present day by men of all creeds, ideas and doctrines.'

The city states of Greece and republican Rome not only admitted, but defended, the meting-out of violent death to tyrants.

In the Middle Ages, John Salisbury in his Book of the Statesman says that when a prince does not govern according to law and degenerates into a tyrant, violent overthrow is legitimate and justifiable. He recommends for tyrants the dagger rather than poison.

Saint Thomas Aquinas, in the Summa Theologica, rejects the doctrine of tyrannicide and yet upholds the thesis that tyrants should be overthrown by the people.

Martin Luther proclaimed that when a government degenerates into a tyranny that violates the laws, its subjects are released from their obligations to obey. His disciple, Philippe Melanchton, upholds the right of resistance when governments become despotic. Calvin, the outstanding thinker of the Reformation with regard to political ideas, postulates that people are entitled to take up arms to oppose any usurpation.

No less a man that Juan Mariana, a Spanish Jesuit during the reign of Philip II, asserts in his book, De Rege et Regis Institutione, that when a governor usurps power, or even if he were elected, when he governs in a tyrannical manner it is licit for a private citizen to exercise tyrannicide, either directly or through subterfuge with the least possible disturbance.

The French writer François Hotman maintained that between the government and its subjects there is a bond or contract and that the people may rise in rebellion against the tyranny of government when the latter violates that pact.

About the same time, a booklet—which came to be widely read—appeared under the title Vindiciae Contra Tyrannos, and it was signed with the pseudonym Stephanus Junius Brutus. It openly declared that resistance to governments is legitimate when rulers oppress the people and that it is the duty of Honorable Judges to lead the struggle.

Scottish reformers John Knox and John Poynet upheld the same points of view. And, in the most important book of that movement, George Buchanan stated that if a government achieved power without taking into account the consent of the people, or if a government rules their destiny in an unjust or arbitrary fashion, then that government becomes a tyranny and can be divested of power or, in a final recourse, its leaders can be put to death.

John Althus, a German jurist of the early seventeenth century, stated in his Treatise on Politics that sovereignty as the supreme authority of the State is born from the voluntary concourse of all its members; that governmental authority stems from the people and that its unjust, illegal or tyrannical function exempts them from the duty of obedience and justifies resistance or rebellion.

Thus far, Honorable Judges, I have mentioned examples from antiquity, from the Middle Ages and from the beginnings of our times. I selected these examples from writers of all creeds. What is more, you can see that the right to rebellion is at the very root of Cuba's existence as a nation. By virtue of it, you are today able to appear in the robes of Cuban Judges. Would it be that those garments really served the cause of justice!

It is well known that in England during the seventeenth century two kings, Charles I and James II, were dethroned for despotism. These actions coincided with the birth of liberal political philosophy and provided the ideological base for a new social class, which was then struggling to break the bonds of feudalism.

Against divine right autocracies, this new philosophy upheld the principle of the social contract and of the consent of the governed and constituted the foundation of the English Revolution of 1688, the American Revolution of 1775 and the French Revolution of 1789.

These great revolutionary events ushered in the liberation of the Spanish colonies in the New World—the final link in that chain being broken by Cuba. The new philosophy nurtured our own political ideas and helped us to evolve our Constitutions, from the Constitution of Guáimaro up to the Constitution of 1940. The latter was influenced by the socialist currents of our time; the principle of the social function of property and of man's inalienable right to a decent living were built into it, although large vested interests have prevented fully enforcing those rights.

The right of insurrection against tyranny then underwent its final consecration and became a fundamental tenet of political liberty.

As far back as 1649, John Milton wrote that political power lies with the people, who can enthrone and dethrone kings and have the duty of overthrowing tyrants.

John Locke, in his essay on government, maintained that when the natural rights of man are violated, the people have the right and the duty to alter or abolish the government. "The only remedy against unauthorized force is opposition to it by force."

Jean-Jacques Rousseau said with great eloquence in his Social Contract: "While a people sees itself forced to obey and obeys, it does well; but as soon as it can shake off the yoke and shakes it off, it does better, recovering its liberty through the use of the very right that has been taken away from it."

"The strongest man is never strong enough to be master forever, unless he converts force into right and obedience into duty. Force is a physical power; I do not see what morality one may derive from its use. To yield to force is an act of necessity, not of will; at the very least, it is an act of prudence. In what sense should this be called a duty?"

"To renounce freedom is to renounce one's status as a man, to renounce one's human rights, including one's duties. There is no possible compensation for renouncing everything. Total renunciation is incompatible with the nature of man and to take away all free will is to take away all morality of conduct. In short, it is vain and contradictory to stipulate on the one hand an absolute authority and on the other an unlimited obedience..."

Thomas Paine said that "one just man deserves more respect than a rogue with a crown."

The people's right to rebel has been opposed only by reactionaries like that clergyman of Virginia, Jonathan Boucher, who said: "The right to rebel is a censurable doctrine derived from Lucifer, the father of rebellions."

The Declaration of Independence of the Congress of Philadelphia, on July 4 1776, consecrated this right in a beautiful paragraph which reads: "We hold these truths to be self-evident, that all men are created equal, that they are endowed by their Creator with certain inalienable rights, that among these are Life, Liberty and the Pursuit of Happiness; that to secure these Rights, Governments are instituted among Men, deriving their just powers from the consent of the governed; that whenever any Form of Government becomes destructive of these ends, it is the Right of the People to alter or abolish it and to institute a new Government, laying its foundation on such principles and organizing its powers in such form as to them shall seem most likely to effect their Safety and Happiness."

The famous French Declaration of the Rights of Man willed this principle to the coming generations: "When the government violates the rights of the people, insurrection is for them the most sacred of rights and the most imperative of duties."

"When a person seizes sovereignty, he should be condemned to death by free men."

I believe I have sufficiently justified my point of view. I have called forth more reasons than the Honorable Prosecutor called forth to ask that I be condemned to 26 years in prison.

'How could anyone call revolutionary a regime which has gathered the most backward men, methods and ideas of public life around it? How can anyone consider legally valid the high treason of a court whose duty was to defend the Constitution?'

All these reasons support men who struggle for the freedom and happiness of the people. None support those who oppress the people, revile them, and rob them heartlessly. Therefore I have been able to call forth many reasons and he could not adduce even one. How can Batista's presence in power be justified when he gained it against the will of the people and by violating the laws of the Republic through the use of treachery and force? How could anyone call legitimate a regime of blood, oppression and ignominy? How could anyone call revolutionary a regime which has gathered the most backward men, methods and ideas of public life around it? How can anyone consider legally valid the high treason of a court whose duty was to defend the Constitution? With what right do the courts send to prison citizens who have tried to redeem their country by giving their own blood, their own lives? All this is monstrous to the eyes of the nation and to the principles of true justice!

Still there is one argument more powerful than all the others. We are Cubans and to be Cuban implies a duty; not to fulfill that duty is a crime, is treason. We are proud of the history of our country; we learned it in school and have grown up hearing of freedom, justice and human rights. We were taught to venerate the glorious example of our heroes and martyrs. Céspedes, Agramonte, Maceo, Gómez and Martí were the first names engraved in our minds. We were taught that the Titan once said that liberty is not begged for but won with the blade of a machete. We were taught that for the guidance of Cuba's free citizens, the Apostle wrote in his book The Golden Age: "The man who abides by unjust laws and permits any man to trample and mistreat the country in which he was born is not an honorable man... In the world there must be a certain degree of honor just as there must be a certain amount of light. When there are many men without honor, there are always others who bear in themselves the honor of many men. These are the men who rebel with great force against those who steal the people's freedom, that is to say, against those who steal honor itself. In those men thousands more are contained, an entire people is contained, human dignity is contained.

We were taught that the 10th of October and the 24th of February are glorious anniversaries of national rejoicing because they mark days on which Cubans rebelled against the yoke of infamous tyranny. We were taught to cherish and defend the beloved flag of the lone star, and to sing every afternoon the verses of our National Anthem: "To live in chains is to live in disgrace and in opprobrium," and "to die for one's homeland is to live forever!"

All this we learned and will never forget, even though today in our land there is murder and prison for the men who practice the ideas taught to them since the cradle. We were born in a free country that our parents bequeathed to us, and the Island will first sink into the sea before we consent to be the slaves of anyone.

It seemed that the Apostle would die during his Centennial. It seemed that his memory would be extinguished forever. So great was the affront! But he is alive; he has not died. His people are rebellious. His people are worthy. His people are faithful to his memory. There are Cubans who have fallen defending his doctrines. There are young men who in magnificent selflessness came to die beside his tomb, giving their blood and their lives so that he could keep on living in the heart of his nation. Cuba, what would have become of you had you let your Apostle die?

I come to the close of my defense plea but I will not end it as lawyers usually do, asking that the accused be freed. I cannot ask freedom for myself while my comrades are already suffering in the ignominious prison of the Isle of Pines. Send me there to join them and to share their fate. It is understandable that honest men should be dead or in prison in a Republic where the President is a criminal and a thief.

To you, Honorable Judges, my sincere gratitude for having allowed me to express myself free from contemptible restrictions. I hold no bitterness towards you, I recognize that in certain aspects you have been humane and I know that the Chief Judge of this court, a man of impeccable private life, cannot disguise his repugnance at the current state of affairs that compels him to dictate unjust decisions.

Still, a more serious problem remains for the Court of Appeals. The indictments arising from the murders of 70 men, that is to say, the greatest massacre we have ever known. The guilty continue at liberty and with weapons in their hands—weapons which continually threaten the lives of all citizens. If all the weight of the law does not fall upon the guilty because of cowardice or because of domination of the courts, and if then all the judges do not resign, I pity Your Honor. And I regret the unprecedented shame that will fall upon the Judicial Power.

I know that imprisonment will be harder for me than it has ever been for anyone, filled with cowardly threats and hideous cruelty. But I do not fear prison, as I do not fear the fury of the miserable tyrant who took the lives of 70 of my comrades. Condemn me. It does not matter. History will absolve me.

Fidel Castro and his brother served just two years in jail before going to Mexico and undergoing military training with 'Che' Guevara in preparation for the overthrow of the Batista government.

Castro formed the 26 July Movement (named after the date of the failed attack) with other Cuban exiles and the backing of the Soviet Union and by November 1956, he was ready to return home to lead a people's revolution under the cover of the Cuban jungle.

Despite Batista's best military efforts, Castro remained out of reach for the next eighteen months while his movement gained popular support in rural and city areas. Following Batista's defeat in the Battle of Yaguajay and the loss of Santa Clara, the provisional capital of revolutionary Cuba, the President fled the country on 1 January 1959.

On 8 January 1959, Castro's army entered Havana. After coming to power, the young lawyer and charismatic revolutionary who had captured the attention of the free world, declined to hold free elections and became the leader of a one-party (Communist) socialist republic.

Castro withstood a CIA-backed invasion (1961), the Cuban Missile Crisis (1962) and numerous failed assassination attempts to remain in office unchallenged for the next 50 years. Despite the imposition of international sanctions and allegations of human rights violations, it was ill-health that finally removed Castro from office.

In 2006, while recovering from stomach cancer surgery, Castro transferred his presidential powers to his brother Raúl.

In February 2008, Fidel Castro retired after almost 50 years as Cuban President (although he remains First Secretary of the Cuban Communist Party) and was succeeded by his brother.

Nelson Mandela

'I Am the First Accused'

Pretoria Supreme Court, 20 April 1964

O n 21 March 1960, South African police opened fire on unarmed anti-apartheid protesters in Sharpeville, killing 69 civilians—most of whom had bullet wounds in the back as they ran away from the police.

The government declared a State of Emergency and banned the African National Congress (ANC) and other opposition minority political parties.

Nelson Mandela (b. 1920) responded to the banning of the ANC by forming the underground Umkhonto we Sizwe ('Spear of the Nation' or 'MK') movement whose policy was to target and destroy government utilities and symbols of apartheid—not people.

In 1961, Mandela illegally escaped the country and studied guerrilla warfare in Africa and Europe. Returning from overseas after a year on the run, he was arrested by South African security police in Rivonia, Johannesburg, and sentenced to five years jail on Robben Island.

In 1964, the government brought further charges against him including 'sabotage, high treason and conspiracy to overthrow the government.'

In Nelson Mandela's statement from the dock at the opening of his defence in 1964's Rivonia Trial, he spoke of his ancestry and the struggle for black equality in his white-dominated homeland.

' I am the First Accused.

I hold a Bachelor's Degree in Arts and practised as an attorney in Johannesburg for a number of years in partnership with Oliver Tambo. I am a convicted prisoner serving five years for leaving the country without a permit and for inciting people to go on strike at the end of May 1961.

At the outset, I want to say that the suggestion made by the State in its opening that the struggle in South Africa is under the influence of foreigners or Communists is wholly incorrect. I have done whatever I did, both as an individual and as a leader of my people, because of my experience in South Africa and my own proudly felt African background, and not because of what any outsider might have said.

In my youth in the Transkei, I listened to the elders of my tribe telling stories of the old days. Amongst the tales they related to me were those of wars fought by our ancestors in defence of the fatherland. The names of Dingane and Bambata, Hintsa and Makana, Squngthi and Dalasile, Moshoeshoe and Sekhukhuni, were praised as the glory of the entire African nation. I hoped then that life might offer me the opportunity to serve my people and make my own humble contribution to their freedom struggle.

This is what has motivated me in all that I have done in relation to the charges made against me in this case.

Having said this, I must deal immediately and at some length with the question of violence. Some of the things so far told to the court are true and some are untrue. I do not, however, deny that I planned sabotage. I did not plan it in a spirit of recklessness, nor because I have any love of violence. I planned it as a result of a calm and sober assessment of the political situation that had arisen after many years of tyranny, exploitation and oppression of my people by the whites.

I admit immediately that I was one of the persons who helped to form Umkhonto we Sizwe and that I played a prominent role in its affairs until I was arrested in August 1962.

In the statement which I am about to make, I shall correct certain false impressions which have been created by State witnesses. Amongst other things, I will demonstrate that certain of the acts referred to in the evidence were not and could not have been committed by Umkhonto. I will also deal with the relationship between the African National Congress and Umkhonto and with the part which I personally have played in the affairs of both organizations. I shall deal also with the part played by the Communist Party. In order to explain these matters properly, I will have to explain what Umkhonto set out to achieve; what methods it prescribed for the achievement of these objects, and why these methods were chosen.

> *'...we felt that without violence there would be no way open to the African people to succeed in their struggle against the principle of white supremacy.'*

I will also have to explain how I became involved in the activities of these organizations.

I deny that Umkhonto was responsible for a number of acts which clearly fell outside the policy of the organization, and which have been charged in the indictment against us. I do not know what justification there was for these acts, but to demonstrate that they could not have been authorized by Umkhonto, I want to refer briefly to the roots and policy of the organization.

I have already mentioned that I was one of the persons who helped to form Umkhonto. I, and the others who started the organization, did so for two reasons. Firstly, we believed that as a result of government policy, violence by the African people had become inevitable and that unless responsible leadership was given to canalize and control the feelings of our people, there would be outbreaks of terrorism which would produce an intensity of bitterness and hostility between the various races of this country which is not produced even by war.

Secondly, we felt that without violence there would be no way open to the African people to succeed in their struggle against the principle of white supremacy. All lawful modes of expressing opposition to this principle had been closed by legislation and we were placed in a position in which we had either to accept a permanent state of inferiority or defy the Government. We chose to defy the law. We first broke the law in a way which avoided any recourse to violence; when this form was legislated against, and when the Government resorted to a show of force to crush opposition to its policies, only then did we decide to answer violence with violence.

But the violence which we chose to adopt was not terrorism. We who formed Umkhonto were all members of the African National Congress and had behind us the ANC tradition of non-violence and negotiation as a means of solving political disputes. We believe that South Africa belongs to all the people who live in it, not to one group, be it black or white. We did not want an interracial war and tried to avoid it to the last minute. If the court is in doubt about this, it will be seen that the whole history of our organization bears out what I have said and what I will subsequently say, when I describe the tactics which Umkhonto decided to adopt.

I want, therefore, to say something about the African National Congress.

The African National Congress was formed in 1912 to defend the rights of the African people which had been seriously curtailed by the South Africa Act and which were then being threatened by the Native Land Act. For 37 years—that is until 1949—it adhered strictly to a constitutional struggle.

It put forward demands and resolutions; it sent delegations to the government

'We did not want an interracial war and tried to avoid it to the last minute. If the court is in doubt about this, it will be seen that the whole history of our organization bears out what I have said...'

in the belief that African grievances could be settled through peaceful discussion and that Africans could advance gradually to full political rights.

But white governments remained unmoved, and the rights of Africans became less instead of becoming greater. In the words of my leader, Chief Lutuli, who became President of the ANC in 1952, and who was later awarded the Nobel Peace Prize:

"Who will deny that thirty years of my life have been spent knocking in vain, patiently, moderately, and modestly at a closed and barred door? What have been the fruits of moderation? The past thirty years have seen the greatest number of laws restricting our rights and progress, until today we have reached a stage where we have almost no rights at all."

Even after 1949, the ANC remained determined to avoid violence. At this time, however, there was a change from the strictly constitutional means of protest which had been employed in the past. The change was embodied in a decision which was taken to protest against apartheid legislation by peaceful, but unlawful, demonstrations against certain laws.

Pursuant to this policy, the ANC launched the Defiance Campaign, in which I was placed in charge of volunteers. This campaign was based on the principles of passive resistance. More than 8500 people defied apartheid laws and went to jail. Yet there was not a single instance of violence in the course of this campaign on the part of any defier. I and nineteen colleagues were convicted for the role which we played in organizing the campaign, but our sentences were suspended mainly because the Judge found that discipline and non-violence had been stressed throughout.

This was the time when the volunteer section of the ANC was established, and when the word 'Amadelakufa' ('death defiance!') was first used. This was the time when the volunteers were asked to take a pledge to uphold certain principles. Evidence dealing with volunteers and their pledges has been introduced into this case, but completely out of context. The volunteers were not, and are not, the soldiers of a black army pledged to fight a civil war against the whites. They were, and are, dedicated workers who are prepared to lead campaigns initiated by the ANC, to distribute leaflets, to organize strikes, or do whatever the particular campaign required. They are called volunteers because they volunteer to face the penalties of imprisonment and whipping which are now prescribed by the legislature for such acts.

During the Defiance Campaign, the Public Safety Act and the Criminal Law Amendment Act were passed. These Statutes provided harsher penalties for offences committed by way of protests against laws. Despite this, the protests continued and the ANC adhered to

'We believed in the words of the Universal Declaration of Human Rights, that "the will of the people shall be the basis of authority of the Government..."'

its policy of non-violence. In 1956, 156 leading members of the Congress Alliance, including myself, were arrested on a charge of high treason and charges under the Suppression of Communism Act.

The non-violent policy of the ANC was put at issue by the State, but when the court gave judgement some five years later, it found that the ANC did not have a policy of violence. We were acquitted on all counts, which included a count that the ANC sought to set up a Communist state in place of the existing regime. The government has always sought to label all its opponents as Communists. This allegation has been repeated in the present case, but as I will show, the ANC is not, and never has been, a Communist organization.

In 1960 there was the shooting at Sharpeville, which resulted in the proclamation of a state of emergency and the declaration of the ANC as an unlawful organization. My colleagues and I, after careful consideration, decided that we would not obey this decree. The African people were not part of the government and did not make the laws by which they were governed. We believed in the words of the Universal Declaration of Human Rights, that "the will of the people shall be the basis of authority of the government", and for us to accept the banning was equivalent to accepting the silencing of the Africans for all time.

The ANC refused to dissolve, but instead went underground. We believed it was our duty to preserve this organization which had been built up with almost 50 years of unremitting toil. I have no doubt that no self-respecting white political organization would disband itself if declared illegal by a government in which it had no say.

In 1960 the government held a referendum which led to the establishment of the Republic. Africans, who constituted approximately 70 per cent of the population of South Africa, were not entitled to vote and were not even consulted about the proposed constitutional change. All of us were apprehensive of our future under the proposed White Republic and a resolution was taken to hold an All-In African Conference to call for a National Convention; and to organize mass demonstrations on the eve of the unwanted Republic, if the government failed to call the Convention.

The conference was attended by Africans of various political persuasions.

I was the secretary of the conference and undertook to be responsible for organizing the national stay-at-home which was subsequently called to coincide with the declaration of the Republic. As all strikes by Africans are illegal, the person organizing such a strike must avoid arrest. I was chosen to be this person and consequently I had to leave my home and family and my practice and go into hiding to avoid arrest.

The stay-at-home, in accordance with ANC policy, was to be a peaceful demonstration. Careful instructions were given to organizers and members to avoid any recourse to violence.

The government's answer was to introduce new and harsher laws, to mobilize its armed forces and to send Saracens—armed vehicles—and soldiers into the townships in a massive show of force designed to intimidate the people. This was an indication that the government had decided to rule by force alone. This decision was a milestone on the road to Umkhonto.

Some of this may appear irrelevant to this trial. In fact, I believe none of it is irrelevant because it will, I hope, enable the court to appreciate the attitude eventually adopted by the various persons and bodies concerned in the National Liberation Movement. When I went to jail in 1962, the dominant idea was that loss of life should be avoided. I now know that this was still so in 1963...

Above all, we want equal political rights, because without them, our disabilities will be permanent. I know this sounds revolutionary to the whites in this country, because the majority of voters will be Africans. This makes the white man fear democracy.

But this fear cannot be allowed to stand in the way of the only solution which will guarantee racial harmony and freedom for all. It is not true that the enfranchisement of all will result in racial domination. Political division, based on colour, is entirely artificial and, when it disappears, so will the domination of one colour group by another. The ANC has spent half a century fighting against racialism. When it triumphs, it will not change that policy.

This then is what the ANC is fighting. Their struggle is a truly national one. It is a struggle of the African people, inspired by their own suffering and their own experience. It is a struggle for the right to live.

During my lifetime, I have dedicated myself to this struggle of the African people. I have fought against white domination and I have fought against black domination. I have cherished the ideal of a democratic and free society in which all persons live together in harmony and with equal opportunities. It is an ideal which I hope to live for and to achieve. But if needs be, it is an ideal for which I am prepared to die. ♪

Nelson Mandela and seven other defendants were found guilty on 11 June 1964. Although Mandela and the other accused escaped execution, they were sentenced to life imprisonment. The future president of a united South Africa would spend a total of 27 years in jail until his release in 1990.

Malcolm X

'The Bullet or the Ballot'

Cleveland, Ohio, 3 April 1964

Malcolm X was born Malcolm Little on 19 May 1925, in Omaha Nebraska. One of eight children of outspoken Baptist Minister Earl Little, the family home in Lansing Michigan was burnt to the ground in 1929 because of Little Senior's support of black nationalist leader, Marcus Garvey.

Two years later, Earl Little's body was found lying on a trolley track—the victim of white supremacist group, the Black Legion—but at the time his death was ruled an accident.

Malcolm's mother suffered the first of several nervous breakdowns and he and his siblings were placed in foster homes and orphanages.

Although he was a bright student, Malcolm drifted into petty crime and, after moving to Boston in 1946, was sentenced to ten years jail on burglary charges. Malcolm used his time in jail to rekindle his interest in education and converted to Islam. By the time he was paroled in 1952, Malcolm was a firm follower of 'Nation of Islam' leader, Elijah Muhammad, and forsook his slave name 'Little' for the letter 'X' to symbolise the loss of his African identity.

His ability to articulate Elijah Muhammad's sternest teachings—to despise the white society that had enslaved African-Americans and was actively working against them in achieving equality and a separate NOI State within America—portrayed Malcolm X as a stark alternative for African Americans to the non-violent leadership of Martin Luther King.

Malcolm X emerged as the Nation of Islam's most important leader in the late 1950s and early 1960s—eventually eclipsing his mentor, Elijah Muhammad, whom Malcolm considered a living prophet. When he discovered that Elijah Muhammad was conducting affairs with as many as six women (and had fathered several children) in his organisation, he broke away from NOI in March 1964 and founded his own religious organisation, the Muslim Mosque, Inc.

In this famous speech in Cleveland, Ohio, the following month, Malcolm X gave a scathing account of democratic politics in the United States as that year's presidential race began. At the end of the speech he reiterated his position—if politicians did not grant equality through the ballot then African Americans should fight for their civil rights with bullets if need be.

...Our gospel is black nationalism. We're not trying to threaten the existence of any organization, but we're spreading the gospel of black nationalism. Anywhere there's a church that is also preaching and practicing the gospel of black nationalism, join that church. If the NAACP is preaching and practicing the gospel of black nationalism, join the NAACP. If CORE is spreading and practicing the gospel of black nationalism, join CORE. Join any organization that has a gospel that's for the uplift of the black man. And when you get into it and see them pussyfooting or compromising, pull out of it because that's not black nationalism. We'll find another one.

And in this manner, the organizations will increase in number and in quantity and in quality and by August, it is then our intention to have a black nationalist convention which will consist of delegates from all over the country who are interested in the political, economic and social philosophy of black nationalism. After these delegates convene, we will hold a seminar; we will hold discussions; we will listen to everyone. We want to hear new ideas and new solutions and new answers. And at that time, if we see fit then to form a black nationalist party, we'll form a black nationalist party. If it's necessary to form a black nationalist army, we'll form a black nationalist army. It'll be the ballot or the bullet. It'll be liberty or it'll be death.

It's time for you and me to stop sitting in this country, letting some cracker senators, Northern crackers and Southern crackers, sit there in Washington, DC and come to a conclusion in their mind that you and I are supposed to have civil rights. There's no white man going to tell me anything about my rights. Brothers and sisters, always remember, if it doesn't take senators and congressmen and presidential proclamations to give freedom to the white man, it is not necessary for legislation or proclamation or Supreme Court decisions to give freedom to the black man. You let that white man know, if this is a country of freedom, let it be a country of freedom; and if it's not a country of freedom, change it.

We will work with anybody, anywhere, at any time, who is genuinely interested in tackling the problem head-on, non-violently as long as the enemy is non-violent, but violent when the enemy gets violent. We'll work with you on the voter-registration drive, we'll work with you on rent strikes, we'll work with you on school boycotts.

I don't believe in any kind of integration. I'm not even worried about it, because I know you're not going to get it anyway. You're not going to get it because you're afraid to die. You've got to be ready to die if you try and force yourself on the white man, because he'll get just as violent as those crackers in Mississippi, right here in Cleveland.

But we will still work with you on the school boycotts because we're against a segregated school system. A segregated school system produces children who, when they graduate, graduate with crippled minds. But this does not mean that a school is segregated because it's all black. A segregated school means a school that is controlled by people who have no real interest in it whatsoever.

Let me explain what I mean. A segregated district or community is a community in which people live, but outsiders control the politics and the economy of that community. They never refer to the white section as a segregated community. It's the all-Negro section that's a segregated community. Why? The white man controls his own school, his own bank, his own economy, his own politics, his own everything, his own community; but he also controls yours.

When you're under someone else's control, you're segregated. They'll always give you the lowest or the worst that there is to offer, but it doesn't mean you're segregated just because you have your own. You've got to control your own. Just like the white man has control of his, you need to control yours.

You know the best way to get rid of segregation? The white man is more afraid of separation than he is of integration. Segregation means that he puts you away from him, but not far enough for you to be out of his jurisdiction; separation means you're gone. And the white man will integrate faster than he'll let you separate. So we will work with you against the segregated school system because it's criminal, because it is absolutely destructive, in every way imaginable, to the minds of the children who have to be exposed to that type of crippling education.

Last but not least, I must say this concerning the great controversy over rifles and shotguns. The only thing that I've ever said is that in areas where the government has proven itself either unwilling or unable to defend the lives and the property of Negroes, it's time for Negroes to defend themselves. Article number two of the constitutional amendments provides you and me the right to own a rifle or a shotgun. It is constitutionally legal to own a shotgun or a rifle. This doesn't mean you're going to get a rifle and form battalions and go out looking for white folks, although you'd be within your rights—I mean, you'd be justified—but that would be illegal and we don't do anything illegal. If the white man doesn't want the black man buying rifles and shotguns, then let the government do its job.

'The only thing that I've ever said is that in areas where the government has proven itself either unwilling or unable to defend the lives and the property of Negroes, it's time for Negroes to defend themselves.'

That's all. And don't let the white man come to you and ask you what you think about what Malcolm says—why, you old Uncle Tom. He would never ask you if he thought you were going to say: "Amen!" No, he is making a Tom out of you.

So, this doesn't mean forming rifle clubs and going out looking for people, but it is time, in 1964, if you are a man, to let that man know, if he's not going to do his job in running the government and providing you and me with the protection that our taxes are supposed to be for, since he spends all those billions for his defense budget, he certainly can't begrudge you and me spending $12 or $15 for a single-shot, or double-action.

I hope you understand. Don't go out shooting people, but any time—brothers and sisters and especially the men in this audience—some of you wearing Congressional Medals of Honor, with shoulders this wide, chests this big, muscles that big—any time you and I sit around and read where they bomb a church and murder in cold blood, not some grown-ups, but four little girls while they were praying to the same God the white man taught them to pray to, and you and I see the government go down and can't find who did it.

Why, this man—he can find Eichmann hiding down in Argentina somewhere. Let two or three American soldiers, who are minding somebody else's business way over in South Vietnam, get killed, and he'll send battleships, sticking his nose in their business. He wanted to send troops down to Cuba and make them have what he calls free elections—this old cracker who doesn't have free elections in his own country.

No, if you never see me another time in your life, if I die in the morning, I'll die saying one thing: The ballot or the bullet, the ballot or the bullet.

If a Negro in 1964 has to sit around and wait for some cracker senator to filibuster when it comes to the rights of black people, why, you and I should hang our heads in shame. You talk about a march on Washington in 1963, you haven't seen anything. There's some more going down in 64.

And this time they're not going like they went last year. They're not going singing "We Shall Overcome." They're not going with white friends. They're not going with placards already painted for them. They're not going with round-trip tickets. They're going with one-way tickets. And if they don't want that non-non-violent army going down there, tell them to bring the filibuster to a halt.

The black nationalists aren't going to wait. Lyndon B. Johnson is the head of the Democratic Party. If he's for civil rights, let him go into the Senate next week and declare himself. Let him go in there right now and declare himself. Let him go in there and denounce the Southern branch of his party. Let him go in there right now and take a moral stand—right now, not later. Tell him, don't wait until election time. If he waits too long, brothers and sisters, he will be responsible for letting a condition develop in this country which will create a climate that will bring seeds up out of the ground with vegetation on the end of them looking like something these people never dreamed of. In 1964, it's the ballot or the bullet.

Thank you. ♪

In May 1964 Malcolm X established the Organisation of Afro-American Unity (OAAU), a secular political group.

A pilgrimage to Mecca that year softened his political approach and upon his return to the United States, he saw integration as the real hope for the future.

Slowly, his message started to reach all races and creeds.

But Malcolm X's denouncement of Elijah Muhammad created powerful enemies with the Nation of Islam and his family home in East Elmhurst, New York, was firebombed in February 1964.

One week later, on 21 February, Malcolm X was shot by three members of NOI as he began an address at the Audubon Ballroom, New York. He was just 39 years old when he died.

Salvador Allende

'Farewell Speech to the People of Chile'

Santiago, Chile, 11 September 1973

When Salvador Allende Gossens (1908–73) was elected President of Chile in 1970, he was the first elected Marxist president of any nation. Allende, a former President of the Chilean Senate, had been defeated in his run for the Presidency in 1952, 1958 and 1964 elections. In 1970, his Popular Action Front party (FRAP) was the major plurality vote winner, narrowly defeating former President Jorge Allesandri and the Christian Democrat Party, but represented slightly more than a third of the population (36–37 per cent, according to different sources). Allende's friendship with Cuban dictator Fidel Castro, his links to the Soviet Union and his Chilean Path to Socialism policies, including the nationalisation of industries owned by US interests (especially copper, the country's main export), made him a threat to American business interests and the Nixon administration.

In September 1973, with inflation running rampant, the economy in chaos and the Supreme Court questioning the government's ability to uphold the law of the land, President Allende suggested a referendum be held on 12 September 1973 to decide his government's future.

On 11 September, he was overthrown by a CIA-backed military coup led by General Augusto Pinochet. In his famous farewell speech to the Chilean people, transmitted live on radio from the La Monde Presidential Palace, Allende was already referring to himself in the past tense.

My friends,
Surely this will be the last opportunity for me to address you. The Air Force has bombed the antennas of Radio Magallanes.

My words do not have bitterness but disappointment. May they be a moral punishment for those who have betrayed their oath: Soldiers of Chile, titular commanders in chief, Admiral Merino, who has designated himself Commander of the Navy and Mr. Mendoza, the despicable general who only yesterday pledged his fidelity and loyalty to the Government, and who also has appointed himself Chief of the Carabineros [paramilitary police].

Given these facts, the only thing left for me is to say to workers: I am not going to resign!

Placed in an historic transition, I will pay for loyalty to the people with my life. And I say to them that I am certain that the seeds which we have planted in the good conscience of thousands and thousands of Chileans will not be shriveled forever.

They have force and will be able to dominate us, but social processes can be arrested by neither crime nor force. History is ours and people make history.

Workers of my country: I want to thank you for the loyalty that you always had, the confidence that you deposited in a man who was only an interpreter of great yearnings for justice, who gave his word that he would respect the Constitution and the law and did just that.

At this definitive moment, the last moment when I can address you, I wish you to take advantage of the lesson: Foreign capital, imperialism, together with the reaction, created the climate in which the Armed Forces broke their tradition, the tradition taught by General Schneider and reaffirmed by Commander Araya, victims of the same social sector who today are hoping, with foreign assistance, to re-conquer the power to continue defending their profits and their privileges.

I address you, above all, the modest woman of our land, the campesina (peasants) who believed in us, the mother who knew our concern for children. I address professionals of Chile, patriotic professionals who continued working against the sedition that was supported by professional associations, classist associations that also defended the advantages of capitalist society. I address the youth, those who sang and gave us their joy and their spirit of struggle. I address

'Surely Radio Magallanes will be silenced and the calm metal instrument of my voice will no longer reach you. It does not matter. You will continue hearing it. I will always be next to you.'

the man of Chile, the worker, the farmer, the intellectual, those who will be persecuted, because in our country fascism has been already present for many hours—in terrorist attacks, blowing up the bridges, cutting the railroad tracks, destroying the oil and gas pipelines. In the face of the silence of those who had the obligation to act, they were committed. History will judge them.

Surely Radio Magallanes will be silenced and the calm metal instrument of my voice will no longer reach you. It does not matter. You will continue hearing it. I will always be next to you. At least my memory will be that of a man of dignity who was loyal to his country.

The people must defend themselves, but they must not sacrifice themselves. The people must not let themselves be destroyed or riddled with bullets, but they cannot be humiliated either.

Workers of my country, I have faith in Chile and its destiny. Other men will overcome this dark and bitter moment when treason seeks to prevail. Go forward knowing that, sooner rather than later, the great avenues will open again and free men will walk through them to construct a better society.

Long live Chile! Long live the people! Long live the workers!

These are my last words and I am certain that my sacrifice will not be in vain, I am certain that, at the very least, it will be a moral lesson that will punish felony, cowardice and treason. ♪

Salvador Allende, the elected President of Chile, then allegedly took his own life with a rifle given to him as a present by Castro.

Considering the threat Allende posed to his own nation (Chile had effectively rebelled against Allende's socialist experiment during the previous three years) and to the United States (declassified documents in 2000 revealed that the CIA plotted with coup organisers), it was later observed that Allende's death was more a case of 'assisted suicide'.

In any regard, the new boss—military dictator Pinochet, whose sixteen-year regime was responsible for the abduction, torture and murder of thousands of ordinary citizens and political opponents—was somewhat worse than the 'old boss.'

Archbishop Óscar Romero

'Stop the Repression!'

San Salvador, El Salvador, 23 March 1980

Óscar Romero y Galdámez (1917–80) became the Roman Catholic Archbishop of San Salvador, the capital of war-torn Latin American country, El Salvador, in 1977.

Following the overthrow of the Carlos Romero (no relation) military dictatorship in 1979, the US-backed Revolutionary Government Junta targeted members of the Catholic Church, trade unionists and the peasant population whom they felt were sympathetic to their left-wing military and political opponents.

In the previous three years, six Catholic priests had been assassinated—others had been jailed, tortured and expelled from the country—and death squads attached to the military dictatorship were responsible for the murder and abduction of thousands of Salvadorean citizens.

Óscar Romero was viewed as a conservative compromise candidate as Archbishop of San Salvador, but once in office he became the voice of the voiceless.

Despite Pope John Paul II's warning to the Latin American Catholic Church not to become involved in social activism in their homelands, Archbishop Romero felt that not to speak out against violence and injustice would be a legitimisation of the military persecution of the innocent.

In his sermon at the Metropolitan Cathedral of the Holy Saviour in San Salvador on Sunday, 23 March 1980, Archbishop Romero reviewed the tragic events of the week and finished with a heartfelt, impassioned appeal to the men of the armed forces on both sides.

'Every country lives its own "exodus". Today El Salvador is living its own exodus. Today we are passing to our liberation through a desert strewn with bodies and where anguish and pain are devastating us. Many suffer the temptation of those who walked with Moses and wanted to turn back and did not work together. It is the same old story. God, however, wants to save the people by making a new history...

History will not fail. God sustains it. That is why I say that insofar as historical projects attempt to reflect the eternal plan of God, to that extent they reflect the kingdom of God. This attempt is the work of the church. Because of this, the church, the people of God in history, is not attached to any one social system, to any political organization, to any party. The church does not identify herself with any of those forces because she is the eternal pilgrim of history and is indicating at every historical moment what reflects the kingdom of God and what does not reflect the kingdom of God. She is the servant of the kingdom of God.

The great task of Christians must be to absorb the spirit of God's kingdom and, with souls filled with the kingdom of God, to work on the projects of history. It's fine to be organized in popular groups; it's all right to form political parties; it's all right to take part in the government. It's fine as long as you are a Christian who carries the reflection of the kingdom of God and tries to establish it where you are working and as long as you are not being used to further worldly ambitions.

This is the great duty of the people of today. My dear Christians, I have always told you, and I will repeat, that the true liberators of our people must come from us Christians, from the people of God. Any historical plan that's not based on what we spoke of in the first point—the dignity of the human being, the love of God, the kingdom of Christ among people—will be a fleeting project. Your project, however, will grow in stability the more it reflects the eternal design of God. It will be a solution of the common good of the people every time, if it meets the needs of the people...

Now I invite you to look at things through the eyes of the church, which is trying to be the kingdom of God on earth and so often must illuminate the realities of our national situation.

We have lived through a tremendously tragic week. I could not give you the facts before, but a week ago last Saturday, on 15

'Now I invite you to look at things through the eyes of the church, which is trying to be the kingdom of God on earth and so often must illuminate the realities of our national situation.'

March, one of the largest and most distressing military operations was carried out in the countryside. The villages affected were La Laguna, Plan de Ocotes and El Rosario. The operation brought tragedy. A lot of ranches were burned. There was looting and inevitably people were killed.

In La Laguna, the attackers killed a married couple, Ernesto Navas and Audelia Mejia de Navas, their little children, Martin and Hilda, thirteen and seven years old, and eleven more peasants.

Other deaths have been reported, but we do not know the names of the dead. In Plan de Ocotes, two children and four peasants were killed, including two women. In El Rosario, three more peasants were killed. That was last Saturday.

Last Sunday, the following were assassinated in Arcatao by four members of ORDEN: Peasants Marcelino Serrano, Vincente Ayala, 24 years old, and his son, Freddy. That same day, Fernando Hernandez Navarro, a peasant, was assassinated in Galera de Jutiapa, when he fled from the military.

Last Monday, 17 March, was a tremendously violent day. Bombs exploded in the capital as well as in the interior of the country. The damage was very substantial at the headquarters of the Ministry of Agriculture. The campus of the national university was under armed siege from dawn until 7.00 pm. Throughout the day, constant bursts of machine-gun fire were heard in the university area. The Archbishop's office intervened to protect people who found themselves caught inside.

On the Hacienda Colima, eighteen persons died, at least fifteen of whom were peasants. The administrator and the grocer of the ranch also died. The armed forces confirmed that there was a confrontation. A film of the events appeared on TV and many analyzed interesting aspects of the situation.

At least 50 people died in serious incidents that day. In the capital, seven persons died in events at the Colonia Santa Lucia; on the outskirts of Tecnillantas, five people died; and in the area of the rubbish dump, after the evacuation of the site by the military, were found the bodies of four workers who had been captured in that action.

Sixteen peasants died in the village of Montepeque, 38 kilometers along the road to Suchitoto. That same day, two students at the University of Central America were captured in Tecnillantas: Mario Nelson and Miguel Alberto Rodriguez Velado, who were brothers. The first one, after four days of illegal detention, was handed over to the courts. Not so his brother, who was wounded and is still held in illegal detention. Legal Aid is intervening on his behalf.

Amnesty International issued a press release in which it described the repression of the peasants, especially in the area of Chalatenango. The week's events confirm this report in spite of the fact the government denies it. As I entered the church, I was given a cable that says: "Amnesty International confirmed today [that was yesterday] that in El Salvador human rights are violated to extremes that have not been seen in other countries."

That is what Patricio Fuentes (spokesman for the urgent action section for Central America in Swedish Amnesty International) said at a press conference in Managua, Nicaragua.

Fuentes confirmed that, during two weeks of investigations he carried out in El Salvador, he was able to establish that there had been 83 political assassinations between 10 and 14 March. He pointed out that Amnesty International recently condemned the government of El Salvador, alleging that it was responsible for 600 political assassinations. The Salvadorean government defended itself against the charges, arguing that Amnesty International based its condemnation on unproved assumptions.

Fuentes said that Amnesty had established that in El Salvador human rights are violated to a worse degree than the repression in Chile after the coup d'etat. The Salvadorean government also said that the 600 dead were the result of armed confrontations between army troops and guerrillas. Fuentes said that during his stay El Salvador, he could see that the victims had been tortured before their deaths and mutilated afterward.

The spokesman of Amnesty International said that the victims' bodies characteristically appeared with the thumbs tied behind their backs. Corrosive liquids had been applied to the corpses to prevent identification of the victims by their relatives and to prevent international condemnation, the spokesman added. Nevertheless, the bodies were exhumed and the dead have been identified. Fuentes said that the repression carried out by the Salvadorean army was aimed at breaking the popular organizations through the assassination of their leaders in both town and country.

According to the spokesman of Amnesty International, at least 3500 peasants have fled from their homes to the capital to escape persecution. "We have complete lists in London and Sweden of young children and women who have been assassinated for being organized," Fuentes stated...

I would like to make a special appeal to the men of the army, and specifically to the ranks of the National Guard, the police and the military.

Brothers, you come from our own people. You are killing your own brother peasants when any human order to kill must be subordinate to the law of God which says; "Thou shalt not kill."

No soldier is obliged to obey an order contrary to the law of God. No one has to obey an immoral law. It is high time you recovered your consciences and obeyed your consciences rather than a sinful order. The church, the defender of the rights of God, of the law of God, of human dignity, of the person, cannot remain silent before such an abomination. We want the government to face the fact that reforms are valueless if they are to be carried out at the cost of so much blood. In the name of God, in the name of this suffering people whose cries rise to heaven more loudly each day, I implore you, I beg you, I order you in the name of God: Stop the repression.

The church preaches your liberation just as we have studied it in the holy Bible today. It is a liberation that has, above all else, respect for the dignity of the person, hope for humanity's common good, and the transcendence that looks before all to God and only from God derives its hope and its strength. ♪

The following day, Archbishop Romero was assassinated while he celebrated mass in the small chapel attached to the Divina Providencia Cancer Hospital which he had called home for several years.

In the sermon just minutes before his death, he spoke of the parable of the wheat. 'Those who surrender to the service of the poor through love of Christ, will live like the grains of wheat that die. It only apparently dies. If it were not to die, it would remain a solitary grain. The harvest comes because of the grain that dies'.

At 6.25 pm, as he prayed over the gifts of bread and wine for Communion, he was shot through the heart by unknown members of a Salvadorean military death squad.

Archbishop Romero's funeral the following week attracted more than 250,000 mourners from all over the world and resulted in more bloodshed when a bomb exploded on the steps of the Cathedral and 44 mourners were shot or trampled to death in the ensuing panic.

The civil war in El Salvador lasted for another twelve years (1980-92) but for Óscar Romero, life, not death, would be the final word.

'I do not believe in death without resurrection,' he once said. 'If they kill me, I will be resurrected in the Salvadorean people.'

Benigno Aquino
'The Sacrifice of the Innocent'
Manila, The Philippines, 21 August 1983

Benigno 'Ninoy' Aquino (1932–83) was a prominent opposition leader in the Philippines during the Marcos regime of the 1970s. When President Ferdinand Marcos declared martial law in 1972, 'Ninoy' Aquino was jailed on trumped up charges of murder and subversion and sentenced to death in November 1977.

Bowing to international pressure, especially from the United States, President Marcos commuted the sentence to life in exile in 1980 to allow Aquino to receive medical attention for a heart problem. Aquino and his wife Corazón (Cory) continued their opposition to the Marcos regime for another three years.

In August 1983, with President Marcos on his sickbed following a kidney transplant, Aquino returned to the Philippines to press the government to lift martial law and, if need be, to 'suffer with his people in this time of crisis'. On 21 August, as his plane sat on the tarmac of Manila International Airport, Aquino had a speech in his hand to deliver to the Filipino people denouncing the Marcos regime. The speech was never read.

In spite of protection by his own bodyguards and the presence of a government military team on the tarmac, 'Ninoy' Aquino was fatally shot in the head as he was escorted off the airplane.

Soldiers immediately shot dead a gunman, Rolando Galman, whom they claimed was responsible for Aquino's murder. The brazen nature of the assassination—committed coldly in front of the world media—shocked international observers and the Filipino people.

In the tragic case of 'Ninoy' Aquino, the mere threat of making a speech cost him his life, but his death would change the course of history for an entire nation.

‘ I have returned on my free will to join the ranks of those struggling to restore our rights and freedoms through non-violence.

I seek no confrontation. I only pray and will strive for a genuine national reconciliation founded on justice.

I am prepared for the worst and have decided against the advice of my mother, my spiritual adviser, many of my tested friends and a few of my most valued political mentors.

A death sentence awaits me. Two more subversion charges, both calling for death penalties, have been filed since I left three years ago and are now pending with the courts.

I could have opted to seek political asylum in America, but I feel it is my duty, as it is the duty of every Filipino, to suffer with his people especially in time of crisis.

I never sought not have I been given any assurances, or promise of leniency by the regime. I return voluntarily armed only with a clear conscience and fortified in the faith that in the end, justice will emerge triumphant.

According to Gandhi, the willing sacrifice of the innocent is the most powerful answer to insolent tyranny that has yet been conceived by God and man.

Three years ago when I left for an emergency heart bypass operation, I hoped and prayed that the rights and freedoms of our people would soon be restored, that living conditions would improve and that blood-letting would stop.

Rather than move forward we have moved backward. The killings have increased, the economy has taken a turn for the worse and the human rights situation has deteriorated.

During the martial law period, the Supreme Court heard petitions for habeas corpus. It is most ironic after martial law has allegedly been lifted, that the Supreme Court last April ruled it can longer entertain petitions for habeas corpus for persons detained under the Presidential Commitment Order, which covers all so-called national security cases and which under present circumstances can cover almost anything.

The country is far advanced in her times of trouble. Economic, social and political problems bedevil the Filipino. These problems may be surmounted if we are united. But we can be united only if all the rights and freedoms enjoyed before September 21 1972 are fully restored.

The Filipino asks for nothing more, but will surely accept nothing less, than all the rights and freedoms guaranteed by the 1935 Constitution—the most sacred legacies from the founding fathers.

Yes, the Filipino is patient, but there is a limit to his patience. Must we wait until that patience snaps?

The nationwide rebellion is escalating and threatens to explode into a bloody revolution. There is a growing cadre of young Filipinos who have finally come to realize that freedom is never granted, it is taken. Must we relive the agonies and the blood-letting of the past that brought forth our republic or can we sit down as brothers and sisters and discuss our differences with reason and goodwill?

'The country is far advanced in her times of trouble. Economic, social and political problems bedevil the Filipino. These problems may be surmounted if we are united.'

I have often wondered how many disputes could have been settled easily had the disputants only dared to define their terms.

So as to leave no room for misunderstanding, I shall define my terms:

Six years ago, I was sentenced to die before a firing squad by a military tribunal whose jurisdiction I steadfastly refused to recognize. It is now time for the regime to decide. Order my immediate execution or set me free.

National reconciliation and unity can be achieved, but only with justice, including justice for our Muslim and Ifugao brothers. There can be no deal with a dictator. No compromise with dictatorship. In a revolution there can really be no victors, only victims. We do not have to destroy in order to build.

Subversion stems from economic, social, and political causes and will not be solved by purely military solution. It can be curbed not with ever increasing repression but with a more equitable distribution of wealth, more democracy and more freedom.

For the economy to get going once again, the working man must be given his just and rightful share or his labor and to the owners and managers must be restored the hope where there is so much uncertainty if not despair.

On one of the long corridors of Harvard University are carved in granite the words of Archibald Macleish: "How shall freedom be defended? By arms when it is attacked by arms; by truth when it is attacked by lies; by democratic faith when it is attacked by authoritarian dogma. Always and in the final act, by determination and faith."

I return from exile and an uncertain future with only determination and faith to offer—faith in our people and faith in God. ♪

'Ninoy' Aquino's funeral on 31 August 1983, drew two million people into the streets during the procession of his body to Manila Memorial Park. After mounting domestic and international pressure, the Marcos government called a snap election in November 1985—the first since martial law had been introduced thirteen years before—in the hope that opposition parties would not have time to mount an organised campaign before the elections in February 1986.

Aquino's widow, who had become the focal point of government opposition since her husband's death, led the unified UNIDO Party into the 1986 elections.

When Marcos declared himself the winner, the Filipino people conducted a People Power bloodless revolution and refused to accept the decision. At the same time Marcos was declaring himself president at Malacañang, Cory Aquino was being inaugurated at Club Filipino in San Juan, Metro Manila.

When he lost the support of his military advisers, Ferdinand Marcos, his wife and staff fled into exile to Hawaii (the 72 year-old former dictator would die there in 1989) and Cory Aquino was officially named the first woman President of the Republic of the Philippines.

Slobodan Milosevič

'Gazimestan Speech'

Gazimestan, Kosovo, 28 June 1989

A t a time when Eastern Bloc Communist countries were in their death throes, in May 1989 Slobodan Milosevic (1941–2006) rode a wave of Serbian nationalism and became the first President of Serbia.

In June, Milosevič marked the 600th Anniversary of the Battle of Kosovo, in which the Christian kingdom of Serbia was defeated by the Islamic Ottoman Empire, with a nationalistic speech in Gazimestan, Central Kosovo.

During the late 1980s, there had been mass demonstrations and strikes from the majority Albanian Serb (Muslim) population in Kosovo and the Serbian population had fallen to less than 10 per cent. Many historians now regard Milosevič's Gazimestan Speech as a precursor to the end of the Socialist Federal Republic of Yugoslavia (1991) and the decade of bloodshed that followed in the Yugoslav Wars (1991–2001).

‘ B y the force of social circumstances this great 600th anniversary of the Battle of Kosovo is taking place in a year in which Serbia, after many years, after many decades, has regained its state, national, and spiritual integrity. Therefore, it is not difficult for us to answer today the old question: how are we going to face Milos*? Through the play of history and life, it seems as if Serbia has, precisely in this year, in 1989, regained its state and its dignity and thus has celebrated an event of the distant past which has a great historical and symbolic significance for its future.

Today, it is difficult to say what is the historical truth about the Battle of Kosovo and what is legend. Today this is no longer important. Oppressed by pain and filled with hope, the people used to remember and to forget, as, after all, all people in the world do and it was ashamed of treachery and glorified heroism. Therefore, it is difficult to say today whether the Battle of Kosovo was a defeat or a victory for the Serbian people, whether thanks to it we fell into slavery or we survived in this slavery. The answers to those questions will be constantly sought by science and the people.

What has been certain through all the centuries until our time today is that disharmony struck Kosovo 600 years ago. If we lost the battle, then this was not only the result of social superiority and the armed advantage of the Ottoman Empire, but also of the tragic disunity in the leadership of the Serbian state at that time. In that distant 1389, the Ottoman Empire was not only stronger than that of the Serbs but it was also more fortunate than the Serbian kingdom.

The lack of unity and betrayal in Kosovo will continue to follow the Serbian people like an evil fate through the whole of its history. Even in the last war, this lack of unity and betrayal led the Serbian people and Serbia into agony, the consequences of which in the historical and moral sense exceeded fascist aggression.

Even later, when a socialist Yugoslavia was set up, in this new state the Serbian leadership remained divided, prone to compromise to the detriment of its own people. The concessions that many Serbian leaders made at the expense of their people could not be accepted historically and ethically by any nation in the world, especially because the Serbs have never in the whole of their history conquered and exploited others.

Their national and historical being has been liberational throughout the whole of history and through two world wars, as it is today. They liberated themselves and, when they could, they also helped others to liberate themselves. The fact that in this region they are a major nation is not a Serbian sin or shame; this is an advantage which they have not used against others. But I must say that here, in this big, legendary field of Kosovo, the Serbs have not used the advantage of being great for their own benefit either.

Thanks to their leaders and politicians and their vassal mentality, they felt guilty before themselves and others. This situation lasted for decades, it lasted for years and here we are now at the field of Kosovo to say that this is no longer the case.

Disunity among Serb officials made Serbia lag behind and their inferiority humiliated Serbia. Therefore, no place in Serbia is better suited for saying this than the field of Kosovo and no place in Serbia is better suited than the field of Kosovo for saying that unity in Serbia will bring prosperity to the Serbian people in Serbia and each one of its citizens, irrespective of his national or religious affiliation.

Serbia of today is united and equal to other republics and prepared to do everything to improve its financial and social position and that of all its citizens. If there is unity, cooperation and seriousness, it will succeed in doing so. This is why the optimism that is now present in Serbia to a considerable extent regarding the future days is realistic, also because it is based on freedom, which makes it possible for all people to express their positive, creative and humane abilities aimed at furthering social and personal life.

Serbia has never had only Serbs living in it. Today, more than in the past, members of other peoples and nationalities also live in it. This is not a disadvantage for Serbia. I am truly convinced that it is its advantage. National composition of almost all countries in the world today, particularly developed ones, has also been changing in this direction. Citizens of different nationalities, religions, and races have been living together more and more frequently and more and more successfully.

Socialism in particular, being a progressive and just democratic society, should not allow people to be divided in the national and religious respect. The only differences one can and should allow in socialism are between hard working people and idlers and between honest people and dishonest people. Therefore, all people in Serbia who live from their own work, honestly, respecting other people and other nations, are in their own republic.

After all, our entire country should be set up on the basis of such principles. Yugoslavia is a multinational community and it can survive only under the conditions of full equality for all nations that live in it.

The crisis that hit Yugoslavia has brought about national divisions, but also social, cultural, religious and many other less important ones. Among all these divisions, nationalist ones have shown themselves to be the most dramatic. Resolving them will make it easier to remove other divisions and mitigate the consequences they have created.

For as long as multinational communities have existed, their weak point has always been the relations between different nations. The threat is that the question of one nation being endangered by the others can be posed one day— and this can then start a wave of suspicions, accusations, and intolerance, a wave that invariably grows and is difficult to stop. This threat has been hanging like a sword over our heads all the time. Internal and external enemies of multinational communities are aware of this and therefore they organize their activity against multinational societies mostly by fomenting national conflicts.

At this moment, we in Yugoslavia are behaving as if we have never had such an experience and as if in our recent and distant past we have never experienced the worst tragedy of national conflicts that a society can experience and still survive.

Equal and harmonious relations among Yugoslav peoples are a necessary condition for the existence of Yugoslavia and for it to find its way out of the crisis and, in particular, they are a necessary condition for its economic and social prosperity. In this respect, Yugoslavia does not stand out from the social milieu of the contemporary, particularly the developed world.

This world is more and more marked by national tolerance, national cooperation and even national equality. The modern economic and technological, as well as political and cultural development, has guided various peoples toward each other, has made them interdependent and increasingly has made them equal as well. Equal and united people can above all become a part of the civilization toward which mankind is moving. If we cannot be at the head of the column leading to such a civilization, there is certainly no need for us to be at is tail.

At the time when this famous historical battle was fought in Kosovo, the people were looking at the stars, expecting aid from them. Now, six centuries later, they are looking at the stars again, waiting to conquer them. On the first occasion, they could allow themselves to be disunited and to have hatred and treason because they lived in smaller, weakly interlinked worlds. Now, as people on this planet, they cannot conquer even their own planet if they are not united, let alone other planets, unless they live in mutual harmony and solidarity.

Therefore, words devoted to unity, solidarity and cooperation among people have no greater significance anywhere on the soil of our motherland than they have here in the field of Kosovo, which is a symbol of disunity and treason.

In the memory of the Serbian people, this disunity was decisive in causing the loss of the battle and in bringing about the fate which Serbia suffered for a full six centuries.

Even if it were not so, from a historical point of view, it remains certain that the people regarded disunity as its greatest disaster. Therefore it is the obligation of the people to remove disunity, so that they may protect themselves from defeats, failures and stagnation in the future.

This year, the Serbian people became aware of the necessity of their mutual harmony as the indispensable condition for their present life and further development.

I am convinced that this awareness of harmony and unity will make it possible for Serbia not only to function as a state, but to function as a successful state. Therefore I think that it makes sense to say this here in Kosovo, where that disunity once upon a time tragically pushed back Serbia for centuries and endangered it, and where renewed unity may advance it and may return dignity to it.

Such an awareness about mutual relations constitutes an elementary necessity for Yugoslavia, too, for its fate is in the joined hands of all its peoples. The Kosovo heroism has been inspiring our creativity for six centuries, and has been feeding our pride and does not allow us to forget that at one time we were an army—great, brave, and proud—one of the few that remained undefeated when losing.

Six centuries later, now, we are being again engaged in battles and are facing battles. They are not armed battles, although such things cannot be excluded yet. However, regardless of what kind of battles they are, they cannot be won without resolve, bravery and sacrifice, without the noble qualities that were present here in the field of Kosovo in the days past.

Our chief battle now concerns implementing the economic, political, cultural and general social prosperity, finding a quicker and more successful approach to a civilization in which people will live in the twenty-first century. For this battle, we certainly need heroism, of course, of a somewhat different kind, but that courage without which nothing serious and great can be achieved remains unchanged and remains urgently necessary.

Six centuries ago, Serbia heroically defended itself in the field of Kosovo, but it also defended Europe. Serbia was at that time the bastion that defended the European culture, religion and European society in general. Therefore today it appears not only unjust but even unhistorical and completely absurd to talk about Serbia's belonging to Europe. Serbia has been a part of Europe incessantly, now just as much as it was in the past, of course, in its own way, but in a way that in the historical sense never deprived it of dignity.

In this spirit, we now endeavor to build a society, rich and democratic, and thus to contribute to the prosperity of this beautiful country, this unjustly suffering country, but also to contribute to the efforts of all the progressive people of our age that they make for a better and happier world.

Let the memory of Kosovo heroism live forever!

Long live Serbia!

Long live Yugoslavia!

Long live peace and brotherhood among peoples! ♪

* Milos Obilic, legendary hero of the Battle of Kosovo

The Congress of the League of Communists of Yugoslavia dissolved along republican and ethnic lines in January 1990 and Serbia, sensing an opportunity to re-establish majority power in Kosovo and Vojvodina, revoked several constitutionally guaranteed powers of those states.

Slovenia and Croatia declared independence in June 1991 and a civil war against Yugoslavian and Serbian forces followed. America brokered a peace plan in 1992 but then Macedonia and Bosnia declared independence. The Bosnian-Croat conflict followed but a peace treaty was again arbitrated by the US.

In 1995, however, more than 8000 Bosnian Muslim men and boys were massacred in Srebrenica by Bosnian Serb forces. Only the intervention of NATO forces ended the conflict but by then 100,000 people had been killed or were missing, two million had been displaced and the Yugoslav economy was in collapse.

In 1997, Slobodan Miloseviç became President of Yugoslavia but there were widespread demonstrations in the country's capital, Belgrade, and fighting broke out between Serbian forces and ethnic Albanians in Kosovo. In 1999, NATO intervention restored order in Kosovo which came under the protection of the United Nations.

Miloseviç was voted out of office in 2000 and later stood trial at The Hague for war crimes.

In 2003, Yugoslavia became the State Union of Serbia and Montenegro. Serbia was later found not guilty of genocide by the International Court of Justice (IJC). However, the court found that it failed to prevent the atrocity in Srebrenica or hand over the people responsible for ordering the massacre.

Slobodan Miloseviç died in prison in 2006.

Kosovo, once described as 'the equator of the Serb planet,' declared its independence on 17 February 2008.

Peace
and
Reconciliation

Mustafa Kemal 'Atatürk'

'Message to the Gallipoli Fallen'

Turkey, 1934

Mustafa Kemal (1881–1938)—who was given the honorary title 'Atatürk' in 1934, which means 'Father of the Turks'—was both the hero of the Dardanelles in World War I and the founder of the modern republic of Turkey.

Kemal was born in Salonica (now called Thessaloniki), which is now part of Greek Macedonia, but was part of the Ottoman Empire in the 1880s.

As a young army major he was a central figure in the coup that ousted Sultan Abdülhamid II in 1908 and he played a vital role in defending the Dardanelles in the Balkan Wars (1912–13).

Three years later, with the Ottoman Empire allied to the Central Powers (Germany and Austria-Hungary) in World War I (1914–18) Kemal used his knowledge of the region to save Turkey from invasion by British and ANZAC forces in the ill-fated Gallipoli campaign.

In January 1915, the British Naval Command approved an attack on the Dardanelles to free the narrow strait for shipping into the Black Sea. When naval attacks failed in February and March, the British approved a land invasion on the Gallipoli peninsula.

On 25 April 1915, Australian and New Zealand forces landed at Anzac Cove, British forces landed at Cape Helles to the south and French forces made a diversionary landing at Kum Kale on the Asian side of the strait.

Kemal, however, had been appointed to the command of the 19th Division and had taken position at the top of Gallipoli peninsula. The advance of the Anzac troops was severely checked by the Turkish forces—an estimated 2000 soldiers lost their lives on the first day—and very little ground was captured in the next eight months.

Finally, on 9 January 1916, the Dardanelles Campaign was abandoned and Allied troops withdrawn. The Allied forces lost more than 44,000 men during the campaign with almost 100,000 wounded. The Turks lost even more—almost 56,000 killed and 140,000 wounded—but they had won the battle.

Kemal was promoted to General, put in command of the 16th Army and posted to the Caucuses front in Southern Russia.

Following the armistice of November 1918, he was the inspector of the Third Army in Anatolia and, in opposing both the Sultan's regime in Istanbul and Allied attempts to partition the Ottoman Empire, became the leader of Turkey's national liberation struggle.

In 1920, when the Sultan signed away parts of Anatolia to the Greeks, he set up a rival government in Ankara.

Kemal effectively seized control of the country by defeating the Greeks at Sakarya (1921) and Dumlupinar (1922). On 1 November 1922, the 'Caliphate' (sultanate) was abolished and on 29 October 1923, the Republic of Turkey was declared with Kemal as President.

Within three years, Kemal had imprisoned many of his political rivals, accusing them of assassination conspiracy and established one party rule under the Republican People's Party.

In 1928, a law was imposed which resulted in Islam no longer being the state religion, education became compulsory, the country's Arabic script was abolished and the Latin alphabet was incorporated into the Turkish language. As founding father of the modern Turkish republic and President until his death in 1938, Kemal modelled many of his reforms on the Western democracies. He introduced a broad range of reforms that swept across the country's political, social, legal, economic and cultural life.

Despite his military background, Kemal became a great defender of peace at home and abroad. With the rise of Fascism and Nazism in Europe in the 1930s, Kemal established stronger relationships with World War I enemies, Britain and France.

In 1933 Kemal stated: 'I look to the world with an open heart full of pure feelings and friendship.'

In 1934, the year the Grand National Assembly bestowed the name 'Atatürk' upon him, the Father of Turkey reached out to his former Gallipoli foes with a speech that is today regarded 'among the finest words of reconciliation ever uttered'.

‘ Those heroes who shed their blood and lost their lives... you are now lying in the soil of a friendly country.

Therefore rest in peace.

There is no difference between the Johnnies and the Mehmets to us where they lie side by side in this country of ours...

'You, the mothers who sent their sons from far away countries, wipe away your tears. Your sons are now lying in our bosoms and are in peace.'

You, the mothers who sent their sons from far away countries, wipe away your tears.

Your sons are now lying in our bosoms and are in peace.

After having lost their lives on this land they have become our sons as well. ‚

While it unlikely Atatürk's words were originally spoken in speech form (they were possibly first published in a book and the opening line actually reads, 'Those heroes from England, France, Australia, New Zealand and India who shed their blood...') the above words are carved in stone at the Anzac Cove memorial at Gallipoli.

Today, thousands of Australian and New Zealand travellers—the young and the old —undertake the pilgrimage to the other side of the world to pay homage to the men who lost their lives at Gallipoli almost a century ago. They come away from the memorial at Anzac Cove with Atatürk's words resonating in their hearts and minds for the rest of their lives.

Golda Meir

'For the Attainment of Peace'

Israeli Knesset, Tel Aviv, 26 May 1970

G olda Meir (1898–1978) served as Israeli Minister to Moscow (1948) and Foreign Minister (1956–66) before becoming Prime Minister in 1969 following the death of leader Levi Eshkol.

Her first challenge as Israeli leader was the Six-Day War in June 1967 in which the neighbouring Arab States of Egypt, Syria and Jordan attempted to exact revenge for territories lost in disputes in 1948 and 1956.

Israel struck first and secured control of the Sinai Peninsula after it routed Egyptian and Jordanian forces in less than four days. Jordan and Egypt hastily agreed to the United Nations demand for a ceasefire while Syria struggled on for another two days.

Condemned as the aggressor by the United Nations, Israel refused to return the captured territories to its Arab neighbours.

The continuing quest for peace in the ensuing three years, in which the nation of Israel survived whilst surrounded by hostile enemies, is outlined at the conclusion of this speech by Golda Meir in 1970.

' T oday again, as the guns thunder, I address myself to our neighbours: Stop the killing, end the fire and bloodshed which bring tribulation and torment to all the peoples of the region! End rejection of the ceasefire, end bombardment and raids, end terror and sabotage!

Even Russian pilots will not contrive to destroy the ceasefire lines, and certainly they will not bring peace. The only way to permanent peace and the establishment of secure and recognized boundaries is through negotiations between the Arab States and ourselves, as all sovereign States treat one another, as is the manner of States which recognize each other's right to existence and

> **'Stop the killing, end the fire and bloodshed which bring tribulation and torment to all the peoples of the region!'**

equality, as is the manner of free peoples, not protectorates enslaved to foreign powers or in thrall to the dark instincts of war, destruction and ruin.

To attain peace, I am ready to go at any hour to any place, to meet any authorized leader of any Arab State—to conduct negotiations with mutual respect, in parity and without pre-conditions and with a clear recognition that the problems under controversy can be solved. For there is room to fulfill the national aspirations of all the Arab States and of Israel as well in the Middle East and progress, development and cooperation can be hastened among all its nations, in place of barren bloodshed and war without end.

If peace does not yet reign, it is from no lack of willingness on our part.

It is the inevitable outcome of the refusal of the Arab leadership to make peace with us. That refusal is still a projection of reluctance to be reconciled to the living presence of Israel within secure and recognized boundaries, still a product of the hope, which flickers on in their hearts, that they will accomplish its destruction. And this has been the state of things since 1948, long before the issue of the territories arose in the aftermath of the Six-Day War.

Moreover, if peace does not yet reign, it is equally not because of any lack of "flexibility" on our part, or because of the so-called "rigidity" of our position.

That position is: Ceasefire, agreement and peace. The Arab Governments preach and practise no ceasefire, no negotiation, no agreement and no peace. Which of the two attitudes is stubborn and unyielding? The Arab Governments or ours?

There are some, the Arabs included, who claim that we have not accepted the United Nations Resolution of 22 November 1967 and that the Arabs have. In truth, the Arabs only accepted it in a distorted and mutilated interpretation of their own, as meaning an instant and absolute withdrawal of our forces, with no commitment to peace. They were ready to agree to an absolute Israeli withdrawal, but the Resolution stipulates nothing of the kind. According to its text and the exegesis of its compilers, the Resolution is not self-implementing. The operative clause calls for the appointment of an envoy, acting on behalf of the Secretary-General, whose task would be to "establish and maintain contact with the States concerned in order to promote agreement and assist efforts to achieve a peaceful and accepted settlement in accordance with the provisions and principles in this Resolution."

On I May 1968, Israel's ambassador at the United Nations announced as follows:

"In declarations and statements made publicly and to Ambassador Jarring, the Government of Israel has indicated its acceptance of the Security Council's Resolution for the promotion of an agreement to establish a just and durable peace. I am authorised to reaffirm that we are willing to seek an agreement with each Arab State, on all the matters included in that Resolution. More recently, we accepted Ambassador Jarring's proposal to arrange meetings between Israel and each of its neighbours, under his auspices, and in fulfillment of his mandate under the guidelines of the Resolution to advance a peace agreement. No Arab State has yet accepted that proposal."

'The Arab Governments preach and practise no ceasefire, no negotiation, no agreement and no peace. Which of the two attitudes is stubborn and unyielding? The Arab Governments or ours?'

This announcement of our Ambassador was reported to the House by the Foreign Minister on 29 May 1968 and to the General Assembly in September 1969. It opened the way for Ambassador Jarring to invite the parties to discuss any topic which any of them saw fit to raise, including issues mentioned in the Resolution. The Arabs and those others who assert that we are preventing progress towards peace in terms of the Resolution have no factual basis for so asserting. They seek merely to throw dust in the world's eyes, to cover up their guilt and deceive the world into thinking that we are the ones who are retarding peace.

It is also argued that, by creating facts on the ground, we are laying down irrevocable conditions which render negotiations superfluous or make it more difficult to enter into them. This contention, too, is wholly mistaken and unfounded. The refusal of the Arab States to enter into negotiations with us is simply an extension of their long drawn out intransigence. It goes back to before the Six-Day War, before there were any settlements in the administered territories.

After that fighting, we said—and we left no room for doubt—that we were willing to enter into negotiations with our neighbours with no pre-conditions on either side. This willingness does not signify that we have no opinions, thoughts or demands, or that we shall not exercise our right to articulate them in the discussions, as our neighbours are entitled to no less.

Nasser and Hussein, for example, in their official replies to Dr Jarring, said that they saw the partition borders of 1947 as constituting definitive frontiers. I do not have to explain our attitude to that answer, but we do not insist that, in negotiating with us, the Arab States forfeit their equal right to make any proposal that they think fit, just as they cannot annul from the outset our right to express, in the discussions, any ideas or proposals which we may form. And there assuredly is no moral or political ground for demanding that we refrain from any constructive act in the territories, even though the Arab Governments reject the call for peace and make ready for war.

There is yet another argument touching on our insistence on direct negotiations. It is as devoid as are the others of any least foundation in the annals of international relations or of those between our neighbours and ourselves. For we did sit down face-to-face with the representatives of the Arab States at the time of the negotiations in Rhodes, and no one dare profess that Arab honour was thereby affronted.

There is no precedent of a conflict between nations being brought to finality without direct negotiations. In the conflict between the Arabs and Israel, the issue of direct negotiations goes to the very crux of the matter. For the objective is to achieve peace and co-existence, and how will our neighbours ever be able to live with us in peace if they refuse to speak with us at all?

From the start of the conversations with Ambassador Jarring, we agreed that the face-to-face discussions should take place under the auspices of the Secretary-General's envoy. During 1968, Dr Jarring sought to bring the parties together under his chairmanship in a neutral place. In March 1968, he proposed that we meet Egypt and Jordan in Nicosia. We agreed, but the Arabs did not. In the same year, and again in September 1969, we expressed our consent to his proposal that the meetings be held in the manner of the Rhodes talks, which comprised both face-to-face and indirect talks. A number of times it seemed that the Arabs and the Soviets would also fall in with that proposal, but, in the end, they went back on it.

Only those who deny the right of another State to exist, or who want to avoid recognizing the fact of its sovereignty, can develop the refusal to talk to it into an inculcated philosophy of life which the pupil swears to adhere to as to a political, national principle. The refusal to talk to us directly is damning evidence that the unwillingness of the Arab leaders to be reconciled with the very being of Israel is the basic reason why peace is still to seek.

'The ceasefire is necessary not to perpetuate the lines, but to prevent death and destruction, to make progress easier towards a peace resting upon secure and recognized boundaries.'

I am convinced that it is unreal and utopian to think that using the word "withdrawal" will pave the way to peace. True, those among us who do believe that the magic of that word is likely to bring us nearer to peace only mean withdrawal after peace is achieved and then only to secure agreed boundaries demarcated in a peace treaty. On the other hand, when Arab and Soviet leaders talk of "withdrawal", they mean complete and outright retreat from all the administered territories, and from Jerusalem, without the making of a genuine peace and without any agreement on new permanent borders, but with an addendum calling for Israel's consent to the return of all the refugees.

Israel's policy is clear and we shall continue to clarify it at every suitable opportunity, as we have done in the United Nations and elsewhere. No person dedicated to truth could misinterpret our policy. When we speak of secure and recognized boundaries, we do not mean that, after peace is made, the Israeli Defence Forces should be deployed beyond the boundaries agreed upon in negotiations with our neighbours. No one could be misled—Israel desires secure and recognized boundaries with its neighbours.

Israel's Defence Forces have never crossed its borders in search of conquest, but only when the safeguarding of the existence and bounds of our State demanded it. Nasser's claim that Israel wishes to maintain the ceasefire only so as to freeze the ceasefire lines is preposterous. The ceasefire is necessary not to perpetuate the lines, but to prevent death and destruction, to make progress easier towards a peace resting upon secure and recognized boundaries. It is necessary as a step upwards on the ladder to peace. Incessant gunfire is a step downward on the ladder to war.

The question is crystal clear, and there is no point in clouding it with semantics—or in trying to escape from reality. There is not a single article in Israel's policy which prevents the making of peace. Nothing is lacking for the making of peace but the Arab persistence in denying Israel's very right to exist. Arab refusal to acquiesce in our existence in the Middle East, alongside the Arab States, abides. The only way to peace is through a change in that recalcitrance.

When it changes, there will no longer be any obstacle to peace negotiations. Otherwise, no formulae, sophistry or definitions will avail. Those in the world who seek peace would do well to heed this basic fact and help to bring about a change in the obdurate Arab approach, which is the real impediment to peace. Any display of "understanding" and forgiveness, however unwitting, is bound to harden the Arabs in their obstinacy and hearten them in their gainsaying of Israel's right to exist and will, besides, be exploited by Arab leaders to justify ideologically the continuance of the war against Israel.

Nothing unites our people more than the desire for peace. There is no stronger urge in Israel, and on joyful occasions and in hours of mourning alike it is expressed. Nothing can wrench out of our hearts or out of our policy this wish for peace, this hope of peace—not even our indignation over the killing of our loved ones, not even the enmity of the rulers of the Arab world.

The victories that we have won have never intoxicated us, or filled us with such complacency as to relinquish the wish and call for peace—a peace that means good-neighbourly relations, cooperation and an end to slaughter. Peace and co-existence with the Arab peoples have been, and are, among the fundamentals of Jewish renaissance. Generations of the Zionist movement were brought up on them. The desire for peace has charted the policy of all Israel's governments, of whatever membership. No government of Israel in power, however constituted, has ever blocked the way to peace.

With all my heart, I am convinced that in Israel, in the future as in the past, there could be no government which would not bespeak the people's cardinal and steadfast aspiration to bring about a true and enduring peace. ♪

In 1973, Israel was involved in another conflict—the 'Yom Kippur War'—in which Egyptian leader Anwar Sadat attempted to enforce the United Nations Resolution 242; Israel's total withdrawal from territories taken in 1967. Although Meir was able to form a government after the December 1973 elections, following the end of the conflict, she had lost the control of her cabinet and resigned as Prime Minister in April 1974. Golda Meir died in Jerusalem on 8 December, 1978.

David Lange

'Nuclear Weapons are Morally Indefensible'

Oxford Union, Oxford, UK, 1 March 1985

David Lange (1942–2005) served as New Zealand Prime Minister from 1984 to 1989. Lange's Labour Party was elected with an anti nuclear mandate when long-serving conservative Prime Minister, Sir Robert Muldoon, misjudged the mood of the people on the issue and called a snap election.

Former lawyer David Lange, a large man with an even larger intellect, was swept into government and led only the fourth Labour government in New Zealand's 130-year parliamentary history.

Although New Zealand's nuclear-free stance did not become law until 1987, US-New Zealand relationships deteriorated rapidly and by the time Prime Minister David Lange ventured to England in February 1985, the postwar ANZUS alliance was effectively over.

A guest at the famous Oxford Union debating society in Great Britain, Lange spoke for the affirmative team in favour of the topic, 'Nuclear Weapons Are Morally Indefensible'. The world was listening.

'Mr President, honourable members of the union, ladies and gentlemen… in fact if I could greet straight away—because I understand there is a direct feed to the White House tonight—if I could greet the President of the United States, who is of course of the very genesis of the proposition we are debating tonight.

A quote in Time magazine last year, an assertion by the President of the United States that nuclear weapons were immoral; his avowal reiterated in January this year in a statement over the space initiative known as SDI.

And there again, he asserted that this system of the nuclear stare-out cannot

'I can say very simply that it is my conviction that there is no moral case for nuclear weapons.' be sustained morally.

May I say to the honourable gentleman who preceded me, there is nothing of what I am about to say which has been conditioned in any way by my meeting with the Prime Minister of the United Kingdom yesterday... I did not meet her yesterday... I am meeting her on Monday. But I know the apprehension that he feels at his constant fear of being summoned to that carpet.

I also feel a considerable sympathy for the members of the opposite side, who have this extraordinary sense of destabilisation at the imminent prospect of peace breaking out.

The character of the argument, sir, is something which I find regrettable. So I can say very simply that it is my conviction that there is no moral case for nuclear weapons. That the best defence which can be made of their existence and the threat of their use is, as we have heard tonight, that they are a necessary evil; an abhorrent means to a desirable end.

I hold that the character of nuclear weapons is such that their very existence corrupts the best of intentions; that the means in fact perverts the end. And I hold that their character is such that they have brought us to the greatest of all perversions: The belief that this evil is necessary—as it has been stated tonight—when in fact it is not.

And I make my case against nuclear weapons the more vigorously because I distinguish between them and all other forms of coercive or deterrent power. I've got no case to make against the policeman's truncheon. And the people tonight who have argued that you must go to the ultimate in force every time you seek to embark upon it, is of course a surrender to the worst of morality.

I accept, and do not wish to be heard arguing here against any proposition that the state must arm itself with military force to protect its citizens against aggression or to defend the weak and the helpless against aggression.

But I do not accept that the state must for those reasons arm itself with nuclear weapons. That is a case I do not easily or lightly make in Europe where governments have held it their duty to arm themselves with nuclear weapons. I do not doubt for one moment the quality of the intention which led to that decision or that series of decisions.

And I freely acknowledge that that decision is pursued in good conscience with the honourable intention of preserving the life and freedom of the people of Western Europe. Because those governments are faced with the close presence of an alien and relentlessly oppressive regime and obviously feel it their duty to prepare for their own defence by membership in what for most governments' policy now is straightforwardly a nuclear alliance. That is an assessment I understand and I do not come here to argue for any proposition in favour of unilateral disarmament.

And if I make that acknowledgement, I must then deal with the argument that it is the intention which determines the moral character of the action. My contention is very simply that the character of nuclear weapons is such that it is demonstrably the case that they subvert the best of intentions. And the snuggling up to the nuclear arsenal which has gone on with my friends on the opposite side tonight shows at what level of sophistication and refinement that subversion takes place.

There is, Mr President, a quality of irrationality about nuclear weapons which does not sit well with good intentions. A system of defence serves its purpose if it guarantees the security of those it protects. A system of nuclear defence guarantees only insecurity. The means of defence terrorise as much as the threat of attack. In Europe, it is impossible to be unaware of the intensity of military preparedness. In New Zealand, the visitor must make an effort to find a military installation or indeed any sign of military activity, although it does exist. There is no imperative in New Zealand to prepare for war. The result is that I feel safer in Wellington than I ever could in London or New York or Oxford.

The fact is that Europe and the United States are ringed about with nuclear weapons and your people have never been more at risk. There is simply only one thing more terrifying than nuclear weapons pointed in your direction and that is nuclear weapons pointed in your enemy's direction. The outcome of their use would be the same in either case, and that is the annihilation of you and all of us. That is a defence which is no defence; it is a defence which disturbs far more than it reassures. The intention of those who for honourable motives use nuclear weapons to deter is to enhance security. Notwithstanding that intention, they succeed only in enhancing insecurity. Because the machine has perverted the motive.

The President of the United States has acknowledged that, notwithstanding that my honourable friend opposite does not, and the weapon has installed mass destruction as the objective of the best-intentioned.

The weapon simply has its own relentless logic and it is inhuman. It is the logic of escalation, the logic of the arms race. Nuclear weapons make us insecure and to compensate for our insecurity we build and deploy more nuclear weapons. We know that we are seized by irrationality—and every now and then

'It makes no sense for a country to surround its waters or to invite into its ports or country, nuclear weapons, when there is no balance to be achieved.'

some new generation technology comes in, the argument for which is that it will cause us to draw back from the nuclear precipice. And we are seeing right now another initiative, under a new title. The title of course in dispute as much as its efficiency will be. And that, Mr President, is the story of the whole saga of the nuclear escalation.

We know, all of us, that it is wholly without logic or reason, any sense at all, to have the means at the disposal of two particular sets of powers to turn this world into rubble time and time again. And yet in spite of that awareness, the world watches as two enormous machines enhance, refine their capacity to inflict destruction on each other and on all of us.

Every nuclear development, whatever its strategic or tactical significance, has only one result, and that is to add to an arsenal which is already quite beyond reason.

There is an argument in defence of the possession of nuclear weapons which holds that the terror created by the existence of those weapons is in itself the fulfilment of a peaceful purpose. The argument advanced here tonight that that 50 million killed over four years by concerted war in a conventional sense in Europe and the argument that somehow the existence of this mutually assured destruction phenomenon has since that time preserved this planet from destruction.

It is, I think, probably an example of northern hemisphere or European arrogance that we overlook now the 30 million people in this world who have died in wars since then—while we are apparently beset from the two superpowers by a system designed to have people stop killing each other.

I believe that the fear they inspire is not a justification for their existence.'

There were then a number of interjections in which questions were put to Mr Lange from the audience. Would New Zealand do the honourable thing and pull out of the ANZUS alliance, they wanted to know. Lange answered them with wit and humour:

'…I'm going to give (an answer) to you if you hold your breath just for a moment… I can smell the uranium on it as you lean forward!

I want to pass over here the preparations which are constantly being made for the winnable or even survivable nuclear war. I would ignore those and wholeheartedly embrace the logic of the unthinkable war if it could be established that the damage which could result from the collapse of that logic could be confined to nuclear weapon states. Unfortunately and demonstrably, it would not. We in New Zealand, you know, used to be able to relax a bit, to be able to think that we would sit comfortably while the rest of the world seared, singed, withered. We were enraptured!

'We know that if the nuclear winter comes, we freeze, we join the rest of you. And that means that there is now a total denouement as far as any argument in favour of moral purpose goes.'

And the fact is that we used to have the reputation of being some kind of an antipodean Noah's Ark, which would from within its quite isolated preserve, spawn a whole new world of realistic human kind. Now, the fact is that we know that that is not achievable. We know that if the nuclear winter comes, we freeze, we join the rest of you. And that means that there is now a total denouement as far as any argument in favour of moral purpose goes. It is a strange, dubious and totally unaccepted moral purpose which holds the whole of the world to ransom.

There is another assertion of the good moral character of nuclear weapons which holds that they are the armour of good against evil. The argument of the Crusaders; the people who took to arms. The evil which cannot be defeated by persuasion or example must need be suppressed by annihilation. The obvious difficulty here is that evil has declined to be subdued; evil has not accepted annihilation.

The church and its representatives have been going at it now for 2000 years—and it persists. Every attempt to subdue it strengthens its resolve to arm itself further. And the will of the good in weaponry's terms is corrupted by the terrible force of the weapon, into the will of the evil.

And all of us, wherever we are, whatever we believe, live in fear of nuclear weapons. There is a community of interest which binds us all to common ground, which is there so that we all wish to see the elimination of nuclear weapons.

The President of the United States speaks in terms of the elimination of nuclear weapons. Yet nuclear weapons proliferate. The budgets for their creation expand. They in fact govern us. Their existence diverts attention from the fact that there are other ways of resolving the difficulties and tensions which will always abound in the world. Nuclear weapons are not needed.

All the arguments which can be brought forward in support of this evil come to nothing in the fact of its ultimate irrelevance. I don't make that assertion because I have some simple South Pacific—as you put it, grand gesture—answer to the question of the existence of nuclear weapons. All of you in Europe know that negotiating an end to nuclear weapons could hardly be more difficult. And then you have the hide to come here and say that New Zealand's stance is somehow threatening the strength of the West in Geneva. And then others criticise us because they say our position has not reduced by one the number of nuclear weapons in the world. You can't have it both ways!

Either the West goes to Geneva girt about with the hardware it had a month ago, or it doesn't. And it does—and in that nuclear stare-out, there will be a blink—I pray—and there can be a climb-back. But you know you can't wholeheartedly support the argument in favour of the superpowers negotiating control of them while nuclear powers embrace the logic of escalation...

The simple fact is that I make no pretence that the problem which confronted New Zealand is the same as that which confronts Western Europe. And you point out—and you have the right to point out and I am glad that you did, notwithstanding that you allege that you oppose me—that people from New Zealand, a country which has never been attacked, have willingly taken up arms in Europe. They have died in African campaigns, they have their bones bleaching in deserts, they are buried in Italy. They have fought in Vietnam. We have forces right now in Sinai. We have a battalion in Singapore where the British used to be!

And the fact is we do not shrink from that responsibility. We never have and we are not going to. The fact is that we do not choose, we do not choose to be unilateral armers. It makes no sense for a country to surround its waters or to invite into its ports or country, nuclear weapons, when there is no balance to be achieved. The balances there now, there are none. And we don't propose to deter enemies which do not yet exist.

And I ask you to consider that as a fundamental reality of the New Zealand position. And the people of New Zealand reached a very straightforward conclusion: That nuclear weapons which would defend them, they believed, caused them more alarm than any which threatened them and, accordingly, they deem it pointless to be defended by them. And the speakers for the negative who asked the question, are we prepared to have a nuclear umbrella from the United States in terms of an ANZUS arrangement... the answer to that is very simply, very definitely, is not only are we [not] prepared to accept it, we deny it, we refuse it and we specifically say—we do not want to be defended by nuclear weapons!

Because we, by that, avoid the risk of escalating our area into a nuclear zone. You see, in the South Pacific, it's not difficult to achieve the balance of force which allows you with that cheerfulness to dispense with nuclear weapons...

'The only nuclear weapons which presumably were brought by our allies to New Zealand in the past have been tactical weapons. We decided we didn't want to be part of someone's tactical nuclear battle.'

This country, New Zealand, is not going to contribute to a nuclear alliance. This country, New Zealand, never has. New Zealand was declared by the former government to be no part of a nuclear alliance—and we will pick up the tab by conventional defence. And one of the immoralities of nuclear weaponry, surely, is that it creates such a level of depersonalisation that the infinite capacity of destruction is unleashed by a few. Much more is there a moral posture in the conventional event where the humanity of a situation has to be constantly assessed and where there is always a possibility of restraint, because individual people say, dammit, I'm not going to go ahead and do that, because it is absolutely immoral, contrary to the whole ethos of humankind, to do that. You don't get the checks and balances along the nuclear trail.

And in my country, we pay our tab. We are not creating a policy for imitation or export. We can't even deport it to Australia! It's 1200 miles away! And if you think that Belgium and Holland and Greece developed a certain posture, an undercurrent, a surge, because of the New Zealand position, you do us a considerable flattery about our omnipotence, because, you know, we didn't even know they were even thinking about it! And we are no threat to that.

I say to you, we are prepared to pay that price. We have a long history of being anti-nuclear. One of my predecessors in office sent those ships to Mururoa. We've had the fight in the legal areas. We are constantly at issue with France. We proposed in 1975 a South Pacific Zone. We are going to work to protect that this year. We have honoured our long-standing commitments. We've not welshed on any deals for defence. We are in Singapore with a battalion where Britain was, and we are going to see that we contribute to regional security and stability.

And what has happened to New Zealand since the Labour government was elected last year and began to implement its long-established policy— you know—one of the most amazing things about the expectations of world governments, is that first they assume that the opposition's policy is infinitely flexible and then they immediately assume that when you get into government you'll do a u-turn. Well, we are not infinitely flexible and we've done no u-turn and we've done exactly what we've said we'd do. And that of course is terribly destabilising...

Because it makes it so difficult to read all the signs. But what essentially has happened is a demonstration of how nuclear weapons have assumed a moral life of their own.

We have never been part of strategic defence. The only nuclear weapons which presumably were brought by our allies to New Zealand in the past have been tactical weapons. We decided we didn't want to be part of someone's tactical nuclear battle. It's just about as bad as being part of somebody else's strategic nuclear battle. But that has not in any way diminished the deterrent power of the Western alliance. We have not given comfort to the Soviet bloc. We have not undermined the West.

But the result has been that we have been told by some officials in the United States administration that our decision is not, as they put it, to be cost-free; that we are in fact to be made to pay for our action. Not by our enemies, but by our friends. We are in fact to be made an example of; we are to be ostracised, we are to be convicted of some form of heresy and put on probation. We are going to be kept there until we are compelled to resume our seat in the dress circle of the nuclear theatre.

We have been told that because others in the West—and their advocates are here tonight—carry the fearful burden of a defence which terrorises as much as the threat it counters, we too must carry that burden. We are actually told that New Zealanders cannot decide for themselves how to defend New Zealand, but are obliged to adopt the methods which others use to defend themselves.

Lord Carrington [the Secretary-General of NATO] made a case in Copenhagen recently against the creation of nuclear weapon free zones. He argued that if the people of the United States—as advocated by my friend over there—found themselves bearing the burden alone, they would tire of bearing it. Now that is exactly the point. Genuine agreement[s] about the control of nuclear weapons do not cede the advantage to one side or the other: They enhance security, they do not diminish it. And if such arrangements can be made and such agreements reached, then those who remain outside those arrangements might well and truly tire of their insecurity. They will reject the logic of the weapon and they will assert their essential humanity. They will look for arms control agreements which are real and verifiable.

And there's no humanity at all in the logic which holds that my country, New Zealand, must be obliged to play host to nuclear weapons because others in the West are playing host to nuclear weapons. That is the logic which refuses to admit that there is any alternative to nuclear weapons, when plainly there is.

It is self-defeating logic, just as the weapons themselves are self-defeating. To compel an ally to accept nuclear weapons against the wishes of that ally is to take the moral position of totalitarianism, which allows for no self-determination, and which is exactly the evil that we are supposed to be fighting against.

Any claim to a moral justification for the West's possession of nuclear weapons is thereby eliminated. In those circumstances we would be no better than they are.

The great strength of the West, in fact, lies not in the force of arms—although some would seek under the cover of a benign democracy to argue that it is in fact the force of arms—but it lies in its free and democratic systems of government.

That is why, in spite of all the difficulties and disagreements which we have amongst friends and allies, I am not disheartened. I came to Great Britain by way of the United States, where I put my case to the American people through the news media without any kind of hindrance from the United States Administration.

Members of Her Majesty's Government have made it plain to me that they do not hold with the views I am committed to. I, in fact, have heard those before. The other night I heard them from Washington. They were compelling. They were a restatement of the United Kingdom position, and they were said with such candour and frankness that they seemed to persist even after the volume had been turned off. They were done with a strength and a purpose and a vigour.

I want to say that notwithstanding that difference, I have felt welcome here. I have been freely able to express my views. I can say freely whatever I please. Just as any member of Her Majesty's Government in the United Kingdom would be welcome in New Zealand to expound any line of argument in any forum she cared to use. That is the true strength of the West.

And that is a strength which is threatened, not defended, by nuclear weapons. The appalling character of those weapons has robbed us of our right to determine our destiny and subordinates our humanity to their manic logic. They have subordinated reason to irrationality and placed our very will to live in hostage. Rejecting the logic of nuclear weapons does not mean surrendering to evil; evil must still be guarded against. Rejecting nuclear weapons is to assert what is human over the evil nature of the weapon; it is to restore to humanity the power of the decision; it is to allow a moral force to reign supreme. It stops the macho lurch into mutual madness.

And for me, the position of my country is a genuine long-term affirmation of this proposition: that nuclear weapons are morally indefensible.

And I support that proposition. ♩

With his booming voice and idiosyncratic, commanding phrasing, David Lange was accorded a standing ovation from both sides of the house and his team went on win the debate.

But Lange and the people of New Zealand won a larger moral victory on the world stage for their intractable stance against the proliferation of nuclear weapons and the banning of US warships in New Zealand waters. As New Zealand's 'Public Address' noted some years later: 'After decades of knowing our place... suddenly we had a Prime Minister who could stride the international stage with insouciance. And briefly, we seemed to matter.'

Ronald Reagan

'The Challenger Disaster'

White House, Washington DC, 8 January 1986

Ronald Wilson Reagan (1911–2004) was the 40th President of the United States of America. Sportsman, radio broadcaster, movie actor and a conservative Governor of California during the tumultuous 1960s, Reagan was almost 70 years old when he came to the White House, but proved to be one of the country's most popular Presidents.

In March 1981, just six weeks after his inauguration, Reagan barely survived an assassin's bullet. The following year he became the first US President to be invited to speak directly to members of the British Parliament in the Royal Gallery at the Palace of Westminster in London.

Reagan outlined his staunch opposition to Communism and encouraged the British to aid the US in the worldwide struggle for freedom—evoking memories of former British Prime Minister Winston Churchill and the fight against Germany in World War II.

A masterful communicator, in 1986 Reagan delivered arguably the most powerful speech of his Presidency in response to one of the most dramatic disasters of the modern age.

NASA's 'Space Shuttle' program—to create and operate a reusable craft for transportation into space—was successfully launched in 1981 with the maiden flight of Columbia. Challenger came next the following year, followed by Discovery (1983) and Atlantis (1985). Space Shuttle Challenger flew nine successful missions before it took off from Cape Canaveral (formerly Cape Kennedy) on 28 January 1986 with seven astronauts on board. Among them was the first member of the Teacher in Space Program (TISP), Christa McAuliffe, who was selected from 11,000 applicants.

Challenger's lift-off was delayed five times in the week leading up to the eventual launch, which was at 11.38 am (EST) on Sunday 28 January. Seventy-three seconds into Mission 51L, Challenger exploded killing the entire crew. The astronauts' families, a large crowd at Cape Canaveral and the rest of the nation watching on television were transfixed by the destruction that they had just witnessed. A special commission formed to investigate the cause of the accident (which included former astronaut Neil Armstrong) found that an 'O' ring seal in the solid fuel rocket on the Challenger's right side was faulty and that in the cold conditions, booster rocket flames burned through the shuttle's external fuel tank and broke loose a booster rocket which then pierced the tank's side. The mixture of liquid hydrogen and liquid oxygen caused the Challenger to literally tear apart.

But on Sunday night, the American public was not looking for answers, only comfort. In trying to find the right tone for a national address, Reagan's speechwriter, Peggy Noonan, recalled a poem she had been taught in school, 'High Flight' written by 19-year-old pilot, John Gillespie McGee, in the early days of World War II.

McGee, an American serving in England with the Royal Canadian Air Force, had sent the poem to his parents several months before his death in a Spitfire crash in December 1941.

The poem was published and became a source of inspiration for many pilots during the war:

Oh! I have slipped the surly bonds of earth
And danced the skies on laughter-silvered wings;
Sunward I've climbed, and joined the tumbling mirth
Of sun-split clouds — and done a hundred things
You have not dreamed of — and wheeled and soared
And swung high in sunlit silence.
Hov'ring there, I've chased the shouting wind along,
And flung my eager craft through footless halls of air.
Up, up the long, delirious, burning blue
I've topped the windswept heights with easy grace
Where never lark, or even eagle flew
And, while with silent, lifting mind I've trod
The high untrespassed sanctity of space,
Put out my hand, and touched the face of God.

Ronald Reagan also remembered the poem as one fellow actor Tyrone Power had recited to him on his return from World War II. Noonan linked the first and last lines of McGee's poem to construct a speech that touched the hearts of the world:

Ladies and gentlemen:
I'd planned to speak to you tonight to report on the state of the Union, but the events of earlier today have led me to change those plans. Today is a day for mourning and remembering. Nancy and I are pained to the core by the tragedy of the shuttle Challenger. We know we share this pain with all of the people of our country. This is truly a national loss.

Nineteen years ago, almost to the day, we lost three astronauts in a terrible accident on the ground. But we've never lost an astronaut in flight; we've never had a tragedy like this. And perhaps we've forgotten the courage it took for the crew of the shuttle. But they, the Challenger Seven, were aware of the dangers, but overcame them and did their jobs brilliantly. We mourn seven heroes: Michael Smith, Dick Scobee, Judith Resnik, Ronald McNair, Ellison Onizuka, Gregory Jarvis, and Christa McAuliffe. We mourn their loss as a nation together.

For the families of the seven, we cannot bear, as you do, the full impact of this tragedy. But we feel the loss, and we're thinking about you so very much. Your loved ones were daring and brave and they had that special grace, that special spirit that says: "Give me a challenge, and I'll meet it with joy." They had a hunger to explore the universe and discover its truths. They wished to serve and they did. They served all of us.

We've grown used to wonders in this century. It's hard to dazzle us. But for 25 years the United States space program has been doing just that. We've grown used to the idea of space and perhaps we forget that we've only just begun. We're still pioneers. They, the members of the Challenger crew, were pioneers.

And I want to say something to the schoolchildren of America who were watching the live coverage of the shuttle's takeoff. I know it is hard to understand, but sometimes painful things like this happen. It's all part of the process of exploration and discovery. It's

'It's all part of taking a chance and expanding man's horizons. The future doesn't belong to the faint hearted; it belongs to the brave. The Challenger crew was pulling us into the future and we'll continue to follow them.'

all part of taking a chance and expanding man's horizons. The future doesn't belong to the faint hearted; it belongs to the brave. The Challenger crew was pulling us into the future and we'll continue to follow them.

I've always had great faith in and respect for our space program and what happened today does nothing to diminish it. We don't hide our space program. We don't keep secrets and cover things up. We do it all up front and in public. That's the way freedom is and we wouldn't change it for a minute. We'll continue our quest in space. There will be more shuttle flights and more shuttle crews and, yes, more volunteers, more civilians, more teachers in space. Nothing ends here; our hopes and our journeys continue.

I want to add that I wish I could talk to every man and woman who works for NASA or who worked on this mission and tell them: "Your dedication and professionalism have moved and impressed us for decades. And we know of your anguish. We share it."

There's a coincidence today. On this day 390 years ago, the great explorer, Sir Francis Drake, died aboard ship off the coast of Panama. In his lifetime, the great frontiers were the oceans, and an historian later said: "He lived by the sea, died on it, and was buried in it." Well, today we can say of the Challenger crew: Their dedication was, like Drake's, complete.

The crew of the space shuttle Challenger honored us by the manner in which they lived their lives. We will never forget them, nor the last time we saw them, this morning, as they prepared for their journey and waved goodbye, and "slipped the surly bonds of earth" to "touch the face of God." ♪

The Challenger disaster grounded NASA's space shuttle program for another two years, but it was not the only tragedy to confront the Space Agency.

On 1 February 2003, Space Shuttle Columbia, again with seven astronauts on board, was re-entering Earth's atmosphere after a 16-day mission when the craft disintegrated at 12,500 mph—18 times the speed of sound—some 39 miles above Texas. It was an eerie echo of Challenger's fate 17 years before; only the eloquence of Peggy Noonan's comforting words—and the masterful delivery of Ronald Reagan, long retired but bedridden with the Alzheimer's disease that would claim his life the following year—were missing.

Paul Keating

'Eulogy for the Unknown Soldier'

War Memorial, Canberra, 11 November 1993

Paul Keating (b. 1944) was Australia's 24th Prime Minister (1991–96). He entered Parliament at the age of 25 as the Labor member for the NSW seat of Blaxland and was briefly the Minister for Minerals and Energy in the final days of the Gough Whitlam government in 1975.

As Bob Hawke's Treasurer from 1983 to 1991, Keating earned a reputation as an intelligent and somewhat abrasive political speaker who was not afraid to take on an opponent, boots and all, or to tell the Australian public, or his own party for that matter, what he was thinking.

Speechwriter Don Watson wrote of Keating: '(his language) served as the raw instrument of his intelligence… when he was on a roll he could remind you what language can be and what it could do.'

In July 1991, after more than eight years as Deputy Prime Minister, Keating unsuccessfully challenged Bob Hawke for the ALP leadership and the Prime Ministership of Australia. After several months as a backbencher, Keating launched another challenge on 19 December 1991 and was successful in removing Hawke, who was the longest serving Labor Prime Minister in the nation's history.

In March 1993, Keating led Labor in an election victory many thought unwinnable after ten years in power and governed his Party in his own right for the next three years.

In his five years as Prime Minister, Paul Keating introduced the Native Title legislation in wake of the High Court's 'Mabo' ruling regarding the formal recognition of the land rights of indigenous peoples; promoted economic and political relations with Asia; and initiated moves towards

Australia becoming a republic.

Although he was never far from a political stoush if one was required, Keating surprised many with his statesmanship as Prime Minister (for example, his famous Redfern Speech in 1992), his ability to get to the heart of a national matter (most notably his commonsense approach of the potentially divisive republic issue) and his clear vision for the country's future prosperity as a trading partner for Asia—not America or Europe.

On 11 November 1993—on the 75th anniversary of the signing of the armistice that ended World War I—Paul Keating eloquently and articulately spoke at the Tomb of the Unknown Soldier in the Hall of Memory of the Australian War Memorial.

The remains of the Australian soldier, exhumed from the Adelaide Cemetery in Villers-Bretonneux in France, had been interred at the specially constructed 'Stone of Remembrance' memorial in the heart of the nation's capital. Keating's eulogy, delivered during the funeral service for the Unknown Soldier, was described by The Age journalist, Michael Fullilove, as 'composed of good, plain words, elegantly arranged' by speechwriter Don Watson—but movingly delivered by the Prime Minister.

'We do not know this Australian's name and we never will. We do not know his rank or his battalion. We do not know where he was born, or precisely how and when he died. We do not know where in Australia he had made his home or when he left it for the battlefields of Europe. We do not know his age or his circumstances—whether he was from the city or the bush; what occupation he left to become a soldier; what religion, if he had a religion; if he was married or single. We do not know who loved him or whom he loved. If he had children we do not know who they are. His family is lost to us as he was lost to them. We will never know who this Australian was.

Yet he has always been among those we have honoured. We know that he was one of the 45,000 Australians who died on the Western Front. One of the 416,000 Australians who volunteered for service in the First World War. One of the 324,000 Australians who served overseas in that war, and one of the 60,000 Australians who died on foreign soil. One of the 100,000 Australians who have died in wars this century.

He is all of them. And he is one of us.

This Australia and the Australia he knew are like foreign countries. The tide of events since he died has been so dramatic, so vast and all-consuming; a world has been created beyond the reach of his imagination.

He may have been one of those who believed the Great War would be an adventure too grand to miss. He may have felt that he would never live down the shame of not going. But the chances are that he went for no other reason than that he believed it was his duty—the duty he owed his country and his King.

Because the Great War was a mad, brutal, awful struggle distinguished more often than not by military and political incompetence; because the waste of human life was so terrible that some said victory was scarcely discernible from defeat; and because the war which was supposed to end all wars in fact sowed the seeds of a second, even more terrible, war—we might think that this Unknown Soldier died in vain.

But in honouring our war dead as we always have, we declare that this is not true.

For out of the war came a lesson which transcended the horror and tragedy and the inexcusable folly.

It was a lesson about ordinary people—and the lesson was that they were not ordinary.

On all sides they were the heroes of that war: Not the generals and the politicians, but the soldiers and sailors and nurses—those who taught us to endure hardship, show courage, to be bold as well as resilient, to believe in ourselves, to stick together.

The Unknown Australian Soldier we inter today was one of those who, by his deeds, proved that real nobility and grandeur belongs not to empires and nations but to the people on whom they, in the last resort, always depend.

That is surely at the heart of the Anzac story, the Australian legend which emerged from the war. It is a legend not of sweeping military victories so much as triumphs against the odds, of courage and ingenuity in adversity. It is a legend of free and independent spirits whose discipline derived less from military formalities and customs than from the bonds of mateship and the demands of necessity.

It is a democratic tradition, the tradition in which Australians have gone to war ever since.

This Unknown Australian is not interred here to glorify war over peace; or to assert a soldier's character above a civilian's; or one race or one nation or one religion above another; or men above women; or the war in which he fought and died above any other war; or of one generation above any that has or will come later.

The Unknown Soldier honours the memory of all those men and women who laid down their lives for Australia.

His tomb is a reminder of what we have lost in war and what we have gained.

We have lost more than 100,000 lives, and with them all their love of this country and all their hope and energy.

We have gained a legend: A story of bravery and sacrifice and with it a deeper faith in ourselves and our democracy and a deeper understanding of what it means to be Australian.

It is not too much to hope, therefore, that this Unknown Australian Soldier might continue to serve his country—he might enshrine a nation's love of peace and remind us that in the sacrifice of the men and women whose names are recorded here, there is faith enough for all of us. ♪

In the federal election of 1996, Keating's Labor government was defeated after a record 13 years in power. In retirement, Keating remained an outspoken opponent of the government policies led by his successor, Liberal leader John Howard; was an occasional critic of his own political party in opposition; and continued to be a fierce advocate for indigenous rights, social reform and the move towards an Australian Republic.

On 13 February 2008, Keating joined three other former Australian Prime Ministers—Gough Whitlam (1972–75), Malcolm Fraser (1975–83) and Bob Hawke (1983–91)—as newly elected government leader Kevin Rudd opened Federal Parliament and formally apologised to indigenous Australians of the 'stolen generation' for years of social abuse and political mismanagement.

Boris Yeltsin

'Yekaterinburg Apology'

St Petersburg, Russia, 17 July 1998

Boris Yeltsin (1931–2007) was an abrasive, erratic and unpredictable Russian President—he famously suspended parliament in 1993, sacked two prime ministers and two premiers in 18 months and fired his entire cabinet in 1999.

Boris Nikolayevich Yeltsin was born in Yekaterinburg, Ukraine, in 1931. After joining the Communist Party of the Soviet Union in 1961, he was inducted into the Central Committee of the party by newly-elected general secretary Mikhail Gorbachev in 1985.

Yeltsin served as Moscow Party Chief in 1985 and was a member of the party Politburo before being replaced for criticising the slow rate of change. He was the first popularly elected President of the Russian Federation in 1990, at a time when the Soviet Union was crumbling.

After the dissolution of the Soviet Union in 1991, he was regarded as a hero and saviour in Russia, but a buffoon and a liability internationally.

However, there were signs of a great man trying to escape mounting health problems and an alcoholic haze. Yeltsin had become a national hero in August 1991 when he led a people's protest against a coup and mobilised the Russian army to surround public buildings resulting in the surrender of the plotters.

After the break-up of the Soviet Union in 1991, Yeltsin remained Russian President and following his re-election in 1994, continued to press for reform.

In 1998, Yeltsin made an impassioned speech in the cathedral of Peter and Paul at Yekaterinburg—the place of his birth—acknowledging the previously unspoken fate of Tsar Nicholas II, his wife Alexandria and their five children. DNA and forensic technology had only recently confirmed to the world the shameful secret—covered up by the Soviet

Union for decades—of the execution of the Russian Royal Family there by Red Army soldiers on 17 July 1918.

On the eightieth anniversary of their death, a noticeably ill President Yeltsin addressed millions of Russians—and the world media—and officially apologised for the atrocity via this televised speech.

'It's an historic day for Russia. Eighty years have passed since the slaying of the last Russian emperor and his family. We have long been silent about this monstrous crime. We must say the truth: The Yekaterinburg massacre has become one of the most shameful pages of our history.

By burying the remains of innocent victims we want to expiate the sins of our ancestors. Guilty are those who committed this heinous crime and those who have been justifying it for decades—all of us.

We must not lie to ourselves, explaining this senseless cruelty with political goals. The execution of the Romanov family was the result of an irreconcilable split in Russian society. Its results are felt to this day. The burial of the victims' remains is an act of human justice, an expiation of common guilt.

We all bear responsibility for the historical memory of the nation; and that's why I could not fail to come here. I must be here as both an individual and the President.

I bow my head before the victims of the merciless slaving.

While building a new Russia we must rely on its historical experience.

Many glorious pages of our history are linked with the Romanovs. But also connected with their name is one of the most bitter lessons—that attempts to change life by violence are doomed.

'We must finish this century, which has become the century of blood and lawlessness for Russia, with repentance and reconciliation irrespective of political and religious views and ethnic origin.'

We must finish this century, which has become the century of blood and lawlessness for Russia, with repentance and reconciliation irrespective of political and religious views and ethnic origin. This is our historic chance. On the eve of the third millennium, we must do it for the sake of our generation and those to come. Let's remember those innocent victims who have fallen to hatred and violence.

May they rest in peace.

By the end of the decade and with Russia on the brink of financial collapse (the rouble lost 75 per cent of its value during the 1990s), Yeltsin went into semi-retirement while the government was run by Prime Minister Yevgeny Primakov.

Yeltsin refused to resign as President and hand over Russia to former Communist Party interests and sacked Primakov in June 1999.

When parliamentary elections were held in December 1999 Yelstin stood down in favour of his new Prime Minister, Alexander Putin.

On 1 January 2000, Boris Yeltsin exited the world stage when he voluntarily resigned his position of President and Putin was subsequently elected to the position in March of that year.

After Boris Yeltsin died in April 2007 of heart failure, he became the first Russian statesman in more than a century to be buried in a church ceremony. President Putin declared the day of Yelstin's funeral a national day of mourning

Tony Blair

'Farewell to Politics'

Trimdon Labour Club, Sedgefield, England, 19 May 2007

Tony Blair (b. 1953) was Labour's longest-serving Prime Minister and the only person to lead the Party to three consecutive general election victories (1997–2005).

Blair, who came to the leadership upon the sudden death of John Smith in 1994, helped modernise the Labour Party after more than a decade in opposition.

While many believed Labour abandoned the very policies that made them the socialist alternative to conservative rule, 'New Labour' was swept to power on 2 May 1997 and 44-year-old Tony Blair commenced a tumultuous decade as British Prime Minister.

Almost immediately, Tony Blair was confronted with national and international events that would punctuate his time at 10 Downing Street. The death of Diana, Princess of Wales, in August 1997 stunned the nation and shocked the world. Blair can draw much credit for the quiet, yet forceful, manner with which he confronted the Royal family's cold reaction to the tragedy and united the British people in their grief.

Although Blair won his second general election, in 2001, just as easily as his first, he was already drawing criticism for the perceived pursuit of popular appeal at the expense of real policies. In the words of the greatest pop culture heroes of his generation, Blair was in danger of becoming British politics' Nowhere Man—neither socialist nor conservative—but lost somewhere in between.

The events of 11 September 2001 called for a response and, right or wrong, Tony Blair fell in behind US President George W. Bush. Britain's involvement in the invasion of Afghanistan (2001) and Iraq (2003) polarised personal and political support for Blair. Despite increasing political and media pressure that Blair had taken Britain into Iraq on 'faulty judicial advice and inaccurate intelligence information', in 2005 Labour won a third general election.

But by September 2006, following pressure from his own party, Blair announced that he would step down as Prime Minister within the next twelve months.

On 19 May 2007, ten years after his party gained power, Tony Blair announced his resignation as Prime Minister:

' I have come back here, to Sedgefield, to my constituency, where my political journey began and where it is fitting it should end.

Today I announce my decision to stand down from the leadership of the Labour Party. The Party will now select a new leader.

On 27 June, I will tender my resignation from the office of Prime Minister to the Queen. I have been Prime Minister of this country for just over ten years. In this job, in the world today, that is long enough, for me but more especially for the country. Sometimes the only way you conquer the pull of power is to set it down.

It is difficult to know how to make this speech today. There is a judgment to be made on my premiership. And in the end that is for you, the people, to make. I can only describe what I think has been done over these last ten years and perhaps more important why. I have never quite put it like this before.

I was born almost a decade after the Second World War. I was a young man in the social revolution of the 60s and 70s. I reached political maturity as the Cold War was ending and the world was going through a political, economic and technological revolution.

I looked at my own country. A great country... wonderful history... magnificent traditions... proud of its past but strangely uncertain of its future... uncertain about the future ... almost old-fashioned. All of that was curiously symbolised in its politics.

You stood for individual aspiration and getting on in life or social compassion and helping others. You were liberal in your values or conservative. You believed in the power of the State or the efforts of the individual. Spending more money on the public realm was the answer or it was the problem.

None of it made sense to me. It was twentieth century ideology in a world approaching a new millennium. Of course people want the best for themselves and their families but in an age where human capital is a nation's greatest asset, they also know it is just and sensible to extend opportunities, to develop the potential to succeed for all, not an elite at the top.

People are today open-minded about race and sexuality, averse to prejudice and yet deeply and rightly conservative with a small 'c' when it comes to good manners, respect for others, treating people courteously. They acknowledge the need for the State and the responsibility of the individual. They know spending money on our public services matters and that it is not enough. How they are run and organized matters too.

So 1997 was a moment for a new beginning, for sweeping away all the detritus of the past.

Expectations were so high. Too high. Too high in a way for either of us. Now in 2007, you can easily point to the challenges, the things that are wrong... the grievances that fester.

But go back to 1997. Think back. No, really, think back. Think about your own living standards then in May 1997 and now. Visit your local school, any of them round here, or anywhere in modern Britain. Ask when you last had to wait a year or more on a hospital waiting list, or heard of pensioners freezing to death in the winter unable to heat their homes. There is only one government since 1945 that can say all of the following:

More jobs... fewer unemployed... better health and education results... lower crime... and economic growth in every quarter.

This one.

But I don't need a statistic. There is something bigger than what can be measured in waiting lists or GSCE results or the latest crime or jobs figures. Look at our economy... at ease with globalization. London, the world's financial centre. Visit our great cities and compare them with ten years ago. No country attracts overseas investment like we do.

Think about the culture of Britain in 2007. I don't just mean our arts that are thriving. I mean our values. The minimum wage... paid holidays as a right... amongst the best maternity pay and leave in Europe ... equality for gay people.

Or look at the debates that reverberate round the world today. The global movement to support Africa in its struggle against poverty... climate change... the fight against terrorism. Britain is not a follower. It is a leader. It gets the essential characteristic of today's world: its interdependence.

This is a country today that for all its faults, for all the myriad of unresolved problems and fresh challenges, is comfortable in the twenty-first century. At home in its own skin, able not just to be proud of its past but confident of its future. I don't think Northern Ireland would have been changed unless Britain had changed. Or the Olympics won if we were still the Britain of 1997.

As for my own leadership, throughout these ten years, where the predictable has competed with the utterly unpredicted, right at the outset one thing was clear to me. Without the Labour Party allowing me to lead it, nothing could ever have been done. But I knew my duty was to put the country first. That much was obvious to me when just under 13 years ago I became Labour's Leader. What I had to learn, however, as Prime Minister, was what putting the country first really meant.

Decision-making is hard. Everyone always says: Listen to the people. The trouble is, they don't always agree. When you are in Opposition, you meet this group and they say why can't you do this? And you say: It's really a good question. Thank you. And they go away and say: It's great; he really listened. You meet that other group and they say: Why can't you do that? And you say: It's a really good question. Thank you. And they go away happy you listened.

In government you have to give the answer. Not an answer, the answer. And, in time, you realise putting the country first doesn't mean doing the right thing according to conventional wisdom or the prevailing consensus or the latest snapshot of opinion.

It means doing what you genuinely believe to be right. Your duty is to act according to your conviction. All of that can get contorted so that people think you act according to some messianic zeal. Doubt, hesitation, reflection, consideration and re-consideration: These are all the good companions of proper decision-making. But the ultimate obligation is to decide.

Sometimes the decisions are accepted quite quickly. Bank of England independence was one, which gave us our economic stability. Sometimes, like tuition fees or trying to break up old monolithic public services, they are deeply controversial, hellish hard to do, but you can see you are moving with the grain of change round the word. Sometimes like with Europe, where I believe Britain should keep its position strong, you know you are fighting opinion but you are content with doing so. Sometimes, as with the completely unexpected, you are alone with your own instinct.

In Sierra Leone and to stop ethnic cleansing in Kosovo, I took the decision to make our country one that intervened, that did not pass by, or keep out of the thick of it. Then came the utterly unanticipated and dramatic. September 11 2001 and the death of 3000 or more on the streets of New York. I decided we should stand shoulder to shoulder with our oldest ally. I did so out of belief.

So Afghanistan and then Iraq… the latter, bitterly controversial. Removing Saddam and his sons from power, as with removing the Taliban, was over with relative ease. But the blowback since, from global terrorism and those elements that support it, has been fierce and unrelenting and costly. For many, it simply isn't and can't be worth it.

For me, I think we must see it through. They, the terrorists, who threaten us here and round the world, will never give up if we give up. It is a test of will and of belief. And we can't fail it.

So… some things I knew I would be dealing with. Some I thought I might be. Some never occurred to me on that morning of 2 May 1997 when I came into Downing Street for the first time. Great expectations not fulfilled in every part, for sure. Occasionally people say, as I said earlier, they were too high; you should have lowered them. But, to be frank, I would not have wanted it any other way. I was, and remain, as a person and as a Prime Minister, an optimist. Politics may be the art of the possible; but at least in life, give the impossible a go.

So of course the vision is painted in the colours of the rainbow; and the reality is sketched in the duller tones of black, white and grey. But I ask you to accept one thing. Hand on heart, I did what I thought was right. I may have been wrong. That's your call. But believe one thing if nothing else. I did what I thought was right for our country.

I came into office with high hopes for Britain's future. I leave it with even higher hopes for Britain's future. This is a country that can, today, be excited by the opportunities, not constantly fretful of the dangers. People often say to me: It's a tough job.

Not really.

A tough life is the life the young severely disabled children have and their parents who visited me in Parliament the other week. Tough is the life my Dad had, his whole career cut short at the age of 40 by a stroke. I have been very lucky and very blessed. This country is a blessed nation. The British are special. The world knows it. In our innermost thoughts, we know it.

This is the greatest nation on earth.

It has been an honour to serve it. I give my thanks to you, the British people, for the times I have succeeded, and my apologies to you for the times I have fallen short.

Good luck. ♪

'I came into office with high hopes for Britain's future. I leave it with even higher hopes for Britain's future. This is a country that can, today, be excited by the opportunities, not constantly fretful of the dangers'

Tony Blair resigned as Prime Minister on 27 June, 2007 and was succeeded by Gordon Brown, who had served in the Blair government as Chancellor of the Exchequer for the previous ten years.

While the ink is still drying on Blair's legacy to British and World politics, a series of controversies in Gordon Brown's first year as Prime Minister (most notably his failure to hold a referendum regarding the constitution of the European Union and to call a general election) has quickly assured him that the love affair the public and media once enjoyed with the Blair Government is well and truly over.

Kevin Rudd

'Apology to Indigenous Australians'

Parliament House, Canberra, 13 February 2008

O n 13 February 2008, Australian Prime Minister Kevin Rudd opened the first sitting of the newly elected Labor Government by fulfilling one of his key election promises—to apologise to Indigenous Australians for the stolen generations, where thousands of children were removed from traditional communities under a government-sponsored policy.

Fifty-year-old Rudd, the son of a Queensland dairy farmer and a former State Labor Party Chief of Staff, led his party's sweep to power in the November 2007 federal elections which ended more than 11 years of conservative party rule under Liberal Prime Minister, John Howard. Bright, personable, but described as being almost 'nerdish' in his appearance and quiet manner (and perfectly fluent in the Chinese dialect of Mandarin) when he began his term as Australia's 26th Prime Minister, Rudd showed that he possessed that unique leadership quality of grasping the mood of the people with a symbolic act that had been long overdue.

At Canberra's Parliament House, Kevin Rudd became the first Australian Prime Minister since Federation in 1901 to invite the traditional owners of the area, the Ngunnawal people, to take part in a 'welcome to country' ceremony to open the 41st Australian Federal Parliament. Accompanied by Aboriginal dancers and musicians, members of the Ngambri people, who have a traditional connection to the Canberra and Yass areas, presented Mr Rudd with an Aboriginal 'message' stick.

At 9.30am in the House of Representatives, on behalf of the elected government and televised live to an audience of millions, Kevin Rudd read his own message of national reconciliation:

Today we honour the Indigenous peoples of this land, the oldest continuing cultures in human history.

We reflect on their past mistreatment. We reflect in particular on the mistreatment of those who were stolen generations—this blemished chapter in our nation's history.

The time has now come for the nation to turn a new page in Australia's history by righting the wrongs of the past and so moving forward with confidence to the future.

We apologise for the laws and policies of successive parliaments and governments that have inflicted profound grief, suffering and loss on these our fellow Australians.

We apologise especially for the removal of Aboriginal and Torres Strait Islander children from their families, their communities and their country.

For the pain, suffering and hurt of these stolen generations, their descendants and for their families left behind, we say sorry.

To the mothers and the fathers, the brothers and the sisters, for the breaking up of families and communities, we say sorry.

And for the indignity and degradation thus inflicted on a proud people and a proud culture, we say sorry.

We the Parliament of Australia respectfully request that this apology be received in the spirit in which it is offered as part of the healing of the nation.

For the future we take heart; resolving that this new page in the history of our great continent can now be written.

We today take this first step by acknowledging the past and laying claim to a future that embraces all Australians.

A future where this parliament resolves that the injustices of the past must never, never happen again.

A future where we harness the determination of all Australians, Indigenous and non-Indigenous, to close the gap that lies between us in life expectancy, educational achievement and economic opportunity.

A future where we embrace the possibility of new solutions to enduring problems where old approaches have failed.

A future based on mutual respect, mutual resolve and mutual responsibility.

A future where all Australians, whatever their origins, are truly equal partners, with equal opportunities and with an equal stake in shaping the next chapter in the history of this great country, Australia.

Kevin Rudd 297

British and Australian government institutions dating back more than a hundred years before the 1970s had entered into a policy of the systematic removal of Aboriginal and Torres Strait Islander children from remote communities and suburban homes if there was a belief that children were at a social, physical or even a religious risk.

Thousands of Aboriginal children were placed into orphanages and foster homes, with parents often not informed of the reasons for the removal of their children, or the implications. Many indigenous families did not see their children again.

However well-intentioned the policy may have been as a dubious or even preventative form of child protection, there is evidence today that a primary government agenda was to breed the Aboriginal race into extinction through a program of removal from traditional communities and forced assimilation into mainstream Australia.

The practice was widely and indiscriminately applied throughout the country, often without having established cases of neglect or mistreatment and regardless of the impact on individuals, Aboriginal families or whole communities. Succeeding generations of Indigenous Australians suffered from the practice and stories from the stolen generations became an integral part of the Aboriginal experience.

The 'National Inquiry into the Separation of Aboriginal and Torres Strait Islander Children from their Families' was established by Paul Keating's Labor Government in 1995 in response to requests from key Indigenous welfare agencies and communities.

The inquiry was set up to hear submissions and personal stories to determine the extent of the stolen generations and to formally recognise the hurt caused to victims and their families by this policy.

A 700-page report entitled 'Bringing Them Home' was tabled in federal parliament in May 1997, by which time John Howard's Liberal Party had come to power.

Although individual states and territotories fulfilled a key recommendation of the report and issued formal apologies to the stolen generations, Prime Minister Howard ignored an apology and issued instead a statement of 'deep and sincere regret.'

Fearing compensation claims that could have amounted to hundreds of millions of dollars and speaking, perhaps, to 'middle Australia' which had remained largely ignorant of these issues for decades, John Howard said this he was more concerned with 'practical reconcilaition' than symbolic acts.

Famously, and without the slightest hint of irony, the second longest serving Prime Minister in Australian history (1996–2007) remarked that he refused take a 'black armband view of history'… Howard's government would not apologise for past injutices.

After Kevin Rudd claimed electoral victory on 24 November 2007, he imediately indicated that Australia would ratify the Kyoto Protocol regarding limiting greenhouse emissions, wind back the previous government's controversial workplace relations legislation and inform US President George Bush that Australia would be withdrawing its troops from Iraq.

But the following February in Canberra, Prime Minister Rudd turned an important page in Australian history when he took the first step towards national reconciliation. His formal apology and the twenty-minute speech that followed were generally met with tears, joy and widespread applause.

Although Mr Rudd ruled out any retrospective compensation for the stolen generations—committing to improve the living conditions and health of today's Indigenous communities—in just 361 words he did more for healing past injustices for all Australians than a century of government policies.

Bibliography

Print

Abrams, Irwin, Aung San Suu Kyi of Burma: The Nobel Peace Prize Annual, 1991 (New York: IMG, 1992)

Anderson, Louis E., John F. Kennedy (Bison Books, London, 1986)

Bernstein, Carl and Woodwood, Bob, All the President's Men (Simon and Shuster, New York, 1973)

Boys, Sir Michael Hardie, Remembrance Day Service, Auckland (12 November, 2000)

Cathcart, Michael and Darian-Smith, Kate, Stirring Australian Speeches (Melbourne University Press, Melbourne, 2004)

Crystal, David, The Cambridge Biographical Encyclopedia (Cambridge University Press, Cambridge, 1994).

Fisher, Jack, Stolen Glory: The McKinley Assassination (Alamar, New York, 2000)

Fraina, Louis C, Brest-Litvosk: What Is a Peace Programme? (Lanka Samasamaja Publications, Colombo, Ceylon, 1956).

Fullilove, Michael, 'When the Right Words Matter' (The Age, 11 November 2006)

Golden Renny; Wright, Scott and Dennis, Marie, Oscar Romero: His Life and Teachings (Orbis Books, New York 2004)

Haslam, Jonathan, The Nixon Administration and the Death of Allende's Chile: A Case of Assisted Suicide (Verso, New York, 2005)

Lenethal, Albert V., War: A Visual History (Ridge Press, New York, 2003)

MacArthur, Brian, The Penguin Book of Twentieth Century Speeches (Penguin, London, 1999)

McPherson, James M., The Best of My Ability: The American Presidents (DK Press, New York, 2000)

Rayner, Ed and Stapley, Arthur, Debunking History (The History Press, London, 2006)

'RFK: For Perspective and Determination' (Time magazine, 14 June 1968)

Riding, Alan, 'The Prisoner of Vichy Prison Journal', New York Times (1995)

Royal, Robert 'Catholic Martyrs of the 20th Century Copyright' (Arlington Catholic Herald, Inc. 2000)

Sell, Louis, Slobodan Milosevic and the Destruction of Yugoslavia (Duke University Press, USA, 2003)

Watson, Don, Recollections of a Bleeding Heart (Knopf, Sydney, 2002)

Whiticker, Alan, Crimes of the Century (New Holland Publishers, Sydney, 2006)

Whiticker, Alan, Speeches That Shaped the Modern World (New Holland Publishers, Sydney, 2005)

Electronic

AAP 'CIA acknowledges involvement in Allende's overthrow, Pinochet's rise' September 19, 2000. www.cnn.com

The American Presidency Project, www.presidency.ucsb.edu

'American Rhetoric' www.amercianrhetoric.com

Atatürk, www.mkemalataturk.net

Balkan Timeline, www.time.com, www.bbc.co.uk

BBC Online, 'On This Day: 4 April 1968' www.bbc.co.uk

Bhutto, Benazir, www.pigeonproject.wordpress.com

Blair, Tony, www.guardian.co.uk

Bond, Julian, www.democracynow.org

'Bringing Them Home: The "Stolen Children" Report', (Human Rights and Equal Opportunity Commission, 2005).

Brown, Hillary, 'The Romanov Dynasty' (ABC News, www.west.net, 1998)

Brown, Russell and Rae, Fiona, 'Public Address: Great New Zealand Argument' www.publicaddress.net/default

Castro, Fidel, www.marxists.org

Chavez, Cesar, www.aztlan.net, www.lasculturas.com

Churchill, Sir Winston, www.especches.com

Darrow, Clarence. www.federalobserver.com

De Klerk, FW, www.fwdklerk.org.za

Dewes, Kate, 'Legal Challenges to Nuclear Weapons from New Zealand' www.disarmsecure.org

Frier, Professor Bruce W, 'The Defense of Henry Sweet' National Association for the Advancement of Colored People (1927), www.law.umkc.edu

Gandhi, MK 'Selected works of Mahatma Gandhi; "Mahatma" Vol. II,' (1951) www.mkgandhi.org

Guevara, Che, www.marxists.org

Herzog, Chaim, 'Israeli Ambassador Herzog's Response To Zionism Is Racism

Resolution' www.jewishvirtuallibrary.org

Historic Speeches, www.sojust.net

Hitchinson, Elfie Ofari, 'Revisiting the Malcolm X Assassination' www.alternet.org

Kennedy, Ted, www.jfklancer.com, www.airsafe.com

Kurti, Beth 'Obra Revolucionaria, Ano 1960, No. 24' (Official English translation

Che Guevara Internet Archive www.marxists.org, 1999)

Lewis, Charles and Reading-Smith, Mark, 'False Pretences' (The Centre for Journalistic Integrity, 2006 www.public.intetgrity.org)

Magee, John Gillespie, 'High Flight,' www.deltaweb.co.uk

McCarthy, Joe, www.mnstate.edu

'The McKinley Assassination Historical Site', www.geocities.com

'The Obersalzberg Speech', Modern History Sourcebook www.fordham.edu

'Mussolini Justifies War Against Ethiopia' www.dickinson.edu

'Nelson Mandela' www.nobelprize.org

'On the Rivonia Trial', www.anc.org.za

Queen Elizabeth II, www.qmmemorial.gov.uk

Quirk, Robert E. 'Fidel Castro' www.fiuedu

'Reflections on Russia', www.racu.org

Richards, Ann, www.tsl.state.tx.us

Rogers, Will, www.federalobserver.com

Rudd, Kevin, www.smh.com.au (18 February, 2008)

Scarborough, Megan, 'A Voice That Could Not Be Stilled: Barbara Jordan's Legacy of Equality and Justice' www.utexas.edu

Sun Star Davao (1983), www.sunstar.com.ph

Truman, Harry S. www.trumanlibrary.org

Thatcher, Margaret, www.margaretthatcher.org

Various Speeches, www.youtube.com, www.historyplace.com

Weshba, Joseph, 'Edward R. Murrow and the Time of His Time' www.evesmag.com

'Women's Library: Women's Internet Information Network' www.thelizlibrary.org

X, Malcolm, 'The Bullet or the Ballot' (1964) www.historicaldocuments.com

Will Rogers' speech provided by The Federal Observer, http://www.federalobserver.com

Helen Keller's Speech from Helen Keller: Her Socialist Years (International Publishers, 1967)